DATE DUE			

Reporters and Officials

Reporters and Officials

The Organization and Politics of Newsmaking

Leon V. Sigal

D.C. HEATH AND COMPANY
Lexington, Massachusetts   Toronto   London

Clothbound edition by Lexington Books

Library of Congress Cataloging in Publication Data

Sigal, Leon V.
　　Reporters and officials.

　　Includes bibliographical references.
　　1. Government and the press—United States.
I. Title.
PN4738.S5　　　　070.4'0973　　　　73-8524
ISBN 0-669-85035-7

Second printing August 1974.

Published simultaneously in Canada.

Printed in the United States of America.

Paperbound International Standard Book Number: 0-669-89276-9
Clothbound International Standard Book Number: 0-669-85035-7

Library of Congress Catalog Card Number: 73-8524

To Anne

Contents

List of Tables

Preface

An American Assistant Secretary of State meets with the Japanese Prime Minister to discuss the results of the President's talks with Chinese leaders in Peking. The Nixon Administration debates deployment of a new generation of tactical nuclear weapons in Western Europe. A bus pulls into Chicago carrying an ex-tenant farmer and his family to their new home. A U.S. fighter-bomber roars off the bombing deck of an aircraft carrier en route to bomb a suspected enemy supply dump in North Vietnam. For nearly every American these events would pass unnoticed were it not for a news report about them. Yet the four events differ greatly in their accessibility to newsmen. Which, if any, will be reported in the press?

Officials in the American government may learn of these events from a cable put in their in-box or a telephone call from a subordinate the next morning, but quite often, even they find out only when they read a newspaper over breakfast. Which stories make the news and which do not can affect what officials as well as citizens of the United States know about current political developments. What the press reports about these developments can often shape how the government responds to them. A page-one story can create expectations that make it difficult for officials to avoid a response. Information in the press can gradually alter the perceptions of policy-makers, the array of politically viable options for dealing with a situation, or the arguments they make in behalf of these options, ultimately affecting what the United States government does. Relationships between press and government may explain not only the news but also some actions of the government.

Classical democratic theory suggests that the press influences the electorate, and through them, the officials who act in behalf of the government. A variant of the theory portrays the press as surrogate for public opinion directly affecting the makers of policy inside the government. Another way of viewing press-government relations ignores the public and concentrates on the interaction between men in the government and those in the press and the effects on governmental outcomes. This approach artificially but usefully narrows the investigator's concern to two sets of questions. *First, how does the press cover the nation and the world? How does it process the information it gathers? Second, why do officials make use of the press? How do they accomplish their aims through it?* If the answers to these two sets of questions turn out to be closely related, then focusing on the interactions of newsmen and officials will be justified, for it will shed light on both news content and policy outcomes.

The research strategy that I adopted represented a series of compromises. First, instead of doing a set of case studies, I culled memoirs of newsmen and officials and the political science literature for specific examples of their dealings and followed up some of these incidents by interviews with some of the participants. I then observed the interactions in the newsrooms of the *New York Times* and the *Washington Post* and the Washington bureau of the *Times*, and instead of trying to record what I saw, I drew on the examples from written sources as illustrations. I reexamined a case study done by others, the Skybolt controversy, and compared the study with the news stories at the time of the controversy to see what light I could shed on the case and coverage of it. Finally, I attempted to collect and analyze whatever systematic data I could get on sources and channels of national and foreign news in the *Times* and *Post*.

Many people have assisted me along the way, and I am grateful to all of them. In particular, I wish to thank Ben Bagdikian, Max Frankel, and Robert Phelps for their cooperation in letting me see the *Post* and the *Times* from the inside; the Institute of Politics at Harvard, the Brookings Institution, and the Rockefeller Foundation for their generosity in affording me a place to think about what I saw; George B. Washington for his research efforts; and Graham Allison, David Forrester, Alexander George, Leslie Gelb, Arnold Kantor, Henry Owen, Murray Rossant, John Steinbrunner, Charles Stevenson, and Richard Ullman for their comments and criticisms of various drafts. Finally, I owe special thanks to Mort Halperin and Herb Kaufman for their help and insights, to Dick and Bert Neustadt for their advice and encouragement over the years, and to my wife Anne, who endured many a distraction and refused to let me take it all too seriously.

LVS
New York City
March, 1973

It is senseless to talk of an absolute or objective reality without connecting with the procedures through which such a reality could be established as real by us.

— Hegel

1

What the News Means Depends on How the News Gets Made

But don't you see that the whole trouble lies here. In words, words. Each one of us has within him a whole world of things, each man of us, his own special world. And how we ever come to an understanding if I put in the words I utter the sense and value of things as I see them, while you who listen to me must inevitably translate them according to the conception of things each one of you has within himself. We think we understand each other, but we never really do.

Luigi Pirandello, *Six Characters in Search of an Author*

One big trouble with news is that nobody knows what it is. The other trouble is that nobody knows what it means.

That nobody knows what news is implies the absence of universally shared criteria for distinguishing news from non-news. Much of the controversy between the press and its critics turns on the issue of standards.

One conceivable way of resolving that issue is to define news as what newsmen say it is. But there are as many definitions of news as there are newsmen. *New York Sun* editor John B. Bogart offered a classic formulation to a cub reporter: "When a dog bites a man, that is not news; but when a man bites a dog, that *is* news."[1] To others, what sets news apart from other information is the quality of the reaction it produces: "News is something that will make people talk."[2] Talk was not enough for the Hearst editor who stipulated that news is "anything that makes a reader say, 'Gee whiz!' "[3] A version more suitable for a newspaper of record is the one proposed by Turner Catledge, former managing editor of *The New York Times*: "News is anything you find out today that you didn't know before."[4] Nevertheless, examination of the various criteria implicit in the definitions that newsmen have offered quickly disabuses the optimist. The disparity among newsmen's standards is as wide as among their critics'. The criteria are mutually, if not internally, inconsistent. Nor is any single criterion sufficient to delineate the boundaries between news and non-news.

Another way of defining news is to look at what newsmen do. News, in this operational sense of the term, is whatever the news media publish or broadcast. Even a cursory glance at a newspaper or transcript reveals that there is not much relationship between what newsmen say news is and what the news media transmit. The newsmen's criteria fail a crucial test: they do not describe what their proponents do in practice.

1

Defining news operationally as what the news media transmit sidesteps the irresolvable issue of identifying criteria for news. Concern over what makes the news leads directly to the question of how the news gets made. Before considering that question, though, it is worth recalling the other trouble with news—that nobody knows what it means.

Uncertainty about what the news means confounds newsmen and their critics alike. Even in a relativist age, two points that may need reemphasis are the subjectivity of all knowledge and the inevitability of conflict over what truth is. Every man has within himself, in Pirandello's words, "his own special world." Consequently, every newsman confronts an epistemological enigma not unlike that of a historian or social scientist seeking to establish the validity of his interpretation of events. How each accomplishes that task determines what each "knows."

Two aspects of that task are especially noteworthy. First, all seeing is theory-laden. Historical events, in particular, cannot be interpreted apart from a framework of meaning, a framework which necessarily determines how "facts" are sorted out, interpreted, and emphasized. The observer supplies that framework.[5] Yet the framework is not entirely subjective. It is the product of a time, a culture, and, most immediately, a worklife shared with others. Second, information about events comes from other men, sources with their own frameworks of meaning and their own interests to protect. The sources a newsman talks to largely shape what he reports. Not only does theory color his view of events but also men intervene to screen his line of sight.

One crucial premise therefore guides all that follows: in order to comprehend what news is and, even more, what news means, it is essential to understand how news gets made.

Making the News

What makes the news depends largely on the choices that newsmen make. *Choices*, as used here, differ from *decisions* in that they need not emerge from either a conscious weighing of issues by an individual or a formal meeting of a group, whereas decisions necessarily do. Most news results from choice, not decision. News is, moreover, the product of the choices of many rather than the decisions of a few. A small number of news media executives are ultimately responsible for news content, just as the President ultimately bears responsibility for the actions of the government under his administration. This does not mean, however, that they decide exactly what gets published or broadcast, any more than the President decides what every government official does at every point in time. A sizable number of reporters, editors, and media executives are involved in making the choices that shape the content of the news.

More than the result of the choices of many, news is intrinsically "consensible."[6] As Ziman has pointed out about science, the newsmaking enterprise is corporate. No single newsman, no single news organization, not even the news community as a whole alone determines the final product. The audience for news, particularly the attentive elite and potential news sources, by their response to information made public, actively shapes the substance of the communications that it receives. The process of consensus formation, then, is critical to the newsmaking endeavor.

Consensus formation does not take place in a vacuum but within a context of shared values and inside organizational structures, both of which help to shape the result.

Journalistic Conventions

The context of shared values does not refer simply to the personal political predilections of newsmen themselves. More important are those attitudes widely shared among reporters and editors in the news community, attitudes which might properly be called *the journalist's creed*, or ideology. Much of this creed derives from the imperatives of organization in an earlier journalistic era. Most significant among the tenets of the creed is a set of *conventions* for choosing which information to include in the news and which to ignore.

Conventions perform for the reporter the function that rules of evidence do for the scientist: they are his epistemological premises, the criteria accepted in the field for assessing validity, the argumentation for defending his findings. Unlike those rules of evidence, however, conventions are rarely subject to conscious scrutiny by newsmen; they are just the way things are done around the newsroom.

The Reporter As Organization Man

The Washington correspondent, in Douglass Cater's words, "clings to the image of the reporter as the supreme individual in the age of the organization man."[7] Yet the era of individualism in reporting in Washington and elsewhere is long past, and the image of the lone reporter doggedly "nosing out the news" obscures the extent to which newsmen, like most of the people they cover, are organization men.

The larger news organizations have all the principal attributes of bureaucracies. They have a division of labor along functional and geographic lines. Functionally, newsmen specialize as editors, general assignment reporters, or reporters covering a specific substantive area such as economics, sports, society, or the arts. Geographically, they are arranged in bureaus in various parts of the world and on beats in various parts of major cities like Washington. They have a hierarchy of authority, at least in a formal sense. They operate with a system of rules for both gathering and transcribing information. Lastly, they have a measure of impersonality: men interact with each other not simply according to who they are as people but to what they are inside the organization.

Outside their organizations, reporters are by no means lone wolves either; they travel in packs. A reporter seldom covers a news development by himself. Most beats or locations regularly covered by a reporter also have others on assignment there from rival news organizations.

The proposition that bureaucratic organizations and multimanned beats structure newsgathering has important implications for explaining how news gets made. These implications are often overlooked by those who say that a publisher lays down his editorial line and newsmen follow it; or that newsmen are increasingly recruited from an intellectual elite whose attitudes reflect an "adversary culture" predominant in those circles; or that news responds to economic imperatives, particularly to circulation, to pressure from large advertisers, or to the class interests of owners or executives. Whatever the merits of each of these views, they share a common perspective. They all treat news as if it were the product of a single value-maximizing individual. They vary in what—or whose—values they emphasize. In other words, they agree with the proposition, "Who pays the piper calls the tune." They disagree mainly about who the piper is and who pays him, and what their tastes in music are. By contrast, a focus on newsmen within the context of their organizations emphasizes that the piper is not a soloist and that the ensembles in which he plays critically affect his repertoire.

The organizational perspective brings two aspects of newsmaking into focus. First, newsmaking, and particularly newsgathering, is routine behavior. Reporters follow *routines* for collecting information. These have a counterpart in the routines of their sources, especially government officials, for releasing information to the press. From the standpoint of organizational processes, then, a good deal of the news is a product of the coupling of two information-processing machines: one, the news organization; the other, the government.

Secondly, the division of labor within news organizations does more than reflect organizational processes. Along it crystallize lines of cleavage. Men in one position in the organization see the world from perspectives that differ from men elsewhere in the organization. Conflicts often arise between reporters and editors, between an overseas bureau and the home office, among reporters covering different beats, or between an editor on the national desk and one on the foreign desk. These conflicts are not simply the petty bickering of proud, even vain men who happen to work in a news organization at any point in time; they are jurisdictional disputes built into all large news organizations by the division of labor necessary for covering the news. What passes for office politics, or more precisely, *bureaucratic politics*, can have important consequences for news content.[8]

Similarly on the beat, bargaining enters the relationships among reporters and between the reporter and his sources of information. In these relationships, motives are mixed; overt competition coexists with tacit cooperation. Among his sources, too, bargaining affects what information they pass along. Inside the government, for instance, men struggle to shape the outcomes of public policy. The ability to get information into the news and to prevent rivals from doing so is at once a tactic and a stake in that fight.

Four bargaining games run concurrently: those among newsmen inside their organizations, among reporters on the beat, between the reporter and his news sources, and among those sources, mostly officials in various government positions. Outcomes in one game can affect outcomes of the others. From the standpoint of bureaucratic politics, then, news is an outcome of the bargaining interplay of newsmen and their sources.

The assumption that underlies what follows is that organizational processes and bureaucratic politics account for more of news content than, say, the political proclivities of individual newsmen. In short, what newsmen report may depend less on who they are than on how they work.

Scope and Summary

For economy of effort, the focus of this discussion will be on news, as distinct from editorial comment; on newspapers, rather than other news media; and on the coverage of national and foreign news, particularly in Washington. The conclusions may not apply equally to other content, media, or locales, but a premise of the study is that the conclusions will point in the right direction for understanding the other elements as well.

The New York Times and *The Washington Post* were singled out for examination. There were several reasons for this choice. First, virtually alone among American newspapers, they have sizable staffs assigned to Washington and to bureaus around the country and the world, to gather news firsthand instead of relying primarily on news services to supply them with stories. Second, in Washington, nearly everyone reads the *Post* and the *Times*; this applies to newsmen as well as to officials and the attentive public. Third, the two papers have considerable influence on the news that readers of other newspapers obtain, both because they have an extensive audience in the journalism community and because many of the leading regional newspapers in the country subscribe to their news services. Fourth, because of the size and quality of their staffs, the *Times* and the *Post* enjoy a distinguished reputation in the field of journalism for their energetic and thorough coverage.

With the scope of the study in mind, it may be useful to lay out an outline of the rest of the book. Chapter 2 traces the formal organization of the *Times* and the *Post*, the constraints that the structure imposes on newsmen, the procedures they follow in transcribing the information they receive, and the organizational in-fighting that results. Chapter 3 focuses on the beat and its impact on the news consensus and the selection of news sources. Chapter 4 examines elements in the journalist's creed, conventions of newsmaking, and newsmen's conceptions of their role, and then how these aspects affect the news. Chapter 5 describes the routines of newsgathering and Chapter 6, their impact on news content. Chapter 7 looks at officials and the uses they make of the news for their own tactical purposes in governmental policy disputes. Chapter 8 takes up the question of how newsmaking affected Anglo-American relations during the Skybolt controversy. The final chapter summarizes the findings and draws some implications both for news content and for policy-making.

Notes

1. Frank Luther Mott, AMERICAN JOURNALISM (New York: Macmillan, 1950), p. 376.
2. Charles Dana, quoted in Robert E. Park, "News As a Form of Knowledge," in Ralph H. Turner (ed.), *Robert E. Park on Social Control and Collective Behavior* (Chicago: University of Chicago Press, 1967) p. 43-44.
3. Arthur McEwan, San Francisco CHRONICLE editor, quoted in Mott, AMERICAN JOURNALISM, p. 475.
4. Catledge, quoted in Herbert Brucker, JOURNALIST (New York: Macmillan, 1962), pp. 116-17.
5. Reinhold Niebuhr, among others, has argued the similarity of the newsman's and the historian's work in "The Role of the Newspaper in America's Function As the World's Greatest Power," THE PRESS IN PERSPECTIVE, ed. by Ralph D. Casey (Baton Rouge: Louisiana State University Press, 1963), p. 45.
6. The term, "consensible," was coined by John Ziman, PUBLIC KNOWLEDGE: THE SOCIAL DIMENSIONS OF SCIENCE (Cambridge: Cambridge University Press, 1968), Ch. 1.
7. Douglass Cater, THE FOURTH BRANCH OF GOVERNMENT (New York: Houghton Mifflin Company, 1959), p. 2.
8. The concepts "organizational processes" and "bureaucratic politics" as used here, owe much to the work of Graham T. Allison, ESSENCE OF DECISION (Boston: Little, Brown, 1971), Allison and Morton H. Halperin, "Bureaucratic Politics: A Paradigm and Some Policy Implications," WORLD POLITICS 24 (Spring 1972) pp. 40-79, and Richard E. Neustadt, ALLIANCE POLITICS (New York: Columbia University Press, 1970).

2

Organizational Politics at the *Times* and the *Post*

Those of us on the outside looking in at government assume that policy is the product of rational decision-making by a handful of men, just as those outside newspapers looking in assume that news is the product of rational decision-making by a handful of men.

Ben Bagdikian[1]

Newspapers originated as newsletters. The first weekly published in the Colonies, like its predecessors in the Old World, was essentially a medium for broadening the dissemination of what citizens had previously communicated primarily by word of mouth. Appropriately named the *Boston News-Letter*, the paper was the handiwork of the town postmaster, a person whose social location made him uniquely qualified to circulate local gossip.[2] It is still useful to conceive of news as a selected sample of gossip that gains currency, if not credence, through publication. The origin of the gossip has by now become global; its audience, nearly so. Meanwhile, the organization that selects what gossip makes the news has undergone major transformation.

A century ago, newsmongering was mostly a one-man operation. The publisher was at once reporter and editor, advertising manager, production supervisor, and circulation director. Today, only a handful of weeklies survive that bygone era. By contrast, *The New York Times* currently employs over 6,000 people—more than 500 as editors, reporters, and copyreaders in the news department. The rest work in the production, advertising, and promotion departments. The *Times* has bureaus in fifteen cities across the United States and in twenty-eight capitals abroad, supplemented by a worldwide network of 500 stringers.[3] *The Washington Post* with fifteen bureaus, eleven of them overseas, and about 2,100 employees, 400 of them newsmen, looms small only in comparison to its giant competitor.

With the growth of news organizations has come division of labor and specialization of function. With burgeoning complexity have come elaborate networks for internal communication, both formal and informal. Now, as in the past, economic organization dictates the necessity for choice in newsmaking by imposing constraints, principally on available money, space, staff, and time. The economics of newsmaking thereby sets the stakes of the politics inside newspapers. But now, unlike a century ago, bureaucracy shapes the patterns of choice by structuring political interaction among choice-makers. Newsmaking has become enmeshed in bureaucratic politics.

7

First, the newspaper's organization imposes economic constraints, which constitute the stakes of its internal politics; second, it establishes a formal chain of command, and alongside that, informal lines of communication, which together form the internal procedures for choice-making by the newspaper; and third, it structures patterns of intra-organizational conflict along the lines of the division of labor. Each of these aspects of newspaper organization affects the content of news.

Economic Constraints:
The Stakes of Newspaper Politics

Newspapers are business firms trying to turn a profit. They compete with other newspapers and news media in two oligopolistic markets—one for the sale of news and the other for the sale of advertising space. How well they do in the first market affects how well they do in the second over the long run. For firms in major regional markets such as New York and Washington, revenues accrue primarily from advertising and secondarily from circulation, both of which vary with the competitiveness of the news industry in a particular locale and with general economic conditions. Within these broad parameters, profits are a function of costs: the cost of producing the first copy of the day's paper, including the operation of the news and editorial departments and typesetting and composing; and the cost of printing and selling all additional copies, including newsprint, ink, distribution, and promotion. Since the cost of producing additional copies is relatively inflexible within a given level of technology, control of costs, and hence the management of earnings depends on the newspaper's control over the costs of producing the first copy.

Yet to analyze the newspaper as a profit-making enterprise by applying economists' models of the firm to its behavior seems less fruitful an explanation of news content than viewing economic factors as constraints on organizational behavior and as stakes of internal bargaining.

The News Business

Far more than in most business enterprises, the profit motive alone is an inadequate explanation for the behavior of the *Post* and the *Times*. These news organizations, like some large corporations, relegate profitability to the place of ultimate—and remote—test of success or failure. So long as revenues are sufficient to ensure organizational survival, professional and social objectives take precedence over profits, particularly for the management of firms like the *Post* and the *Times*, where a single family maintains financial control. Adolph Ochs, the patriarch of the *Times* publishing dynasty, was perhaps the best exemplar of this ethic in the news business. "The craftsman's intrinsic incentives rather than the extrinsic incentives of the entrepreneur were the important ones for Ochs," writes Paul Weaver. "The corporate interests of the *Times* therefore lay not so much in maximizing profits or power as in providing the security that the practice of pure craftsman-like journalism required."[4] Ochs' heirs have kept faith with his legacy. "If we did things differently," Mrs. Iphigene Ochs Sulzberger has said, "the paper might earn more money in the short run. But our way is the best in the long run. You know, we are not the sort of people who feel we must have yachts."[5] Profits do count, but enough is enough.

Both the *Times* and the *Post* usually make enough. The *Times* has consistently ranked among the leading newspapers in advertising linage, in part because of its circulation among the nation's elite, in part because of New York's role as the nation's cultural trend-setter. Charging the comparatively high rates it does, the *Times* has usually operated at a profit even in hard times. The *Post*'s domination of the Washington metropolitan market is the bedrock of its financial security. With a sizable lead in circulation over its afternoon rival, the *Star*, it has won the duel for advertising linage. In addition, diversification has helped to solidify the financial positions of both newspapers.

Diversification has also made profit figures hard to distill from those of the parent company, but rough approximations are available. In 1970 the *Post* had about $77 million in revenues, $64 million of it from advertisers. The $13 million it took in from readers was not worth the paper the *Post* was printed on—$20 million worth of wood pulp. From its total revenues, the *Post* took in about $9 million in operating income, or income before deductions for "other expenses," mostly interest payments. The Washington Post Company, which embraces not only the newspaper but also *Newsweek*, three television and two radio stations, and other subsidiaries, reported after-tax profits of $4.9 million on revenues of $178 million.[6]

That same year, the *Times* saw its advertising revenue shrink by $15 million to $159 million. Even with a small gain in circulation revenue, its total revenue came to $210 million in 1970, down $10 million from a record high the previous year. Operating income, in turn, fell to about $9 million from $17 million. The New York Times Company and its subsidiaries showed total revenues of $269 million and after-tax profits of $13.7 million.[7]

Both firms are nonetheless economically vulnerable. Underlying conditions contribute to vulnerability: the gradual dispersion of readers to the suburbs, with local merchants hard on their heels, raises the costs of distribution while reducing advertising revenue. "It is hard to imagine anything worse," a *Times* executive has said, "than a manufacturing operation which is supplied by almost a third of a million tons of raw materials every year shipped into the middle of a large metropolitan city, and which distributes its products to a market that is rushing away from the city like an exploding galaxy."[8] The *Times* in particular, must face competition for local advertising dollars not only from suburban newspapers, but also from magazines and broadcasting.

Temporary events lend this vulnerability a poignancy which longer run changes may not. The 116-day strike that hit the *Times* in 1962-63 put it in the red for the first time since 1895. The recession of 1970-71 cut deeply into the profits of both newspapers. Diversification of the parent companies has also hurt at times. Adding subsidiaries has not always improved the *Times'* profit picture. The *Post*'s broadcasting properties have left it open to challenges at license renewal time, threatening to run up sizable legal fees and stimulating a sharp drop in the price of its stock. It is in times of financial stringency that constraints on resources impinge most noticeably on newsmen: the profit motive matters most when profits are least.

Extra staff, space, and time always cost newspapers money, whatever their economic circumstances. Scarcity makes economizing necessary. At the *Times* and the *Post*, however, explicit comparison among alternative uses for resources is rare. Part of the reason for this lies in the difficulty of relating even gross changes in costs of newsgathering to marginal changes in revenue. Reader demand, and hence advertising revenue, do not appear particularly sensitive to changes in quality of national and foreign news coverage. The number of subscribers to *The New York Times* or *The Washington Post/Los Angeles Times* news service may respond somewhat more directly to qualitative changes, but not enough to affect revenue significantly.

For the most part, though, the lack of economic analysis is intrinsic to the budgetary procedures inside the two newspapers. Instead of formal decisions and systematic plans, the *Times* and *Post* allocate resources through decentralized choice-making and bargaining among organizational components. Each news desk, for instance, has its own budget for travel and other expenses, in effect, allowing editors to use their own discretion but imposing a ceiling on discretionary activity. Editors receive statements periodically monitoring the flow of expenditures. Hiring new staff, as well as other major outlays, requires the approval of the managing or executive editor and sometimes the publisher. In the absence of measures of cost-effectiveness, these outlays are the subject of negotiation and log-rolling among the desks.

Between the lack of conscious cost-benefit calculation and the difficulty of determining what the trade-offs are, economic explanations of newspaper behavior lose much of their force. If the cost of stationing a correspondent overseas, for example, runs about $55,000 a year, exclusive of communications costs,[9] and his presence there hardly registers in the revenue column, then the expansion of overseas staff may have a noneconomic explanation. At the *Times* and the *Post*, profit maximization provides no guidepost, only constraints.

Staff, Space, and Time:
The Stakes of Newspaper Politics

Whether or not to add personnel and where to locate them are far from the only hard choices posed by the constraint on staffing. Knowing that he lacks the manpower even to cover all of Washington, let alone the country, a national editor tries to assign most men to cover the key beats, relying on the wire services to fill in the gaps and to cue him in on the stories his men might overlook. Whenever he gets word of a story breaking elsewhere, he must decide whether to leave coverage up to the wire services or a stringer working for the newspaper part-time, or to dispatch an available staff man to the scene. He has little time to deliberate if his man is to arrive there in time to file a story the same day, and often he has only the sketchiest details on which to base his judgment.

In 1970, for instance, the *Post*'s national staff consisted of four reporters in bureaus scattered around the United States, twenty-six reporters in Washington mainly covering the federal establishment, and a nationwide network of stringers. It had little secretarial or research help: two news assistants were assigned to the desk to take messages, run errands, and check out occasional details. When the first reports of a shooting at Kent State clattered across the Associated Press wire on the afternoon of May 4, national editor Ben Bagdikian knew that one of his most experienced reporters, Haynes Johnson, was free to go to Ohio, but Johnson had just stepped out to lunch. The only national news reporter in the newsroom at the time was another veteran, Richard Harwood. Harwood was already working on a story, but he wanted to cover Kent State. Was the AP report accurate, they wondered. If so, AP had to have a man on the scene by now, and the *Post* had a reliable stringer in Cleveland capable of covering the story. Bagdikian might need Harwood in Washington: the Cambodian invasion was just under way and the capital was full of speculation about it. Fragmentary reports of student unrest were coming in from around the country. Would Kent State prove unique? Harwood felt it would and pressed Bagdikian to let him go. The next plane to Cleveland did not leave for two hours, and by that time the AP had a preliminary report that some students had been killed at Kent State. That persuaded Bagdikian; both Harwood and Johnson would go, one to concentrate on tomorrow's story and the other to begin piecing together the background for a longer story the following day. The *Times*, meanwhile, was more fortunate. One of its reporters, John Kifner, happened to be on the Kent State campus compiling a story on campus unrest and witnessed the shootings. His dispatch won a Pulitzer Prize.

Newspapers seldom have enough reporters to go around. Adding a few men to the staff can facilitate more thorough coverage of fast-breaking events, but a larger staff only poses the customary dilemma in a new way. Should the editor send his best reporters out to cover a routine story or hold them in the newsroom in the event that a more significant story should come along? How many reporters should he relieve from spot news coverage to work on in-depth stories? Under conditions of scarcity, staff location becomes crucial.

Staff is one economic constraint; space, another. In order to show a profit, newspapers over time must devote a certain proportion of space to advertising. Moreover, the mechanics of production makes it efficient to add to or subtract from the overall size of the newspaper in units of four pages. In the case of the *Times*, the capacity of the presses ordinarily limits the size of the daily editions to 96 pages. Within these parameters, there is some room for maneuver, but not much.

From time to time, rising costs force management to reduce the ratio of news to advertising. Page one fortunately has not shrunk, but the possibility of freeing space elsewhere in the paper for full-page display of stories, perhaps by printing the paper in four sections instead of two, as the *Times* does on occasion, is usually limited by the need to run enough advertisements to cover costs. Even when editors displace ads with important or late-breaking news, as they can at the *Times* and the *Post*, the ads removed seldom entail a loss of revenue, only a contraction of news space on the day that they eventually run.

Space has always been at a premium in newspapers. Until the 1920s, *Times* reporters were paid, like today's stringers, by the number of words they got into the paper. This gave them an incentive to pad their stories with details. "All the news that fits it prints," became the byword if not the motto of *Times*men. Newsmen still compete for scarce space. For reporters, making page one is a primary motivation in newsgathering. For editors, increasing their share of the newshole is a daily preoccupation. It comes as little surprise, then, that newsmen at the *Times* would begrudge a decision to turn over nearly eight full columns to the editorial department for an "Op Ed" page devoted to opinions by *Times* columnists and outside contributors; the news department's loss is editorial's gain. It also takes space to be a newspaper of record: pages must be freed in order to print the texts of addresses, reports, and news conferences. As news space contracts, it is harder to make room for such documents.

The constraints on space are most keenly felt on page one. It is a belief widely shared among newspapermen that few readers ever have the time to read stories on the inside pages. Apart from this belief, there is a mystique about getting a byline on page one that has long motivated men in the trade. As a sign of its importance, *Times* reporters overseas, who might have to wait several days before seeing today's paper, receive a telegram informing them about the placement of their stories in the first edition. Known as a "fronting cable," it lists the two lead stories; all other stories "fronted," or placed on page one; the rest of the foreign desk's stories "insided," or relegated to the inside pages; and those held over for the next day.[10]

Yet the number of stories that page one can accommodate on any given day is limited. In 1970, it ranged from 8 to 16 on the *Times* with a median of 12, and from 6 to 13 on the *Post* with a median of only 9. The small number of slots for stories on page one sharpens the competition to get on it.

Time, too, is an economic constraint on newsmaking. To distribute news-papers throughout a metropolitan area and beyond means putting delivery trucks on the road and meeting trains on schedule. Newsgathering, editing, and production must be completed on time or distribution—and eventually circulation—will suffer. The composing room needs a steady flow of copy throughout the day to avoid evening bottlenecks, and deadlines are set accordingly. Still, disputes over allocation of time between the news and production departments break out intermittently: every extra minute it takes to set type, lock up pages, and cast page plates leaves less time for filing stories and editing them.

The extensive monitoring of staff, space, and time provides some indication of their importance as constraints inside newspapers. Every day, a schedule of reporter's locations, their story assignments, and their progress on longer projects is updated and circulated at the desks. Every day, the desks receive a space budget and records of the previous day's allowances, the space actually filled, and the copy set in type but not used for lack of space. Every day, too, the desks get reports of the number of column inches sent to the composing room after copy deadlines and of the penalty costs assessed for late copy. These records lend the constraints of staff, space, and time a quantifiable hardness otherwise uncommon to newsmaking.

Staff, space, and time constitute at once measures of performance and stakes of bargaining for the men inside news organizations. By a process of goal displacement characteristic of many large-scale bureaucracies, a rule or index of performance devised initially as a means of attaining the goals of the organization in the end supplants those goals.[11] Just as the desire to maximize a share of the budget or the number of subordinates motivates many officials in government agencies, so, too, the desire to maximize the share of available space and the length and play of stories, while minimizing penalties for missing deadlines, comes to impel newsmen in their daily endeavors.

Formal Hierarchy and Action Channels

Besides setting constraints, the organization of newspapers superimposes a formal hierarchy of authority on relations among newsmen. Atop the hierarchy at both the *Times* and the *Post* sits the publisher, formally responsible to a board of directors of the parent company on which he serves. Beneath him are the managing editor and the editorial page editor, formally in charge of the news and editorial sections respectively, and the men supervising advertising, production, circulation, and business matters. At the *Post* all these men report to an executive editor, Benjamin Bradlee. At the *Times* a vice president, James Reston, and the Sunday editor have a somewhat ambiguous but roughly co-equal relationship to the managing editor and the editorial page editor. Responsible, in turn, to the managing editor are a night editor, who oversees headline-writing and makeup and takes over from the managing editor in the evening, and various editors in charge of the news desks—national, foreign, metropolitan, financial, sports, and culture (or "style" as it is known at the *Post*). Below them are assistant news editors and copy editors on the desks and reporters in the field.

The formal hierarchy, however, does not necessarily correspond to the distribution of influence over news content at either the *Times* or the *Post*. In a book on the *Times* entitled *The Kingdom and the Power*, a former *Times* reporter, Gay Talese, characteristically discovers neither "kingdom" nor "power" there. Instead of a kingdom, there are only feudal domains; instead of power, never-ending struggle:

The *Times*, with Ochs dead, soon became splintered into several small office empires, little dukedoms, with each duke having his loyal followers and special territory to protect. . . . [T]hey competed with one another in an amazing variety of ways, often influencing how a news story was covered, who covered it, how much space it was allotted, where it appeared in the paper . . . .[12]

When it comes to specifying the links between internal hierarchy and influence over news choices, Talese finds himself perplexed:

High power at the *Times* is a vaporous element—energy is harnessed, pressure is built, decisions emanate from a corporate collective, but it is difficult to see which man did what, and it often seems that nobody really did anything. Decisions appear to ooze out of a large clutch of executive bodies all jammed together, leaning against one another, shifting, sidling, shrugging, bending backwards, sideways, and finally tending toward some tentative direction; but whose muscles were flexed? whose weight was decisively felt? The reporters in the newsroom do not know.[13]

Why are the men who shape news content so hard to pinpoint? Coordinating the vast amount of activity necessary to put out a daily newspaper under pressure of deadlines requires a division of labor and specialization of function. A necessary concomitant is decentralization of control.

Nevertheless, action in any organization does not occur at random. Cable traffic inside the State Department passes along certain prescribed routes intersecting with particular officials, those with a "need to know." Budget preparation within government departments involves some officials and not others at each point along the route. These procedural paths for producing outcomes are called *action channels*. News organizations have action channels, too. Hierarchical lines of communication form some of the channels; so, too, do the preestablished routes along which news copy flows inside newspapers. Together, they determine who is in a position to make choices and who can intervene to reverse them, who must sit in on decisions and who may get involved if he wishes.

Reporters and editors do not work for the *Post* or the *Times*; they work for the national, foreign, or metropolitan desk. The national editor and his subordinates on that desk supervise the everyday work of reporters in bureaus around the country and on beats throughout the federal government. The foreign desk does the same for bureaus overseas and at the United Nations; the metropolitcan desk, for local coverage. In the course of newsgathering and writing, reporters continually consult with the desk. Manning each desk are a day editor and a night editor; a handful of assignment or originating editors who suggest ideas for stories, information to include, and angles to play; and roughly six copy editors.

Assigning Stories

Some ideas for stories filter down to the desks from the top of the newspaper hierarchy and from elsewhere in the news and editorial departments. Others emerge from periodic story conferences mapping longer-run strategies for covering news. The vast majority originate in the course of daily conversations among reporters and between reporters and the desk.

For the man on a beat, following up yesterday's news and attending to the routine flow of information through press releases and press conferences circumscribe his choice of stories to pursue. Usually he can tell the desk what he intends to cover, then go off and do it. In the course of the day, news editors may call him with queries that come into the newsroom from other beats, bureaus, and news organizations.

Editors have greater say over men on general assignment. Reporters not stationed on beats are available for deployment to cover events elsewhere or to help out on an especially busy beat, and occasionally to spell beat correspondents from the drudgery of spot news coverage so that they can research an in-depth feature.

While keeping up with spot news, reporters may be engaged in researching and writing as many as two or three lengthier articles. The ideas for these features are mainly self-generated, but the scope and details of each are worked out in concert with the desk. Lists of work in progress keep editors and other reporters abreast of the features under way. Yet the pressure of putting out a daily newspaper leaves little time to develop topics for features, to map out strategies for future coverage, to anticipate upcoming events—in short, to make the plans that are essential for in-depth reportage and assessment of social trends.

The *Times* has instituted two procedures to facilitate planning. The first is one James Reston initiated when he took over as executive editor in 1968. He convened a daily conference at 11:30 in the morning which brought together the managing editor, the assistant managing editor, and the national, foreign, metropolitan, and picture editors to exchange ideas on stories worth exploring. The 11:30 conference has had a fitful existence since its inception. The second procedure was adopted by Max Frankel after he became Washington bureau chief. He formed two clusters, one among the four reporters in the bureau covering urban affairs, another among the half dozen dealing with national security. The clusters institutionalize the informal note-trading found in the *Post* newsroom. They meet from time to time in order to plot coordination of coverage, arranging for some reporters in the bureau to keep up with spot news and freeing others to work on features.

Gathering News

Information-gathering is largely left to a reporter's own initiative. Editors occasionally telephone or cable suggestions to men on the beat or pass on leads picked up elsewhere. They monitor the wire services constantly throughout the day and feed reporters incoming information to incorporate in their stories or to pursue with their sources on the beat.

Autonomy for reporters in newsgathering extends so far that editors may not even know the identity of the sources their own reporters are relying on—and may even refrain from asking for specifics.

When deadlines and location permit, reporters do their writing in the newsroom, giving editors an opportunity to discuss a story before it is set down on paper, to suggest new angles to play and sources to tap. Reporters in foreign and domestic bureaus outside of Washington interact at a distance with editors back in the home office. The necessity of communicating long distance by cable or telephone leaves reporters freer of newsroom influences, yet more at the mercy of editors handling copy under pressure of deadlines. The same applies somewhat for men covering the Pentagon, where workdays begin early in the morning and editors are a twenty-minute taxi ride away.

Editing Copy

Once the reporter has transcribed the news into a dispatch and filed it, editors at the desk read it over both for questions of substance and for an assessment of its importance relative to other stories. The dispatch then passes to the copy editors, who examine it for style, grammar, and emphasis, as well as for any errors of fact or infractions of libel law they can detect. They cut the dispatch to fit the space available. They also "neutralize" explicit value judgments in the copy, toning down the affect-laden vocabulary, excising any adjectives with pejorative or approbative connotations.

A large volume of copy flows quickly across the desks, surging as the deadline approaches. Sometimes, the national or foreign editor will pore over a story himself, rewriting it, verifying information, cutting some details, adding others. Shortage of time precludes his scrutiny of all the stories that cross the desk. He may look at the stories he intends to recommend for page one; but he confines his editing to the few stories that catch his attention or arouse his suspicions, especially those stories resulting from leaks. Stories scheduled to receive prominent play or expected to arouse bitter controversy may get yet another reading from the managing editor or the executive editor. The rest are left to subordinates on the desk, occasionally whomever the reporter chooses to hand the story to as he completes it.

On the copy desks, the chief copy editor or "slot man" hands available editors the stories as they come from the news desks. He tries to keep special interests and knowledge in mind as he distributes the stories, but the pressure of time often interferes. Any substantive questions on content the copy editors take up with editors at the desk, who in turn may consult the reporter if he is accessible and if time is available.

Relations on the desk are informal, though not unstructured. They are based largely on shared expectations. The national or foreign editor lets his desk men and copy editors handle the editing, occasionally voicing objections or making changes to facilitate their gradual adjustment to his own preferences. The relationship depends on the editor's trust in the judgment of his subordinates; their mutual adjustment is never complete.

The flow of copy along the desks, the action channels for editing, allow considerable leeway for subordinates to choose what makes the news. The national or foreign editor may intervene; so, too, may the managing or executive editor. But most of the time they are too busy with other tasks to monitor more than a small sample of copy. Although they can get involved whenever they want, they do so mostly in the event of disagreements among their subordinates.

When a story does not fit a desk man's expectations, he may try to alter it. Peremptory changes in copy are the exception rather than the rule, however. Reporters resent them as direct affronts to their professional judgment. Instead of fueling their resentment and exacerbating future dealings with them, the experienced desk man tries whenever possible to contact them on substantive disagreements. Distance aggravates the problem, however. So do deadlines. When reporters are inaccessible and stories cannot wait, the practice is to edit first and apologize later.

'Killing' Stories

Editing copy is less effective in shaping the content of the stories reporters file than "killing" them—withholding publication altogether. Control over writing, the phraseology and metaphor of a story rather than the precise wording, is a jealously guarded reportorial prerogative. Free-handed blue-pencilling, desk men find, only breeds discontent without modifying behavior among reporters at the *Times* and the *Post*. The choice of stories for publication, on the other hand, reporters do regard as a legitimate function of the editor. However strenuous their objections, they gradually adjust themselves to his preferences, and he to theirs, mainly in bargaining over inclusion or exclusion, not phraseology.

Bureaucratic Layering

Geography complicates action channels at the *Times* by adding a bureaucratic layer between the national desk and the Washington bureau. The national desk in New York has a smaller equivalent in Washington under the aegis of the bureau chief. His deputy, who supervises the operation of the desk there, must coordinate the hour-by-hour editing by telephone with his New York counterpart, the deputy national editor. A similar intervening layer of editors for foreign news is set up in London.

In the case of national news, the intervening layer at the *Times* insulates the national desk in New York somewhat from the pressure of reporters covering Washington. This insulation probably gives rise to newsmen's perceptions of the *Times* as an "editor's paper," in contrast to the *Post*, which is seen as a "reporter's paper." When reporters work in the newsroom, as most Washington correspondents at the *Post* do, they can follow their story as it is edited, and even read the galley proofs or the first edition. They can then take their grievances directly to the offending editor. For their own part, editors find it desirable, if not essential, to raise any objections with the reporter face to face. New York is too remote to allow this feedback at the *Times*. Distance can preserve the anonymity of the desk men at the home office. Editorial changes are usually faits accomplis; complaints can be registered only after the reporter sees the next morning's edition. Instead of the face-to-face airing of disagreement at the *Post*, a reporter's complaint at the *Times* must pass through channels, sometimes in writing, from the bureau chief or his deputy in Washington to the national editor or his deputy in New York, then down to the man on the national or copy desk, losing much of its steam in the process.

Some *Times* veterans become inured to the treatment of their copy at the hands of editors. On March 29, 1972, Homer Bigart filed a dispatch on the conviction of Lieutenant William Calley. It contained a contrast to another court martial Bigart had covered previously:

Although he had just been found guilty of 22 murders, Calley was treated far more gently than was Army doctor Captain Howard B. Levy four years ago after receiving a sentence for refusing to give medical training to Green Berets on the grounds that the training would be used unlawfully in Vietnam.

Unlike Levy, Calley was not handcuffed and left the court unfettered. An officer explained: "His conduct has been exemplary throughout and he'll continue to be treated as an officer."

By the time the desk finished revising it, the passage read, "Lieutenant Calley was not handcuffed when driven to the stockade." Bigart, about to retire after forty-five years as a reporter, seventeen of them on the *Times*, shrugged off the desk's handling of his dispatch: "I never read my stories in the paper any more. It's a safe way to avoid ulcers. You can't win. You finally come to the point where you either have to take it or quit. People have tried to fight back, but they get nowhere. You can't beat a newspaper bureaucracy any more than you can beat any other kind of bureaucracy."[14]

For the reporter based in a bureau outside the home office, the telephone and the telegraph cannot adequately compensate for face-to-face discussion with editors about stories. A difference in time zones occasionally allows editors to "fire off a rocket" to an overseas correspondent questioning his dispatch and receive a return cable in time to incorporate clarifications into tomorrow's story. Correspondents in most overseas bureaus do not even get to see the paper until days after their stories run. Instead, the foreign desk sends out a "fronting" cable notifying them of the fate of their stories. This helps reporters to file their next story, but it does not undo what has been done to their last. Usually, reporters away from the home office have little recourse but to complain after the fact; the fate of their stories lies in the hands of men on a far-off desk.

The Division of Labor
and Organizational Conflict

As the first reader who can choose whether or not a story will appear in print, the national or foreign editor becomes a crucial audience for the reporter within the news organization. Once he accepts a story, the editor is expected to be its defender, protecting it against the depradations of the copy desk and advocating it for favorable play in conferences with other editors during the afternoon. Failing to fulfill this obligation can undermine his standing among his reporters. The man in charge of the desk thus occupies a pivotal position in the newspaper, having to accommodate to the demands of the other editors while keeping his own staff happy. To do his job effectively, he cannot simply execute the policy preferences of his superiors, the managing editor, the executive editor, and ultimately the publisher, unless he also acts as a bulwark against constant intervention from above in the activities of his staff. Mediation is built into his role.

The bureaucratic demands on the national or foreign editor and their effect on his behavior represent another consequence of the organization of newspapers. More than determining who gets involved in making news choices and decisions, position in the organization affects the choices newsmen are inclined to make and the stands they are likely to take.

The difference in perspective between the desk and the reporter, for instance, are built into the operation of the newspaper. The man on the desk, in reading wire service reports and stories in the evening papers, in chatting with others in the newsroom, with his own news sources, and with reporters on other beats, shapes his expectations of the dispatch that his man on the beat will file. Editors stress their vantage point as intelligent lay readers somewhat removed from, and hence independent of, the beat. One self-proclaimed "unrepentent deskman" at the *Times* expressed it this way:

I suspect that many daily failures of the press—particularly stories that go galloping after trivia—happen because deskmen forget their obligation to maintain an independent viewpoint. . . . A deskman should be equipped for this because (a) he is a generalist, while the reporter may be a specialist, and (b) he is removed from the physicial circumstances of a story, while the reporter may be wading in it hip deep.[15]

The man on the beat has a different vantage point, however. As a correspondent once put it,

You're the man on the scene and you have to call your own shots. In most cases the editor suffers from overreading. He reads too many other stories. . . . He gets preconceptions. The clever reporter used to be the one that satisfied his editor's preconceptions. But it doesn't work that way any more. The competent reporter is now the man who satisfies his editor's urge to know, and the only way to do that is to write stories that answer questions and explain situations for your own mind.[16]

Desk men in the past usually had limited experience as reporters, but even rotating newsmen between the desk and the beat, while it may increase empathy between reporters and editors, does not eliminate the difference in perspective.

Perspectives also vary from beat to beat, from desk to desk, and from bureau to bureau. To the metropolitan editor, a scandal in the mayor's office has the makings of a right-hand lead while the outbreak of civil war in East Bengal may seem like a quarrel in a far-away country between people of whom he knows nothing. After moving from the Washington bureau to the home office in New York, Turner Catledge of the *Times* saw himself as a "reformed sinner":

I could remember vividly my frequent outrages when the New York office dared touch my copy or question, no matter how indirectly or slightly, my "superior" knowledge of Washington or the national scene. Once I got to New York, however, I could see how often my reactions had been mistaken, and sometimes downright silly.[17]

In newspapers, as in government bureaucracies, position helps to define the priorities a man has and the faces of issues he sees. Whether a bureaucrat is a Republican or a Democrat, a liberal or a conservative, a hawk or a dove, may affect the stands he takes on most issues less than whether he is Secretary of Defense or Labor, the national editor of a newspaper, or its London bureau chief. In the words of Rufus Miles, "Where you stand depends on where you sit."[18]

In a broader sense, the division of labor within newspapers forms the lines of cleavage along which organizational conflict crystallizes. At the *Times*, for instance, the metropolitan desk's geographic jurisdiction extends throughout New Jersey, in southern New York as far north as Albany, and in the bedroom suburbs of Connecticut as far east as New Haven; at the *Post*, metropolitan's jurisdiction includes the Virginia and Maryland state houses as well as the suburbs of Washington. The national desks take over beyond those points. The foreign desks cover stories originating overseas and at the United Nations, as well as some news emanating from the State Department, but none from the Department of Defense.

Events, however, do not confine themselves to the geographic or beat boundaries drawn by the organization. As a result, the desks often squabble over assignments. During the Kennedy Administration, the Kennedy family's activities fell under the jurisdiction of the national desk at the *Times*, but after the President's assassination, when his wife and brother began shuttling between Washington and New York, the question of whether the national or metropolitan desk had the right to cover them touched off sporadic disputes. Similarly, in 1965, when David Broder, then based in Washington as a national political correspondent for the *Times*, sought to cover a speech by President Johnson in Princeton, the metropolitan desk succeeded in stymying his plans by insisting that Princeton was part of its territory.[19] Broder and the national desk, more attuned to the nuances of political debate inside Washington if not elsewhere in the country, might have produced a story somewhat different from the one written and edited by metropolitan's personnel.

Boundary wars inside the two newspapers seldom reach a truce. When the President delivers an address on U.S. foreign policy, is it national news to be assigned and edited by the national desk or foreign news to be handled on the foreign desk? If he gives the speech in New York, who should cover the story, someone on the metropolitan staff, or the national desk's White House correspondent accompanying the President on his travels, or the foreign desk's U.N. correspondent? To a degree, the outcome depends on how much play the story is likely to get. Page-one news calls for a fight; less important but nonetheless time-consuming stories get fobbed off to other desks. Precedent also counts: once a desk takes charge of a story, it may exercise proprietary rights in the future, rights which the other desks may seek to deny it at the outset.

Not only the news desks compete in newsgathering. The news department has competition elsewhere within the *Times*. The editorial department has been known to "scoop" the news department, seeking out newsworthy items for its own pages. The Sunday department, which puts out the Sunday magazines and the "News of the Week," bids for the services of reporters in the news department to contribute articles. The inducements it can offer are more than pecuniary; reporters can use the flexibility of the magazine and news analysis formats to insert material that might not get onto the regular new pages. They often save interesting tidbits for the Sunday sections, a matter of some annoyance to news department editors.

Organizational politics affects the choice of who should cover stories in other ways. The *Post* and the *Times* each subscribe to a number of wire services, including Associated Press, United Press International, Dow-Jones, Reuters, and the new services of the *Los Angeles Times, Chicago Daily News, Sunday Times* (London), and *Chicago Tribune/New York Daily News.* On the AP's "A" wire alone, stories clatter across the teletypewriter at a rate of 45 words a minute, 3,000 words an hour, around the clock.[20] Yet wire service stories rarely make page one at either newspaper. Faced with the alternative of using a story off the wires or one filed by a man on their own staff, editors opt for the staff man's version, even if it seems less readable or thorough, and then edit it with the wire service copy in mind. Partly it is a matter of confidence: they know their own man better and place more trust in the reliability of his reporting. One *Times* editor explains his reliance on his own staff: "We try to hire people who bring an extra dimension into their reporting of the news, and that dimension is superior understanding."[21] Partly, though, office politics comes into play. Choosing wire service accounts costs his reporters page-one bylines, which may lower staff morale. The choice may also prove difficult to justify to superiors; why should they pay a man to cover the story if the wire service can do a better job?

Some reporters want to work only on longer in-depth stories, others are content with covering spot news, and nearly all resent doing legwork for someone else's bylines. These considerations weigh on editors trying to make assignments. Young reporters on assignment for the metropolitan desk at both newspapers, for instance, desire few things more than the opportunity to write for the national or foreign desk. At the *Post*, the more aggressive of them will approach these desks with story ideas from time to time, usually to meet with polite refusal. The editors, again, have their own staffs to think of: if one of their reporters sees a man on the metropolitan desk getting an assignment while he has nothing to do, he will need placating. Even when everyone on the desk is busy, borrowing a reporter from metropolitan can arouse jealousy and produce morale problems for the editor there.

Compromise among contending organizational parts is a critical element in news coverage. Following the invasion of Cambodia and the killing of four students at Kent State in May 1970, the *Post* mapped out a strategy for covering an antiwar rally expected for the weekend of May 9-10. For two days the national and metropolitan staffs quarrelled intermittently over who would take charge of the coverage. For the Moratorium rally in Washington the previous

November, an ad hoc arrangement had allowed each desk to make its own assignments and to handle its own copy, but had put an assistant managing editor in charge of coordinating staffing and coverage. National editor Ben Bagdikian now argued for maintaining this arrangement on grounds of autonomy since each editor knew the capacities of his own staff best. Metropolitan editor Harry Rosenfeld proposed instead that his desk handle the coverage with the help of some reporters on loan from the national desk and edit the copy as well. Managing editor Eugene Patterson at first backed Bagdikian, then reversed himself. Metropolitan's staff was larger than national's but less experienced, and some of the young reporters might be more sympathetic to the protesters than their older colleagues on the national staff. Moreover, the police radio, which would help editors stay abreast of events, was located on the metropolitan desk.

Yet Patterson's decision did not rest on the logistics of coverage or on its possible slant: "The national staff is number one on this paper, everyone knows, and this was necessary for Harry's morale."[22] Bagdikian appealed the decision to executive editor Benjamin Bradlee on grounds of territoriality: "The capital is in Washington—how is that a metropolitan story?" All he gained from Bradlee, however, was the assurance that the decision did not constitute a precedent for the future. As a sop to Bagdikian, Patterson later assigned a member of the national staff to write Sunday's right-hand lead wrapping up the events of the weekend. When Bagdikian proposed that Haynes Johnson do an article on the mood of the demonstration, though, Rosenfeld objected. He wanted his own staff to write this story, but Bradlee overruled him: "We've got the best goddamn mood reporter in the country—we've got to send him out." All three front-page stories on the demonstration were eventually assigned to national staff members, but there were still complaints about working for metropolitan.

Besides the assignment of personnel, newsmen bargain out the allocation of space in the next day's paper along bureaucratic lines. At the *Times*, the man who shuffles requests for space from the desks is the news editor; at the *Post*, the managing editor. By early afternoon, each of the desks has drawn up a news budget roughly estimating the number of columns of news it expects to send to the composing room that day. On the basis of these budgets, the news editor at the *Times* and his counterpart at the *Post* give the advertising department an estimate of the total news hole that day. The advertising director, meanwhile, has prepared his own estimate of the total columns of ad copy on hand. Ideally the two figures should add up to a multiple of thirty-two, the number of columns in a four-page unit. Ideally, too, the mix of advertising and news should fall within the profit-yielding range. It rarely works out that way. Keeping in mind the formulas that relate the volume of advertising to the size of the newspaper, the news editor begins consultation with the desks to pare down their requests for space. By 3 p.m. he must fix the overall size of the next day's paper; thereafter, any expansion of the newshole comes at the expense of advertising. While taking into account events of unusual newsworthiness, in practice he bases his decision on a few rules of thumb, depending on the day of the week, the season of the year, and the editors' estimates. While the decision rules help him to act amid uncertainty, the actual flow of news may vary much more than his rules of thumb allow, leaving considerable room for chance to determine whether or not a marginal story will get into the paper that day.

At 4 p.m., the managing editor allocates the newshole among the competing desks. A round of negotiations ensues. Editors, who customarily overstate their needs in their preliminary requests, now begin to adjust. The desks trade space among one another, palm off some stories to other desks with available space, eliminate other stories altogether, and appeal to the news editor for a larger share of space. If they cannot strike a bargain, then they sometimes take their case to a higher court—the managing editor at the *Times* and the executive editor at the *Post*—to trim advertising space or expand the paper. Finally, the desks are forced to reallocate space among their stories, killing some and cutting others, in order to come in under the limit. By this time, the copy has begun flowing across the desks, providing one last chance to cut down or fill out stories to meet the constraint of space.

The rules of makeup adhered to at the *Times*, and less stringently at the *Post*, forbid "jumping" stories from page to page inside the paper. This rule forces editors to negotiate with the news editor in order to open up space for stories with extensive text, photographs, or charts. Often the managing editor's intercession is necessary to get the advertising department to rearrange its makeup to accommodate such stories. His involvement places another hurdle in the way of lengthier articles, in that he will often insist on reading and editing them as the price of fitting them into the paper. Sometimes, editors can sidestep this hurdle by negotiating with other desks for extra space or holding a story for a lighter news day, but often he will put pressure on his staff to keep stories short instead.

Some stories that appear in earlier editions will be killed later in the evening as new material comes in, putting renewed pressure on available space. In addition, copy squeezed out of the city edition under pressure of time may have to be reinserted. The news editor's task includes accommodating conflicting space requirements for later editions. He takes charge of the paper when the managing editor leaves. Each of the desks, too, has a night editor who comes to work about 4 p.m. and stays until the paper goes to bed, around midnight. Relationships among the desks and between the news editor and the editors on the night shift are not unlike those during the day. Yet coordination is essential to avoid stark contrasts between night and day in the newsroom. It requires briefings for the men taking over in the evening and late-night communications in the event of unforeseen difficulties. In the end, just as among various editors on the desk, mutual adjustment between the "day side" and the "night side" is never complete.

Time, too, becomes a stake in bargaining along bureaucratic lines. Distribution schedules and the speed of printing presses impose an inflexible deadline on the activities that precede rolling the presses. The time available for transcription and production of news up to that point, however, is subject to negotiation within and between the newsroom and the composing room. Reporters and editors, typesetters and printers engage in sporadic battles to relieve the pressure of time at each other's expense. Editors exhort their staffs every night to turn in their copy early; reporters hold out, waiting for last-minute developments. Production managers bemoan the torrent of copy around deadline time, and managing editors berate their subordinates for it. Attempts to move copy deadlines back meet with union resistance in the shop. Managerial speed-ups in the composing room only bring worker slowdowns, and occasionally, wildcat strikes. Negotiations usually end in stalemate and in accommodation to existing deadlines.

The bargaining over deadlines affects news content. As distribution schedules have forced deadlines up, reporters have had less time for newsgathering. If a story breaks in Washington around 4 p.m., reporters lack the time to sample reaction around the capital. The next day's paper will thus tend to reflect the views of the source putting out the original information more than the views of his opponents.

Choices of how to allocate scarce resources at the *Times* and *Post* are important determinants of news content. Politics affect these choices, but they are often less the personal politics of individual newsmen than the internal politics of the organization.

Bureaucratic Politics and Page-One Makeup

During the early evenings, after the stories had been turned in and were being edited or set in type, [Abe] Rosenthal and [Arthur] Gelb would wait for the layout sheets that would show which stories had been selected by the bullpen for page one, and if there were five or more by the New York staff, Rosenthal and Gelb would leave the office in a triumphant mood. Once when Rosenthal had left the office before seeing the layouts, he telephoned a subordinate editor and was told five stories had made it. But moments after Rosenthal had hung up, the subordinate editor received a revised layout showing that two New York stories had been replaced by late-breaking stories from out of town. The editor, upset, walked over to the bullpen carrying the revised layout and said, "Look, I already told Abe we had *five* stories on page one."

"Well," one bullpen editor replied casually, "you now have three."

"Yes," the New York man said quickly, "and what's Abe going to say about *that*?"

"You mean Abe is going to get mad at *you*?"

"Well," the New York man said tentatively, "you know Abe."[23]

Talese's description of the importance that Rosenthal and Gelb attached to putting stories on page one when they first took over the *Times* metropolitan desk in 1963 typifies the newsman's concern with that page. Whenever a new man takes over at one of the desks, it is a time of testing. One measure of his skill and will, crucial in the eyes of his staff and colleagues sizing him up, is his ability to maintain or enlarge his desk's share of page-one space. This was the case at the *Post*. When Harry Rosenfeld first assumed the position of metropolitan editor in 1969, he lobbied vigorously for page-one recognition for his staff's reporting. His actions produced reactions in kind from national editor Ben Bagdikian and foreign editor John Anderson, who were hardly content to lose ground and face to the upstarts on the metropolitan desk, and who were quick to point out that the metropolitan desk had its own section of the paper complete with a full display page set aside exclusively for its own use every day.

Page one is the newspaper's showplace. Its primacy is rooted in the reading habits of the public as well as enshrined in the folklore of the Fourth Estate. Not just editors but every newsman takes satisfaction in making page one. Every afternoon some hover nearby as the news editor draws up the "dummy," or layout sheet, for the page. Once he has finished and the managing editor nods his assent, word of story placement circulates rapidly throughout the newsroom. The news service wires transmit the word to other bureaus as well as to subscribing news organizations across the nation, listing the stories that made the right- and left-hand leads and those elsewhere on page one. A cable goes out later from the foreign desk informing reporters abroad of the placement of their stories.

The keenness of competition for page one matches the concern of newsmen with it. The nature of that competition reflects the bureaucratic politics of the organization with lines of cleavage crystallizing along the division of labor. Page-one makeup is perhaps the clearest illustration available of the impact that organizational politics has on news content.

The choice of stories for page one is the product of group decision. That decision proceeds along two action channels, the mid-afternoon story conference and the early evening makeup conference.

The Story Conference

Post editors hold their story conference around 3 p.m.; *Times* editors have theirs an hour later. The format and agenda at each are basically the same. The publisher or executive editor may watch from the sidelines, but the managing editor chairs the meeting. In attendance are representatives of the various desks, often the editor in charge accompanied by his deputy, sometimes one or the other, along with the news editor, who must implement any decisions upon the managing editor's departure for the night. The circulation, promotion, and wire service directors all sit in to familiarize themselves with any particular problems that might affect their areas of responsibility—a story of special concern in one suburb warranting extra deliveries to newsstands there, a feature worth highlighting in radio commercials to boost street sales, an exclusive requiring special transmission by the news service to keep it out of the hands of competitors.

The managing editor calls on the national, foreign, and metropolitan editors to describe in brief the most important stories their desks will have for tomorrow's paper. The financial, culture, or even the sports editor may also offer a story or two from his desk as worthy of page-one play. As each editor runs down his list, the others comment on the substance of the stories and raise issues of newsgathering and makeup, suggesting new angles to check in writing the story and possible links to take into account in making up the paper. The managing editor then makes his selections for page one, relying almost exclusively upon the editors' lists, but once in a while glancing at the news budgets drawn up by the desks and asking editors about a story they did not mention. Discussion follows, some of it heated, as editors try to change his mind. The meeting breaks up after fifteen or twenty minutes, but the fight over page one may rage throughout the rest of the afternoon.

At the time of the story conference, editors may have only the sketchiest notion of what their stories will contain, sometimes little more than the one-word "slug" used to keep track of them as they are processed. The *Times* has tried to meet this problem of uncertainty by requiring reporters to file summaries of their stories by 3 p.m. The summaries provide some basis for evaluating the newsworthiness of stories and the "hardness" or verifiability of the information they contain. They also prevent newsmen from slipping stories onto page one unnoticed. While the summaries do give *Times* editors something to go on, more often than not stories change as reporters gather additional information and sit down to write. Knowing that the summaries become talking points for editors trying to make the case for page-one play, however, reporters may promise more than they can deliver, and their editors may play along more or less unwittingly.

The Makeup Conference

At 6 p.m. at the *Post*, 5:30 at the *Times*, editors regroup briefly to take another look at page one. This gathering is much more exclusive than the earlier one: the managing editor, the news editor, the picture editor, and representatives of each of the three major desks usually attend. By now the news editor may have drafted a tentative makeup based on the managing editor's earlier decision. By now, too, editors know what stories to expect that evening. Any story that develops later will have to wait another day unless it is of obvious importance. Editors have some stories in hand; others, they have discussed with their staff. The additional information makes choices somewhat easier, but editors are still obliged to defend the interests of their staffs by trying to undo the decisions of the story conference.

But the scope of negotiations has narrowed. Whereas an editor may have offered six or seven stories for page one earlier in the afternoon, he must now confine himself to advocating one or two additional stories for page one. Coalitions may form between one editor satisfied with the status quo and another fearful that one of his desk's stories may be supplanted. The managing editor may resort to the tactic of having editors choose between a story they have already placed on page one and another they are now pushing.

After five or ten minutes, the managing editor makes his decision. He may solicit the views of other editors on the candidates for right- and left-hand lead. He then lists his selections for page one and instructs the news editor on which stories to place in the leads, leaving him free to distribute the rest on the page and all other stories inside the paper. At the *Post*, which has fewer slots on page one than the *Times* because of differences in makeup style, the managing editor may resort to the use of "mutt boxes," one- or two-sentence capsules that guide readers to a story inside, thereby, in effect, increasing the slots on page one. Still, editors may continue to press for a reversal, but by now, copy is inundating the desks and they have other work to do.

Within a half hour the news editor has drawn up the page-one dummy and obtained approval for it from the managing editor. Duplicates of the dummy are distributed to the desks, and a list sent out to domestic bureaus over the news service wires. The Washington bureau chief at the *Times* may yet telephone New York to request the replacement of one of his bureau's stories by another, and the national desk and managing editor may agree to the change. At last, the battle for page one is over for another day.

The Three-Way Split

I.F. Stone once remarked that "the *Post* is the most exciting paper in town—you never can tell where you'll find a front-page story."[24] The same might be said of the *Times*. Yet there is an organizational explanation for page-one makeup.

When Turner Catledge first instituted a story conference at the *Times* in 1946, he did so in order to undercut the long-standing autonomy of the news editor and to bring a measure of coherence to the selection and arrangement of stories for publication. While the change injected the managing editor and the desks into the decision-making process, it has produced coherence of a peculiar sort—a coherence dictated largely by bureaucratic politics.

To the extent that all the editors share certain assumptions about the nature of news, coherence through consensus is theoretically possible. Each day's report does contain some stories that every editor can agree belong on page one. Often consensus exists on the most important story of the day. On the Thursday after the Cambodian invasion and the killings at Kent State, with an aroused crowd of antiwar demonstrators en route to Washington for a protest rally, President

Nixon scheduled an evening press conference. When *Post* managing editor Eugene Patterson asked editors assembled at 3 p.m. what the right-hand lead should be for the next morning's edition, they chorused without hesitation, "The President." Added assistant managing editor Howard Simon, "He's still the President of all the people." Nevertheless, shared values leave considerable scope for disagreement, and the division of labor at the *Times* and *Post* and the ensuing bureaucratic politics ensure that these disagreements are aired.

Before the introduction of the story conference at the *Times*, the news editor made up page one by himself according to his own judgment of newsworthiness, subject only to the unwritten rule that at least some national, foreign, and metropolitan news appear on page one. The story conference changed all that. "When you go out that door," Catledge was fond of telling his editors, "everyone is part of our decisions."[25] Now, even though the managing editor bears sole responsibility for the decision, he is constrained by the decision-making process to treat the national, foreign, and metropolitan desks equitably.

Given their uncertainty about newsworthiness, editors take their cues on the news from their positions in the organization. Much as ambassadors come to view the capitals they are accredited to as the center of the world, an editor thinks of national, foreign, or metropolitan news as *the* news depending on where he sits. Even more important, he feels pressure from his own staff to get optimum play for their stories. The arguments of editors in the two conferences range from precedent—a story on that subject was on page one yesterday and rival news organizations are playing it up—to fairness—one side in a controversy had its say on page one previously; now it's another side's turn—to newsworthiness and exclusivity. Beneath these arguments, however, lies an advocacy relationship. Each of the editors pleads in behalf of a client, his own staff, before a managing editor who sits in judgment.

Editors fight long and hard to get stories from their desks onto page one, but all-out conflict on this point day after day could deplete time and energy better devoted to other activities. Like many organization men, newsmen at the *Times* and *Post* take steps to reduce conflict. Gradually over time, the managing editor unintentionally adjusts his decisions to allocate page-one slots equally among the three principal desks competing for them: national, foreign, and metropolitan. The three rival editors adjust their expectations accordingly, offering more stories than he will accept for page one, but not so many that they squander their influence over his choice by widening his options, or risk disrupting the tacit agreement to share and share alike. The three-way split avoids inequities, reducing friction among editors. It minimizes the numbers of appeals to managing editors. Best of all, it promotes good relations between editors on the desks and their staffs: each editor seems to maintain his standing relative to others in competing for page-one space. The negotiated environment persists until a change of personnel undoes it.

There is some evidence to support the proposition that decisions on page one tend to distribute the number of stories equally among the national, foreign, and metropolitan desks. On the assumption that the substance of newsworthy stories varies randomly, probability could account for a balance among the three desks over time, but it could hardly explain a tendency toward equal distribution day after day.

For every page one, regardless of the total number of stories on it, the distribution that most closely approximates equal shares among the three desks can be defined as the *ideal balance*. A page one with twelve stories, for instance, would be in balance if each desk had four stories; a page one with fourteen stories would be in balance with a five-five-four distribution among the desks. An index of the variance from balance can then be constructed. First, the dateline and byline and, in some cases where both are ambiguous, interview data, indicates which desk has handled the story.[a] After excluding from consideration stories from the financial and sports desks and those less than two inches long, the numbers of stories handled by each desk are arranged in descending order. The absolute difference between the actual distribution of stories among the desks and the ideal balance is the *balance variance*. If, for example, the foreign desk had three stories on page one, the national desk, eight, and the metropolitan desk, five, the ideal balance would be six-five-five and the balance variance, $| 8\text{-}6 | + | 5\text{-}5 | + | 3\text{-}5 | = 2 + 0 + 2 = 4$. In addition, whenever one of the three desks failed to place any stories on page one, the day's page was classified as "imbalanced." Table 2-1 sets out the results for 1970. Of the 365

Table 2-1
Balance Variance on Page One, 1970

Balance Variance	*Post* (N=365)[1]	*Times* (N=365)[1]
0	12.9%	16.4%
2	31.0	37.0
4	26.0	24.7
6	13.2	16.4
8	3.0	1.9
10	0.3	1.4
12	–	–
14	–	–
16	–	–
Imbalanced	13.7	2.2
	100.1 %	100.0 %

[1] Percentage of page ones for the year 1970.

[a] Stories are classified not by substance, but according to the desk handling them. There are some anomalies to keep in mind: at the TIMES, for instance, science news falls under the national desk's jurisdiction; cultural news was part of the metropolitan desk until 1960.

page ones that year, 12.9 percent of the *Post*'s and 16.4 percent of the *Times*' were in balance. Another 31.0 percent and 37.0 percent, respectively, deviated from balance by two; that is, one of the desks had one too many stories on page one and another consequently had one too few for the page to be in balance.

If substantial imbalance were said to exist whenever the balance variance exceeded four, only one-fourth of the *Post*'s page ones and one-fifth of the *Times*' qualified as substantially imbalanced. The metropolitan desk's display page at the *Post* could well account for the difference between it and the *Times* on this measure. Of the fifty days on which one of the desks failed to place any stories on the *Post*'s page one, it was the metropolitan desk that failed on thirty-nine. On both papers, the national desk tended to get a disproportionate share of page-one slots when a balance did not exist.

Whatever the variation in world events and news flow, therefore, the front pages of *The New York Times* and *The Washington Post* had a tendency to contain an equal number of stories from the national, foreign, and metropolitan desks. This tendency is a consequence of the action channels and organizational politics of newsmaking.

Publisher Power

In the description of the organizational politics of the *Times* and the *Post*, the publishers have received little mention because, in the ordinary course of newsmaking at the two papers, they play a minor part. Yet two significant qualifications are in order before dismissing the power of the publisher.

First, a publisher, when he chooses to, can exert considerable influence on the contents of his newspaper by suggesting story ideas to newsmen. Publishers differ in their willingness to do so, as Turner Catledge illustrates in contrasting Arthur "Punch" Sulzberger to his predecessor, Orville Dryfoos:

Sulzberger injected himself into editorial matters often, while Dryfoos almost never did. Sulzberger never wanted it forgotten that he was the publisher, while Dryfoos was more apt to tell me: "That's an editorial matter—you decide it."[26]

When the *Times*' labor specialist Abe Raskin turned in a long account of the 1962-63 strike at the *Times* that was critical of the newspaper's own chief negotiator, Dryfoos at first declined even to read it before publication, and when Catledge insisted he do so, he merely added one detail missing in Raskin's draft and left the decision to publish up to his executive editor.[27] The story filled two pages of the April 1, 1963, edition. Katherine Graham of the *Post* comes closer to the Dryfoos than the Sulzberger school of publishing. Her other publishing and broadcasting ventures keep her out of the newsroom most of the time. When she sat in on an editors' conference to discuss *Post* coverage of the nationwide outburst on U.S. campuses following the 1970 invasion of Cambodia, her presence was considered unusual, the token appearance for the month. When she softly counseled, "Do a paper to cool it down," editors could not recall the last time she had intruded as overtly into the editorial process. Her judgment comported with the views already expressed by several editors present, and it had effect on the treatment of the news. Later, when Haynes Johnson began his lead, "An air of unprecedented crisis . . . ," Bagdikian deleted "unprecedented" with the comment, "It is not unprecedented—we did have a civil war and Pearl Harbor once—and I'm worried that the staccato compiling of events makes it look like the end of the world, when the end is still five days away."

Even a whisper from the publisher resounds throughout the newspaper. Those trying to catch his eye can turn an offhand remark of his into a policy pronouncement, a spur-of-the-moment notion into a full-blown campaign. As Edwin James, one-time managing editor of the *Times*, told the wife of his publisher, "Little lady, you don't know the power of your own words."[28] For this very reason, editors take precautions to insulate their staffs from publisher interference. After Arthur Hays Sulzberger had sent a note of criticism to the art critic of the *Times*, for example, Turner Catledge wrote a memorandum setting out rather sharply his stand on the need for professional autonomy from publisher intervention:

It is true, of course, that [the art critic] is theoretically responsible for what goes into the art columns, even when a story is also done by someone else. . . . And it is also true that he is directly responsible to the managing editor, who, in turn, is responsible *for* him. Under all the circumstances I would not want him to have a note of this temper directly from the Publisher.

. . . I would strongly suggest that you send criticisms about the news product directly to me so that I can make the corrections at the spots where they are needed. I think the Publisher keeps himself in a much better position to deal with the staff at arm's length, especially in the matter of criticisms.[29]

Complete insulation is impossible. Even Catledge, while passing along criticism as if it were his own, would forward notes of praise from the publisher to the newsman. "[I]nsofar as possible," he explains, "I wanted our reporters and editors to do their work without feeling that the publisher was constantly looking over their shoulders. In truth, however, he was."[30]

Suggesting ideas for stories to get is one thing; dictating the line for stories to take is quite another. The distinction, however unclear around the edges, is one that newsmen insist on maintaining. A publisher who intervenes overtly and heavy-handedly in newsmaking will provoke a hostile reaction from his staff, at least at the *Times* and the *Post*.

A second qualification to the general point that publishers play a minor part in day-to-day newsmaking at the two papers applies independently of their propensity to intervene. Some decisions require the publisher's authorization; for others, his approval, increases compliance. Publishers *must* intervene in some intra-organizational conflicts in order to achieve a resolution. When senior editors clash, sometimes only the publisher himself can settle the dispute. In other situations, when the managing editor or executive editor has turned down a proposal, editors may feel strongly enough to turn to him as a court of last resort. Getting to the publisher is then a strategy for newsmen trying to get their own way.

Even when he does take sides, the publisher's intervention may not prove decisive. In 1966 Turner Catledge, dissatisfied with Tom Wicker's leadership of the Washington bureau, wrote a memorandum to the publisher proposing a shift of personnel: upon the retirement of Arthur Krock early the next year, Wicker would take his place as columnist but step down as bureau chief. Wicker balked, citing as precedents Krock and James Reston, each of whom had held both positions simultaneously. Catledge nonetheless won Sulzberger's approval. When Catledge proposed Anthony Lewis as Wicker's replacement, however, the Washington bureau members made known their opposition, and Wicker was granted a temporary stay as bureau chief. He was still at his post in early February 1968 when Sulzberger called Catledge and Reston in to discuss the Washington bureau. Their new candidate for bureau chief was James Greenfield, a *Time* magazine diplomatic correspondent who had headed the State Department's Office of Public Affairs during the Kennedy Administration. He had been recently recruited to the *Times* by Abe Rosenthal, who was now boosting his promotion. Before the shakeup could be announced, though, the staff of the Washington bureau again rallied to Wicker's side. They objected to Greenfield as a newcomer and a "Kennedy man," but above all, as an outsider to the bureau forced upon them by New York. Some even hinted at resigning. At this point Reston changed his mind, aligning himself with the Washington bureau. A week after the initial decision Sulzberger reversed himself as well; Wicker would stay on. Before the day had ended, Greenfield quit. In Catledge's assessment,

At first I concluded that [Sulzberger] had bowed to the threat, implied if not real, that leading members of the Washington bureau would resign if he appointed Greenfield as bureau chief. I had no such fear, and I also felt that even if all the aggrieved reporters had quit, *The New York Times* would have still come out. Yet Punch had had a problem which in time I came to understand and appreciate. He had believed he was running the risk of losing Frankel and Wicker and possibly Reston. The possible alternative of losing Greenfield, who was a new recruit, and even Rosenthal and [Clifton] Daniel, was preferable to Punch.[31]

As the power struggle raged, the *Times* continued to cover the Tet offensive and the New Hampshire primary without an indication to readers that anything was amiss.

Even the power of the publisher is sometimes no match for the Washington bureau. Personalities aside, though, it is difficult to see how much effect changes in personnel—at the very top of the *Times* and the *Post* no less than at the bottom—can have on newsgathering under the combined impress of the division of labor and the daily routine of putting out a newspaper.

The Newsman As Bureaucrat

The editor-publisher of the *Boston News-Letter* usually had in hand the news items he would print several days before his paper went to press. He could choose among the stories those he would put on page one, those he would relegate inside, and those he would have to throw away for lack of space. The latest news he might feature prominently, but the choice was his to make. At the *Times* and *Post* of today, editors have to choose the stories to put in tomorrow's paper often with only the vaguest idea of what their news budget will resemble by late afternoon. Late-breaking news, far from getting page-one play, may not make the paper at all. The selection of stories for page one is the outcome of bargaining among the desks.

Decentralization of control and the pace of events only compound the uncertainty endemic to news. What news is, what it means, what the costs and revenue for getting it are—all are to varying degrees unknown or unknowable. Uncertainty permits the concreteness of organizational constraints and the pressure of organizational politics to exert a major influence over the choice of news content.

The division of labor inside newspapers shapes perspectives, vests interests, and defines lines of cleavage for internal conflict. It also provides newsmen with resources, arguments, and maneuvers for waging these conflicts. It thereby affects the outcomes, and hence the content of news.

Organizational politics, in turn, helps to establish new lines of process, new channels of action for gathering and transcribing news in the future.

To appreciate the effect of organizational processes and politics on news-making, then, it helps to view newsmen as they but seldom view themselves—as bureaucrats: "The movies and television traditionally picture a crusading editor running the rascals out of city hall, or facing down a lynch mob, or something equally dramatic," reminisces Turner Catledge. "My career was not without drama, but the hardest decisions tended to be those within the organization, within the family, decisions regarding policy and people, decisions that demanded a crusading spirit less often than a careful balancing of complex issues."[32]

Notes

1. Panel discussion at the Institute of Politics, Kennedy School of Government, Harvard University, May 19, 1970.
2. Mott, AMERICAN JOURNALISM, p. 11-14.

3. Data as of December 31, 1970, according to the New York Times Company's PROXY STATEMENT (February 26, 1971), pp. 21 and 23.

4. Paul Weaver, "The Metropolitan Newspaper as a Political Institution," Ph.D. dissertation, Department of Government, Harvard University, pp. 42-43.

5. Quoted in Roger Kahn, "The House of Adolph Ochs," SATURDAY EVENING POST 238 (October 9, 1965), 32ff.

6. These figures were reported in the WASHINGTON POST August 19, 1971, p. A-20, and August 20, 1971, p. A-23.

7. These figures were reported in the New York Times Company's ANNUAL REPORT–1971, pp. 23 and 27, and in the PROXY STATEMENT (February 26, 1971), p. 19. Operating income for the newspaper alone was calculated in the following way: the net revenue of pooled businesses was subtracted from the net income of the Company as a whole, exclusive of new acquisitions. On the assumption that the newspaper accounted for roughly 90 percent of the income netted by the company as a whole—it had been 92 percent in 1969 and 90 percent for the first three quarters of 1970—the operating income for THE NEW YORK TIMES itself was derived.

8. Quoted in Chris Welles, "Harder Times at 'The Times,' " NEW YORK MAGAZINE 5 (January 17, 1972), p. 38.

9. John Hohenberg, BETWEEN TWO WORLDS (New York: Praeger, 1967), p. 85.

10. A sample of a "fronting cable" appears in Ruth Adler, A DAY IN THE LIFE OF THE NEW YORK TIMES (Philadelphia: J.B. Lippincott, 1971), pp. 206-207.

11. Robert K. Merton, "Bureaucratic Structure and Personality," READER IN BUREAUCRACY, edited by Merton et al. (New York: Free Press, 1952), p. 365.

12. Gay Talese, THE KINGDOM AND THE POWER (New York: World, 1969), pp. 38-39. Reprinted by permission of the World Publishing Company. Copyright © 1966, 1967, 1968, 1969 by Gay Talese.

13. Ibid., p. 121.

14. Quoted in MORE, "Hellbox," 1, 1 (September 1971): 2.

15. John J. Corry, "Confessions of an Unrepentent Deskman," NIEMAN REPORTS, 18, 4 (December 1964): 11.

16. Alexander Kendrick, quoted in William E. Hocking, FREEDOM OF THE PRESS, A Report from the Commission on Freedom of the Press (Chicago: University of Chicago Press, 1947), p. 165n.

17. Turner Catledge, MY LIFE AND THE TIMES (New York: Harper and Row, 1971), pp. 297-98. Copyright © 1971 by Turner Catledge. By permission of Harper & Row, Publishers, Inc.

18. An aphorism attributed to Miles by Herbert Kaufman. Cf., Graham T. Allison, "Conceptual Models and the Cuban Missile Crisis," AMERICAN POLITICAL SCIENCE REVIEW, 63, 3 (September 1969): 711.

19. Talese, THE KINGDOM AND THE POWER, p. 384.

20. Ben Bagdikian, THE INFORMATION MACHINES (New York: Harper and Row, 1971), pp. 98-100.

21. Clifton Daniel, then assistant managing editor of the TIMES, quoted in COLUMBIA JOURNALISM REVIEW 1, 3 (Fall 1962): 60.

22. Interview with Eugene Patterson, May 5, 1970.

23. Talese, THE KINGDOM AND THE POWER, p. 382.

24. Quoted by Howard Simons, then assistant managing editor of the POST, after a particularly hectic story conference, May 5, 1970.

25. Catledge, MY LIFE AND THE TIMES, p. 178.

26. Ibid., p. 272.

27. Ibid., pp. 273-74.

28. Quoted in Catledge, MY LIFE AND THE TIMES, p. 222.

29. Catledge, MY LIFE AND THE TIMES, pp. 241-42.

30. Ibid., p. 190.

31. Ibid., p. 304. Also, this incident is discussed on pp. 301-05 and in Talese, THE KINGDOM AND THE POWER, pp. 492-511. Talese's account appears to have relied heavily on Catledge's testimony.

32. Catledge, MY LIFE AND THE TIMES, p. xii.

3

The Newsroom and the Beat

The talk of the corps of correspondents who follow the candidates is not simply gossip; gossip is only its surface form. It is consensus—it is the tired, emotional measuring of judgments among men whom the weeks on the road have made into a brotherhood that only they understand. And the judgment of the brotherhood influences and colors, beyond any individual resistance to prejudice or individual devotion to fact, all of what they write. For by now they have come to trust only each other.

Theodore H. White, *The Making of the President—1960. Published by Atheneum Publishers*

News is consensible: newspaper audiences, by their responses to news, actively shape its content. Yet the average reader has little impact on the consensual process. If he doesn't like what he reads, he can write a letter to the editor or quit buying the paper, but few readers do either of these things. In practice, feedback comes primarily from those with face-to-face contact with newsmen, especially fellow journalists and news sources.

Within the broad confines of the news consensus, the specific content of news depends on the exchange of information between newsmen and their sources. Social location is the most important determinant in the mutual choice of partners for news trading. Outside the newsroom, Washington is the most important site for newsgathering by *Times* and *Post* reporters. Within Washington, one set of locations is crucial—the beats in government agencies. A relatively large proportion of reporters covering national and foreign news—about one-third at the *Times* and nearly one-half at the *Post*—do so from Washington, and most of them have beats in the American government (Table 3-1).

While news trading in the journalist and official community in Washington is rather haphazard, the beat and the newsroom impose arrays of incentives on newsmen, organizational incentives that structure the consensual process and the exchange of information.

'Shop Talk' and Consensus

In the *Post* newsroom, circa 1970, a glass enclosure sheltered the national editor. Just outside was a horseshoe-shaped arrangement of desks for desk men and copy editors. The furniture demarcated the frontiers of the national staff.

Table 3-1
Allocation of *Times* and *Post* Manpower

	Bureaus		On Beats in U.S. Government	
	Times (N=86)[1]	Post (N=43)[1]	Times (N=86)[1]	Post (N=43)[1]
Washington	34.9	48.8	23.3	37.2
Other U.S.	23.2	16.3	–	–
Foreign	41.9	34.9	1.2	2.3
	100.0	100.0	24.5	39.5

[1] Percentage of full-time reporters on national and foreign staffs.
Note: Figures are based on 1970 data supplied by the TIMES and the POST.

Within these borders, informality seemed to reign. As former national editor Ben Bagdikian sets the scene,

There are no hermetically sealed layers. There is free flowing contact all the time, from top to bottom, and in a physical way. Stand in the aisle for an hour, and you'll talk with everyone from the executive editor to the State Department reporter to someone who will cover the PTA in Hyattsville and a copy boy. The *Post* is a great big village where people are meeting all the time on the village square and talking about their day's work and how to go about it.[1]

Despite appearances, the arrangement has a pattern. Reporters covering beats with considerable overlap, like the White House and the State Department, were seated side by side to facilitate "shop talk."

Compared to the *Post*, the Washington bureau of the *Times* seems much more formal. It applies more formal means, too, to encourage its newsmen to talk shop—through clusters, grouping the four reporters covering various government agencies dealing with urban affairs into one, and the half dozen covering national security affairs into another. The men in each cluster sit at adjacent desks. They hold periodic meetings with editors to plot coverage of major stories, arranging for some to cover spot news while freeing others to work on longer-range projects. Primarily, though, the clusters facilitate the swapping of information. In addition to the clusters, the *Times* has two house organs which formalize shop talk: "Winners and Sinners," begun by Theodore Bernstein in 1953 when he was news editor to publicize exceptional writing, good and bad alike; and "Times Talk," carrying articles on work life on the newspaper, including details on how reporters obtained a particular story, and descriptions of newsgathering in various *Times* bureaus.

Reporters on beats also talk shop. Those covering the same beat for rival news organizations frequently exchange information. Partly, it is a matter of efficiency. Sometimes two events occur simultaneously. Other times, stories break too near a deadline to enable a single reporter to compile a complete account on his own. Most common of all, space limits the access of reporters to an event; pool arrangements among White House correspondents merely formalize the informal exchange of information that goes on at many beats. "The amount of note trading is simply prodigious," reports columnist Russell Baker, who used to cover the White House for the *Times*. "Some of the greatest information trading centers in Washington are the White House lobby, the State Department press room, and the Senate Press Gallery. Forty-five minutes at the press table of the Senate Dining Room is commonly recognized around town as the equivalent of a full day's legwork in the darkest recesses of Capitol Hill."[2]

Yet efficiency by itself does not account for the cooperation among competitors. Shop talk, wherever its location, however formal its structure, performs another function essential to newsmaking. Reporters and editors, exchanging information and interpretation, forming judgments about men and events, almost imperceptibly forge a consensus about what is news. The consensus may have less appreciable effect on spot news than on stories that linger in the headlines over a period of time, but it does alter assessments of news sources and reshape perceptions of events. On the beat, as in the newsroom, reporters do not work alone, but in groups; and in the course of events, the group subtly molds individual values into group judgment.

This group judgment, or consensus, imparts a measure of certainty to the uncertain world of the newsman. If no newsman knows what an event means, whether or not it is news, or who the reliable sources are, then reaching some agreement with colleagues on what is news and how to write a story about it helps to authenticate the news.

The News Community

Consensus formation also takes place beyond the walls of the newsroom and the boundaries of the beat. In conversations with acquaintances in the news community in Washington and around the country, newsmen broaden their horizons and expand the circle in which consensus develops.

A degree of social organization knits the community. Union locals, social clubs, fraternal organizations, and professional associations all form strands in the net. The Newspaper Guild, the National Press Club and the Overseas Press Club, the Gridiron Club, Sigma Delta Chi, and the White House Correspondents Association and the State Department Correspondents Association provide more than good fellowship to members; each is a forum for talking shop, for swapping ideas, for forging consensus among more varied sets of newsmen than those who get together in the newsroom and on the beat. These organizations are the manifestations of a community that sets standards and shapes perspectives for its members.

Those in the community also share a caution bred of uncertainty. This caution perpetuates the herd instinct to follow a few bellwethers who have not led them astray in the past. The bellwethers are opinion leaders in the community. Opinion leadership is exercised not only by those who administer Pulitzer Prizes and Nieman Fellowships but also by a handful of newspapers and columnists. In 1962 William Rivers, replicating a study done by Leo Rosten twenty-five years earlier, polled Washington correspondents about the newspapers that they used in their work and about the newspapers and columnists that they considered "fair" and "reliable." Roughly nine out of ten of the 250 respondents used *The New York Times* and considered it "fair" and "reliable." *The Washington Post* though ranking second in usage, was then in rather ill repute. Among columnists, only Walter Lippmann was highly esteemed.[3]

Ostensibly competitive news organizations cooperate tacitly in shaping the news consensus as well. As *Times* managing editor Turner Catledge acknowledged when he learned of the demise of *The New York Herald-Tribune* in 1966, "We're going to miss the *Trib* over here. It kept us honest."[4] These days, some *Times*men get the news from out of town. On the *Times* national staff, at least, nearly everyone reads the *Post*, and vice versa. Until just recently, each newspaper obtained a facsimile of the other's front page as soon as the first edition appeared. Insofar as each sets the standard for national coverage for the other, moreover, news in one will tend to duplicate news in the other.

The consensible nature of news may even impede the breaking of stories that lack corroboration from opinion-leading newspapers. Once they do break, however, big stories will tend to remain in the news as first one news organization and then another uncovers additional information or a new interpretation.

News of the bombing damage to civilian areas in North Vietnam followed this pattern. On Christmas morning of 1966, Harrison Salisbury began filing a series of dispatches to the *Times* from Hanoi, the first correspondent on a major American newspaper to do so since the United States intervened overtly in the Vietnam War. Until that time, the news media had virtually ignored firsthand reports in *Le Monde* and other foreign news organs describing the bombing damage, reports which in part confirmed Communist news agency allegations that residential areas had been struck and many civilians killed. "Contrary to the impression given by United States communiqués," wrote Salisbury, "on-the-spot inspection indicates that American bombing has been inflicting considerable civilian casualties in Hanoi and its environs for some time past."[5] Salisbury's articles soon drew official reaction in Washington, which was reported widely in the news media and in the *Times* itself. But the frontal assault did not begin until New Year's Day with a story by George Wilson in the *Post*. Based on information supplied by the Pentagon, the defense correspondent wrote that the list of civilian casualties in Salisbury's discussion of the bombing of one town were "identical to those in a Communist propaganda pamphlet issued in November," and described officials of the Johnson Administration as "furious" about the series.[6] Within three weeks, though, William C. Baggs, editor of the Miami *News* went to North Vietnam and wrote a series of dispatches carried by the Associated Press generally confirming Salisbury's findings. Then on January 21, both the *Times* and the *Post* ran an AP story citing "intelligence sources" as saying that aerial reconnaissance had revealed considerable damage to civilian structures as well as to military targets in the North. Thus, Salisbury disrupted what he was to call the "pattern of acceptability" in the news community on stories about bombing damage in North Vietnam.[7] That some prestigious news organizations would carry a series of stories on the civilian casualties inclined other editors to do likewise. Until then, they remained hesitant about running a controversial story that lacked authoritative confirmation.

Seymour Hersh's Pulitzer-Prize winning story of the Mylai massacre replicates the pattern in many ways: stories about allied atrocities in Vietnam had been long overlooked or discounted as enemy propaganda until Mylai made them acceptable. The news actually surfaced first on September 6, 1969, in an AP dispatch datelined Fort Benning, Georgia, which read in full:

An Army officer has been charged with murder in the deaths of an unspecified number of civilians in Vietnam in 1968, post authorities have disclosed.

Col. Douglas Tucker, information officer, said the charge was brought yesterday against First Lt. William L. Calley, Jr., 26 years old of Miami, who was to have been discharged Saturday after two years in the service.

Col. Tucker declined to give details of the case other than to say that the incident had occurred in March, 1968, in Vietnam, and that the charge involves the death of more than one civilian.

Lt. Calley had been assigned to the 23rd Infantry Division.[8]

Although numerous newspapers reprinted the dispatch, none gave it prominence. Five days later, NBC's Pentagon correspondent Robert Goralski telecast news of Calley's arrest to Huntley-Brinkley viewers. Hersh himself, a one-time AP defense correspondent now freelancing for Dispatch News Service, spotted neither the first story nor a subsequent one, which quoted an ex-GI, Ronald L. Ridenhour, as crediting the Army investigation to letters he had sent to the Army and to several Congressmen. The previous spring, Ridenhour had sought to interest *Life, Look*, and *Newsweek* in a story on the massacre, but without success. Now, Pentagon officials aware of the Calley investigation braced themselves for a barrage of press inquiries, but none came. On October 22, six weeks after the AP story, one of Hersh's Pentagon contacts called him to say that the man held at Fort Benning was being charged in connection with seventy civilian deaths. Around the same time, the *Post* and the *Times* also received tips and began following them up.

Having gathered additional information and put together a story on Calley and Mylai, Hersh had an agent attempt to sell it to newspapers around the

United States. Of fifty editors approached, thirty-six decided to buy. On November 13, the *St. Louis Post-Dispatch, Boston Globe, Chicago Sun-Times, Milwaukee Journal,* and *Charlotte Observer,* among others, ran Hersh's story on page one. That same morning, the *Times* published a story of the massacre which, according to its Washington bureau chief, Max Frankel, was independently gathered. The timing was no mere coincidence, however. "I wouldn't doubt for a minute," says Frankel, "that the fact that Hersh was around town peddling the story gave it a competitive edge."[9]

Newsmen also form part of the Washington community, and consequently share many of its values and beliefs. The questions that are on the minds of Washingtonians may not be the same ones that concern New Yorkers, but they do influence the outlooks of *Times* correspondents in the capital. When he was about to quit the *Times* in 1966, David Broder complained about conflicting demands placed on political news out of Washington in a memorandum to his managing editor:

In general, it was my impression that *Times* editors had a certain few stimuli to which they reacted in a political story: Instances of extremism, either of the New Left or the Radical Right; political action by Southern (but not northern) Negroes; Kennedy stories of any variety. These may be the grist of political thought at New York cocktail parties, but, as you know, they do not begin to embrace the variety of concerns that really animate national politics.[10]

The news consensus may similarly vary from beat to beat and from bureau to bureau. Informal shop talk in the newsroom among colleagues from other beats and editors subjects the reporter to cross-pressures by exposing him to different judgments and interpretations of events. Clusters stimulate cross-pressures; team journalism does, too.

'Party Politics' and News Sources

Besides affecting the shape of the consensus within the news community, the pattern of social relations between that community and the rest of Washington helps structure the exchange of information between reporters and news sources. This exchange makes specific the content of news within the general framework of the consensus.

The premium that Washingtonians place on being "in the know" would keep them from excluding newsmen altogether from capital society, but until the New Deal, the reporter's station was a lowly one. By the 1960s, encouraged perhaps by President Kennedy's well-advertised penchant for the company of reporters, Washington society came to lionize a few newsmen. According to columnist Murray Kempton,

The journalists who go to Washington are, in point of fact, an elite. They're people whom their desks regard as the most competent, the brightest, the smartest of all journalists. . . . Journalists can look pretty snazzy in a town like that. I mean the journalists always know what Joe is doing, what everybody else is doing.[11]

No clear line separates work life from social life in the capital. Washington is a one-industry town, and its products can be manufactured and business transacted in its drawing rooms as readily as in its offices. "Party politics" could apply equally well to two aspects of Washington life, partisan wrangling and cocktail chatter. The reporter, if he is to do his job, must partake of both. Not that parties yield much information: simply attending is half the job—seeing officials and being seen, making "contacts" and being contacted. "Although I haven't learned a great deal that's truly vital at a party," comments one defense correspondent, "I have made acquaintances who have proved useful at a later date."[12] It is in the mutual selection of trading partners between reporters and news sources that "party politics" makes itself felt in the news.

Authenticating information is always a problem for reporters. Their assessment rests to some extent on how reliable a source proved in past dealings. Talking to reporters entails some risk to sources as well. If an "inspired" story failed to capture their inspiration adequately or if they were to become identified as the source of inspiration, the repercussions might prove undesirable. Travelling in the same social circles can lay the foundation for trust in each partner's reliability that facilitates exchanging information. Robert Cutler, for example, remembers how he was approached by an old Harvard acquaintance, columnist Joseph Alsop, after taking office as President Eisenhower's Special Assistant for National Security Affairs:

It was on this business that he had come to talk. He spoke of "confidants" in the press whom former Presidents had used to create a favorable background and of the benefit derived from that relationship. Such a person, trusted by a President, could provide an anonymous channel to help shape public opinion. I listened attentively.

In "our" case, he went on, there could be a much closer relation of confidence. His family's tradition was Republican. He and I had known each other during his college days and had shared good times since then at our Cambridge Club. Naturally, he did not contemplate that I would reveal anything of a secret nature. But by periodically outlining background material I could provide enough orientation to make his column an authoritative, but of course anonymous, spokesman for the President without the world being aware of the source of the background. While there was no mention of "exclusive," I sensed that Joe anticipated such a sensible arrangement.[13]

The "old college tie" has similarly been evident in coverage of the Central Intelligence Agency in the recent past.

An affinity of policy views can also help to cement relations. In Saigon during the latter days of the Kennedy Administration, for instance, shared political views affected the flow of information. According to Roger Hilsman,

> Individual members of the embassy and the CIA shared the views of a segment of the press, represented by [the *Times'* David] Halberstam and [AP's Neil] Sheehan, while other members of the embassy and CIA were allied with the opposing segment of the press, represented by [columnists Joseph] Alsop and [Marguerite] Higgins.... And inevitably the activities of a group in one institution supported the activities of its allies in the other—with or without any attempt at connivance. In Saigon, one group leaked to Halberstam and the other to Higgins.[14]

Overly warm relations with an official, however, can tarnish a newsman's reputation for objectivity around the capital and curtail his effectiveness. George Reedy describes sympathetically the plight of William S. White, a man "whose fortunes declined under the Lyndon Johnson Administration simply because of a friendship with the President which dated back more than thirty-five years." Explains Reedy, "White, whose politics were far more conservative than those of the President, found that he could not write as forcefully as he wished on many subjects without embarrassing the White House because his words were interpreted as emanating from the Oval [Office]."[15]

The constant mixing of business with pleasure imposes some restrictions on the flow of information. "Obviously, a reporter cannot make a practice of reporting after working hours," observe Joseph and Stewart Alsop. "If he does so, he will soon achieve the approximate popularity of an insurance agent who takes along a bundle of contracts to every party he goes to."[16] There is the further difficulty of setting boundaries for what is publishable. Information picked up at social gatherings may be fair game for Washington's gossip columnists, but reporters tend to apply broader definitions of privacy to after-hours contact with sources.[17] Most confining of all is the newsman's desire to remain on good terms with friends who occasionally provide him with an item of news. The desire may extend to professional acquaintances he has with the men who count in Washington social circles—mostly officials. Whether or not these friendships are deep and abiding, "popularity"—to take the Alsops' word for it—with sources does matter to reporters both personally and professionally. And self-restraint is the coin of popularity.

Stories emerging a week after the Cuban missile crisis discussing the stands taken by Adlai Stevenson during policy deliberations illustrate some of the dilemmas that "party politics" poses for newsgathering. An article in the *Saturday Evening Post* by Charles Bartlett and Stewart Alsop started the furor. It portrayed Stevenson as the lone dissenter from the consensus reached by the "Executive Committee" of the National Security Council:

> There is disagreement in retrospect about what Stevenson really wanted. "Adlai wanted a Munich," says *a nonadmiring official who learned of his proposal.* "He

wanted to trade the Turkish, Italian, and British missile bases for the Cuban bases." The Stevenson camp maintains that Stevenson was only willing to discuss Guantanamo and the European bases with the Communists after a neutralization of the Cuban missiles. But there seems to be no doubt that he preferred political negotiation to the alternative of military action.[18]

The article misrepresented Stevenson's position as orthodox histories of the period depict it.[19] Exactly where Bartlett and Alsop had obtained their information has never been disclosed, but many in Washington were quick to draw an appropriate conclusion. To quote *Times* columnist Russell Baker,

The reason the *Post* article caused such an explosion was that one of its two authors was . . . one of the President's close personal friends. Every knowledgeable person who read the story wondered if Bartlett's unidentified source was not, in fact, the President. And if the President was, then, in the inexorable logic of the Washington mind, the article could only . . . be construed as an attempt to knife Stevenson.[20]

At his subsequent press conferences President Kennedy implicitly denied that he had been responsible for the disclosure. "It's my judgment," he told reporters, "that this statement or interpretation of Governor Stevenson's position did not come from a member of the National Security Council."[21] His denial notwithstanding, Kennedy had authorized Bartlett and Alsop to gain access to Ex-Com members and had read the galley proofs prior to publication without suggesting any revisions. Instead, he had asked Arthur Schlesinger, Jr., to warn Stevenson of the forthcoming attack. "Everyone will suppose that it came out of the White House because of Charlie," he told Schlesinger. "Will you tell Adlai that I never talked to Charlie or any other reporter about the Cuban crisis, and that this piece does not represent my views."[22] A subsequent press release from the White House expressing full confidence in Stevenson did little to counteract rumors because it lacked any explicit denial of the accusations. Bartlett himself stood by his version, pointing out that "the White House has not denied the story."[23] Stevenson meanwhile became convinced that Bartlett would never have printed such assertions without some indication that they represented views which Kennedy wanted aired.[24]

Now other news organizations took turns at interpreting the affair. *Time* ran a cover story generally supporting Stevenson's own version of the Ex-Com meetings and questioning the accuracy of the *Post* piece. *Time*'s Washington bureau chief, John L. Steele, was considered an old Stevenson friend. "What had probably happened," *Time* concluded, "was that some other New Frontiersman, knowing of the President's lack of deep affection for Adlai, had felt free to knock him. What the whole controversy did was to highlight the huge personal and philosophical differences between Kennedy and Stevenson."[25] It ended up by intimating Stevenson's eventual departure from the Administration. *Newsweek* was the next to hit the streets. It argued against any rift between Kennedy and Stevenson and attributed the *Post* story to sources other than the President;

but it did hold Kennedy blameworthy for knowing about the article and doing "too little and too late" to support his Ambassador to the United Nations.[26] *Newsweek*'s Washington bureau chief at the time, Benjamin Bradlee, was close to Kennedy. The entire controversy prompted Karl Meyer of *The Washington Post* to wonder,

What will some future Trevor-Roper or A.J.P. Taylor make of the oblique and petty vendettas that have followed the striking victory in the Cuban missile crisis? His research materials will be a pile of slick magazines. . . . He then will have to unravel with precision the exact relation of every journalist concerned to different members of the Kennedy Administration.[27]

Kennedy's association with Bartlett posed dilemmas for both men in the performance of their duties. The authority ascribed to the original story was due in large part to their intimacy—Bartlett had introduced Kennedy to Jacqueline Bouvier ten years before.[28] The story was not merely inaccurate; it was damaging to Stevenson's reputation and troubling to the Ambassador's many friends, who urged the President to rebut it. Yet for him to do that would necessarily impute Bartlett's integrity as a journalist—and on a story that Kennedy himself had reviewed in advance of publication. "[T]he President," writes Sorensen, "unwilling either to repudiate his friends or to cause more damage by specifying where they erred, was equally unwilling to take responsibility for what his friends wrote."[29] In the end he rejected both courses of action and instead wrote a letter expressing confidence in Stevenson. He then edited out any references to Bartlett and released the partial text to the press.

The incident highlights some of the difficulties inherent in any "special relationship" between a reporter and his news source. On the one hand, if each is to do his job properly, he may be forced to violate a trust—the reporter by publishing information not meant for release and the source by publicly rebutting it. On the other hand, neither can do his job well without establishing a relationship of trust and exchanging information. The reporter's situation is not the same as the source's, however, for if he violates that trust, he may lose access to information, while his source can always find another reporter to take his information and make it public.

The Beat: Absorption and Parochialism

Shop talk lays the basis for consensus on news judgments. Social location in the news community and the capital affects the specific content of the news. What newsmen know depends to a considerable extent on whom they know, which, in turn, depends on where they are. Yet most Washington correspondents on the *Times* and the *Post* are not as free as columnists to roam around the capital in search of news; they are confined to their beats, usually one or two government agencies. Nor do many travel in the same social circles as senior officials of the government; their contact with much of the official community is limited. While they do spend considerable time in the company of other journalists, much of it is with colleagues on their beat and in the newsroom. Their relations with the rest of the journalistic and official community around Washington may be intermittent, but their interactions on the beat and in the newsroom recur daily. These two locations, above all, are critical for shaping the news consensus.

News sources, past and potential, constitute an important audience for any newsman. While most of his readers remain anonymous, he often must confront his sources face to face. Rarely, if ever, does he know the reactions of most readers to any story: he may get some fan mail and letters to the editor may eventually be relayed to him, but the feedback hardly compares with that from his sources. The impact of this feedback, moreover, is at least in small part a function of social distance. "A reporter," argues one Pentagon correspondent, "may hesitate to take a critical view of regularly tapped sources for the very human reason that he prefers to be greeted pleasantly when he walks into an office, rather than to be treated as though he were poison. His vested interest is in maintaining a pleasant atmosphere."[30]

The importance of the audience of news sources has special significance for *Times* and *Post* newsmen in Washington. Because of their extensive readership among the politically influential, the *Times* and *Post* function as something akin to house organs for the political elite. In particular, use of the two newspapers by officials trying to reach other officials with policy-relevant information may reinforce the tendency of all Washington newsmen to weigh official views heavily in reaching consensus on what is going on in the world. Washington's agenda becomes the newsman's headlines; its outlook, his news content.

In direct daily contact with officials in one department and out of touch with other parts of the government, the reporter on the beat gradually absorbs the perspectives of the senior officials he is covering. This absorption is not as much due to the attitudes he brings to his job as it is necessary to his performance on it. Much of political conversation employs catch phrases and slight shifts in nuance to convey meaning. The reporter with a long-standing relationship with officials on his beat can develop a finely calibrated sensitivity to even the slightest sign of movement on an issue. When tuned in, he can sometimes detect a nuance, and from it, infer a change in policy. Without role-taking, without putting himself in officials' shoes, a reporter might find it somewhat harder to anticipate the outcomes of controversies, or even to understand what a source's comments mean. Yet repeated role-taking may lead him to adopt the official's perspective on issues. The line between role-taking and absorption is a thin one indeed.[31]

Russell Baker claims that role-taking even manifests itself in the personal affectations of reporters covering different beats:

The State Department reporter quickly learns to talk like a fuddy-duddy and to look grave, important, and inscrutable. The Pentagon man always seems to have just come in off maneuvers. The Capitol reporter eschews the raucous spirit of the White House and affects the hooded expression of the man privy to many important deals. Like the politicians he covers, he tends to garrulity, coarse jokes, and bourbon and learns to hate reform.[32]

While any pattern in reporters' mannerisms may be hard to discern, absorption does have quite measurable impacts on their attitudes toward the men they cover. This is especially so when that man is the President of the United States. The trappings of office can be awe-inspiring; the "burdens of the Presidency," depressing. The sympathies they can evoke in reporters emerges from Raymond Clapper's description of a briefing by Franklin Delano Roosevelt:

After lunch he undertook to explain the war budget in order to assist the Washington reporters who would be writing their dispatches about this complicated array of figures. For two hours he tried to reduce the matter to simple terms for us. He patiently answered questions, some intelligent, some not, and some only repetitious. Though he must have been unbelievably tired and pressed with critical business, he never showed impatience and he stayed with it until all questions were exhausted.[33]

By moving reporters out of the anteroom and into the Oval Office, Roosevelt might be expected to have earned their gratitude; but his relations with reporters are hardly unique in the annals of the Presidency. Recalling a rocking-chair conversation of several hours' duration with Lyndon Johnson, James Reston observes, "It is very difficult to sit and listen to a President explaining his terrible problems and narrow options without becoming sympathetic to the man and subjective about his policies."[34]

Absorption culminates in beat parochialism. James McCartney, who has covered the capital for the Knight chain, writes of reporters' developing "vested interests in their beats." The development is by no means confined to the White House alone. "In the Pentagon," notes McCartney, "it is commonplace for reporters to make alliances with one or another of the armed services, presenting, by and large, that particular service's views on highly controversial problems of national defense."[35] For example, Hanson Baldwin, an Annapolis graduate and long-time military correspondent for the *Times*, was commonly thought by Washingtonians to reflect the military's views in fights with Pentagon civilians and the Navy's views in inter-service battles. His *Post* colleague in the 1950s, John G. Norris, carried parochialism one step further; at the time he was covering the Defense Department, he also was serving as a commander in the Naval Reserve. Similarly, the uncritical coverage of the early years of the manned space program may not have been due solely to the National Aeronautics and Space Administration's (NASA) success at news management. Many of the journalists covering Apollo were so caught up in the drama of the space race that they came to regard themselves as part of the NASA "team." The technical language that they used in talking to NASA personnel set them apart from other journalists and contributed to "team" solidarity.[36]

Thus, specialization along beat lines enables reporters to develop proficiency in one area of government policy and process, but at some cost. To quote McCartney again, "[T]he result in extreme form is that reporters become spokesmen for their news sources rather than dispassionate observers. They become sloppy about recognizing that alternative views may exist and about digging out and including alternative views in their stories. Over a period of time some may well be press agents for those they are covering and, indeed, sometimes perform that role, or something very close to it."[37]

The Politics of Newsgathering

While social life in the capital can be somewhat fluid, relations on the beat, by comparison, exhibit a high degree of structure. That structure can be understood as the nexus of three sets of bargaining relations in which the reporter on the beat is intertwined: with his colleagues and editors back in the newsroom, with other reporters on the beat, and with his news sources. These relations, more than shaping the news consensus, influence the choice of news sources and the exchange of information between the reporter and his sources. In particular, they give the reporter incentives to take news passed through routine channels in the government.

Independence from the Newsroom

Formal responsibility for newsmaking is not necessarily the equivalent of deciding what a newspaper publishes. The action channels through which information flows in the *Times* and the *Post* provide reporters on the beat ample opportunity to determine the day-to-day output of news. When a senior editor chooses to intervene in the process, he can alter the outcome; but, even then, reporters retain considerable autonomy in the selection of information for inclusion in their stories.

Editors can assign dull stories to a reporter, reassign him from one beat to another, "lose" a story on his desk, or "bury" it on an inside page. They can also deny him time off from spot news coverage to work on longer in-depth projects, expedite his requests for travel money and allowances, award him bonuses, or—in rare instances—fire him.

An astute editor will endeavor to control resources for manipulating the incentives of his staff. When Turner Catledge took over as managing editor, for instance, he insisted that all salary hikes for members of the news department be made in his name. In an effort to tighten, if not brighten, the ponderous style of the · *Times*, he instituted monthly awards of $100 for exceptional writing to reporters on each of the news desks. Yet the decentralization of the newspaper and its resulting bureaucratic politics are bound to diffuse the impact of any incentive scheme. Even though all raises were made in the managing editor's name, editors on the desks had ways of letting their staffs know who else was responsible for a bigger paycheck. When some editors tried to distribute the writing awards equitably among their staffs, Catledge found himself trying to second-guess their judgments. When copy editors complained that reporters were monopolizing the rewards of shared efforts, Catledge had to make them eligible for writing awards as well. Try as they may to do otherwise, editors ultimately are forced to bargain and persuade in order to work their will on the organization. Editorial power, like Presidential power, is, in Richard Neustadt's phrase, "the power to persuade," with whatever resources and arguments the editor can muster. "The kind of men I wanted in top positions at the *Times*," concedes Catledge, "were independent, creative men, thoroughbreds, and they were not the sort who could be bossed or browbeaten. I had to make them do what I wanted done often by making them think it was what they wanted done."[38]

In conflicts with editors, moreover, reporters have resources, arguments, and maneuvers of their own for getting their way. First, they usually have more detailed knowledge about a story than their editors do. Even when an editor suggests a lead for the story, the reporter can include information that puts a different cast on the story. He can write the story with a semblance of balance among competing points of view, but quote dull statements from one side and colorful lines from another. He can feign an inability to track down an answer to questions the editor raises. He can even refuse to reveal his sources of information to his editor. If challenged, he can appeal on grounds of his expertise and professional ethics, which disapprove of editorial intervention. Editors, themselves ex-reporters, often find these grounds persuasive.

Second, the nature of competition among news organizations covering Washington makes it difficult for a story, once uncovered, to remain unreported. Editors consider themselves obliged to run a story once it "makes the news," regardless of their personal preferences. If a story breaks elsewhere, especially in any of the prestige newspapers, it strengthens the reporter's case for publication. He sometimes helps matters along by slipping some details to a colleague on a rival paper when his own editor seems reluctant to go ahead with publication. The news consensus thus can break down editorial disinterest or resistance.

Third, the editing process arms the reporter with other tactics to slip his story into the newspaper sometimes substantially unaltered. He can turn it in just before the deadline when editors are most distracted by the rush of activity. He can hand his story to a cooperative desk man or copy editor. On national security stories that do not fall neatly into foreign or national news or on economic stories that could be classified as either national or financial news, the reporter may be able to evade a troublesome editor by circumventing one desk entirely and dealing with another.

Fourth, reporters can form tacit alliances against their editors. When a reporter is challenged, his colleagues sometimes rally to his side. Editors need the cooperation of their staffs too much to engage in tests of will. They will try to reach some accommodation.

On the *Times* the remoteness of the Washington bureau from the home office has accentuated in-group loyalties in the past. Reporters usually could win over the bureau chief, and through his intercession, the national editor in New York. When Tom Wicker was bureau chief and Claude Sitton was national editor, reporters in Washington expected the two of them to intervene on their behalf with managing editor Clifton Daniel or assistant managing editor Harrison Salisbury. In Gay Talese's account,

When Wicker's men became angered by the editing or cutting of the copyreaders, or by the imputations from Salisbury or Daniel that a certain Washington story had been inadequately covered, they usually channelled their explanations or objections through Claude Sitton, but they did not often feel he was sufficiently sympathetic; or if he was sympathetic, he seemed powerless to avert the continued second-guessing that emanated from Daniel's office, or from the desk of Harrison Salisbury, or from the bullpen. In the old days when the Washington bureau had such ranking figures as Arthur Krock or Reston to do its bidding, it had been accustomed to getting quick results, and usually favorable results, but now in 1966 it felt mainly frustrated. . . .[39]

To the extent that relations between the bureau chief in Washington and the national desk in New York improve, frictions within the bureaus will increase.

Some Washington correspondents, particularly at the *Times* and the *Post*, have one other special bargaining advantage. Most reporters covet Washington assignments; only the best get them. Once in the capital, a reporter can develop enough of a reputation to provide him a measure of independence from editors. This was not always the case. When he began his career on the *Times*, Turner Catledge remembers, the men on the copy desk had top billing: "They made more money and worked more regular hours than reporters, and were more highly valued by most executives. The shift in status came with the proliferation of bylines in the late thirties. The byline gave the reporter increased prestige."[40] Today, being a star correspondent does carry with it some perquisites of rank, among them, untouchability. His judgment is less open to second-guessing back in the newsroom.

Reporters are quick to complain and slow to forget about restrictions on their newsgathering. Yet the frequency of their complaints about editors' interference on the *Times* and the *Post* are more an indication of reportorial autonomy than of editorial supervision in newsgathering on the beat.

While the outcome may vary from story to story, no individual in the newspaper exercises complete control over the newsmaking process. No reporter can persistently ignore the preferences of his editors without having his copy altered, cut, or withheld altogether. No bureau chief, no national editor, no foreign editor can refuse to support his staff without lowering morale and even worse, coalescing reporters against him. Similarly, no copy editor, even with the support of his superiors, can significantly alter stories day after day without incurring ill will, complaints to higher-ups, and other reprisals. Even managing editors and executive editors find autocratic imposition of policy directives costly to sustain and doomed to frustration. Each man must bargain and seek to persuade the others that what he wants to do would be best for them as well.

Bargaining is not merely the result of the newsman's independence of mind. It is rooted in the processes of gathering and transcribing news. The sheer volume and diversity of information to be handled and the shortage of time in which to do it require a large staff, a division of labor and, above all, considerable autonomy for men on the beat.

Their autonomy is not free of constraint. Their organization's insatiable demand for news dominates the incentives of all newsmen. Every day editors have a sizable news hole to fill. Every day they want something new and original for page one. *The overriding organizational imperatives for reporters are to get news and to get it first.* At first glance these incentives seem obvious. Their consequences, however, are not. There is a fundamental incompatibility between getting news and getting it first. Making inquiries around town, investigating a lead, playing off one source against another absorb time and effort—these are scarce resources that reporters can put to use more efficiently by simply accepting what is handed out. With a daily newspaper to produce, getting news takes primacy over getting it first. What Max Frankel calls "the automatic story" often preempts in-depth coverage. In a larger sense, the tradeoff between getting news and getting it first underlies reporters' relations with news sources on the beat as well as editors' reluctance to scrap the beat system altogether.

Cooperation and Competition on the Beat

One indication of the primacy that getting news takes over getting it first is the cooperation among reporters from rival news organizations on the beat. The methods range from the pool correspondent—one reporter admitted to cover an event who fills in his colleagues on what transpired—to "blacksheeting"— distributing carbon copies of a dispatch to other men on the beat. Cooperation ensures that one story will tend to replicate another, thereby authenticating each man's coverage.

The most prevalent form of cooperative behavior on the beat is also the most significant: the reliance on routine channels of news dissemination in the government, the press release and the press conference. Receiving information through routine channels eases the reporter's task of newsgathering, wherever his beat. It simplifies his job by providing him with newsworthy information at a predictable time and place, and in a form that facilitates transcription. Above all, it gives every reporter the same information.

There are also rules which seek to limit, but not do away with competition on most beats. Reporters on them, while not nearly as clubby as the groups on beats in London or Tokyo, do enforce some of the rules.[41] Recently, Capitol Hill correspondents came close to refusing credentials to a reporter from the underground press.[42] While other motivations doubtless played some part in the action, the reporter under challenge was not someone likely to contribute much to the news consensus. Breaking the rules governing background briefings also brings forth complaints from colleagues. Violating an embargo can warrant exclusion from future briefings. Enforcement of these rules, far from helping reporters to get news first, guarantees that the same information will become news for everyone at the same time.

Some competition nonetheless coexists alongside cooperation on the beat. Except between wire service correspondents, this competition is based not only on speed of transmission but also on originality of information. Getting news first, in practice, means getting exclusives, stories which one reporter alone obtains. There are two channels for getting such exclusives. One is through reportorial enterprise, interviewing and digging up information, cross-checking it with other information, and trying to fit the pieces together. The other, easier by far, is through disclosures supplied by a news source. *Since senior officials probably are the prime source for both channels in Washington, bargaining on the beat turns on the competition for access to them.* In 1946, a report to the Commission on Freedom of the Press summarized the reporter's motives on the beat: "[C]arte blanche is the maximum that newsmen dream about, equality of opportunity the minimum for which they will settle."[43]

Dependence on Officials

Officials, well aware of reporters' need, are not above turning it to their own advantage. The press, says former White House press secretary George Reedy, "seeks continuous access to the President on a 24-hour-a-day seven-day-a-week basis. The clamor is constant and demanding." The clamor for access gives the official in demand a measure of control: "It is impossible to grant everyone access and therefore the access that can be granted must be carefully and painstakingly determined."[44] Other officials are more blunt. Writing of coverage of Saigon in 1963, Roger Hilsman says, "The press, of course, thrived on [the] steady diet of authoritative leaks. Thus [Ambassador Henry Cabot] Lodge was served not only by the stories that put pressure where he wanted it put—and the target was as often an American agency as it was Vietnamese—but by the gratitude of the reporters."[4]

Reporters pay a price for access: they become dependent on their official sources. Dependence combines three elements: some reluctance to offend news sources in the stories they write, considerable willingness to print whatever their sources tell them, and little or no insistence that officials take responsibility for the information they pass along. Reinforcing the pressure to get news, the pressure to get it first makes reporters reluctant to reject information provided through routine channels, lest they jeopardize their access through less formal channels.

The men in charge of government agencies try to centralize the distribution of information through routine channels, thereby preempting a means of influencing governmental outcomes. Although they seek to monopolize outflow of information from their agencies, their subordinates sometimes make their views public without authorization. Senior officials never succeed in sealing leaks altogether, but they do direct most of the outflow through routine channels.

Senior officials employ a variety of tactics against reporters on the beat in order to confine newsgathering to routine channels. One is simply to keep them busy with a steady stream of information through these channels on the premise that the best way to keep the press from peering into dark corners is to shine a light elsewhere. The capacity of officials for inundating reporters may be indicated by the disparity in personnel: in 1969 there were seventy-one correspondents representing forty-three news organizations regularly notified on stories by the Pentagon. Of the regulars, about a dozen worked for daily newspapers or chains and another four for the wire services. By comparison, the Department of Defense alone had 200 authorized positions for public information officers while the services totalled an additional 2500 slots.[46] While public information officers had other things to do apart from keeping correspondents busy, their firepower could be overwhelming when concentrated on discrediting an unfavorable story or just burying it. If the Pentagon does not appreciate the coverage it receives, it can always find itself some other reporters. In response to news out of Vietnam in 1964, the Department's Public Affairs Office initiated Operation Candor, flying newsmen from the United States to Saigon for two-week tours. Many were novices at war correspondence and totally unfamiliar with Vietnam, and hence much more likely than were Saigon veterans to rely on the briefings arranged for them.

Another set of official tactics involves criticizing reporters or going over their heads to complain to editors and publishers. The hortatory approach was common in Vietnam during the early 1960s. When Malcolm Browne, then in Saigon for the Associated Press, asked a probing question of Admiral Harry D. Felt, Commander-in-Chief in the Pacific, at a press conference, Felt snapped, "Why don't you get on the team?"[47] A colleague of Browne's in Vietnam, David Halberstam of the *Times*, was the subject of higher-ranking concern. Ten days prior to Diem's overthrow, Halberstam relates,

On October 22, Arthur Ochs Sulzberger, the new publisher of the *Times*, went by the White House to pay a courtesy call on the President of the United States. . . . Almost the first question from President Kennedy was, "What do you think of your young man in Saigon?" Mr. Sulzberger answered that he thought I was doing fine. The President suggested to the publisher that perhaps I was too close to the story, and too involved—which is the most insidious kind of comment one can make about a reporter. No, said Sulzberger, he did not think that I was too involved. The President then asked if the publisher had been thinking of transferring me to another area. No, said the publisher, the *Times* was quite satisfied with my present assignment. (As a matter of fact, at that particular point I was supposed to go on a breather for a two-week rest, but to its everlasting credit the *Times* immediately canceled the holiday lest it appear to have acquiesced to this pressure.)[48]

If private persuasion fails, as Kennedy's effort did, officials are not loath to resort to public recriminations in order to place newsmen on the defensive. By no means the inventor of the tactic, the Nixon Administration may have been more prone to singling out news organizations for concerted public attack.[49]

Yet behind all the namecalling lies the implicit threat to restrict access. Reporters can be left off a press plane, denied a military accreditation card that would allow them on board military transport in a war zone, barred from a briefing, subjected to harassment and investigation, or simply never granted an interview or a leak.[50] The knowledge that a reporter is in disfavor may make him off-limits even to his friends in government.

In the bargaining, reporters are not wholly without resources or tactics at their disposal. Like bees cross-pollinating in a garden, they do get around their beat and usually have tidbits of information to trade with understanding officials. The official who wants to reach others in the capital needs *Times* and *Post* reporters just as they need him. Particularly in the midst of policy disputes, the savvy reporter can play one official off against another, getting one man's version, trying it on someone else, until he gets a story. Officials can always refuse to comment, but if the reporter intends to write something anyhow, they generally want their side of the story told.

Basically, though, reporters on the beat must bargain for news with sources who hold most of the chips, and newsgathering turns into a series of compromises with the principle of telling everything they know. The way to get exclusives, advises a former White House press secretary,

. . . is to persuade important newsmakers that they can have confidence in the manner in which the reporter will handle a story. The newsman presents himself as one who will not divulge off-the-record material; who will not embarrass his informant by identifying his source; who will not twist the facts to present an event in an unfavorable light. This approach is vital to a successful reporting career and is not to be disdained.[51]

And if the reporter were prone to disdain this approach, he knows others on the beat who will not.

Paradoxically, then, independence from the newsroom spells dependence on the beat. The incentive to get news inclines reporters to rely on routine channels of news dissemination in the government. Paradoxically, too, competition among reporters on the beat reinforces their dependence on their sources. The incentive to get news first makes reporters willing to play along with their sources in order to obtain disclosures on an exclusive basis.

The Newsroom vs. the Beat

Counterpressures to dependence come primarily from the newsroom, not the beat. In the case of leaks, Ben Bagdikian argues,

An important consideration in readiness to use leaked information is the fear of competition. If Correspondent A uses a leak unaltered and in a spectacular way, the managing editor of Correspondent B is not likely to be pleased with the knowledge that his man had the same information and didn't use it. Unless home offices support a policy of care, officials find it easy to play correspondents against each other.[52]

Editors can also exert pressure on their reporters to avoid depending wholly on routine channels. They can try to verify information by checking with their own sources around town and can call into question the competence of reporters who get taken in repeatedly by sources on their beats. They may stop short of transferring men from one beat to another, but they can arrange to free men from the daily grind of spot news coverage in order to track down stories among a broad range of sources in and out of Washington. They can insist on fuller identification of sources. They can persuade reporters not to adhere to ground rules at briefings when officials abuse them.

The reporter on the beat will not take all these steps on his own. One-man rebellion has another name—suicide. When editors encourage him, when colleagues on other papers join in, he may resist being used by the official. But this seldom happens. Editors struggling to get out tomorrow's edition prefer to avoid fights with their staff. Colleagues on other newspapers, as rivals for official attention, are reluctant to join a perhaps losing cause that would adversely effect their own access.

The tension between the newsroom and the beat over newsgathering procedures emerges from an incident that began on December 7, 1971, at the time of the outbreak of full-scale war between India and Pakistan. Flying home from talks between President Nixon and French President Georges Pompidou in the Azores, Henry Kissinger, the national security adviser to the President, held a briefing for the five-man correspondent pool representing the White House press corps on board the President's plane. He told them that "the United States is definitely looking to the Soviets to become a restraining influence in the next few days." Under questioning he warned that "a new look might have to be taken at the President's summitry plans," a reference to talks in Moscow scheduled for late May.[53] That section in the summary of the briefing, compiled by the pool and forwarded to Kissinger's compartment for approval, stipulated, "Lindley rule—deep background: it was the pool's impression that the information in this category could be written on our own without attribution to any administration official—at least that is what we understood Kissinger to have in mind."[54]

When the rest of the White House press corps arrived in Washington and received copies of the pool report, White House press secretary Ronald Ziegler hastily summoned them to a press conference and asserted, "The United States is not considering cancelling the United States-Soviet summit and no United States Government official intended to suggest this."[55]

By evening Benjamin Bradlee, executive editor of the *Post*, which had had no reporter of its own in the pool, decided to identify the source of the briefing by name. The *Times*, after informing the White House of its intentions, attributed the Kissinger statements to "a high White House official" in its early editions. Later, it named Kissinger as the source, justifying the change on the basis of the *Post*'s disclosure.

Editors and reporters at both newspapers had long argued over two aspects of this briefing and others like it. One was the increased use of backgrounding at routine daily briefings by administration officials. The other was the dissemination of information on a so-called "deep background" basis. In statements accompanying publication of stories identifying Kissinger as the source of the news, Bradlee aimed his fire at the first, while *Times* managing editor A.M. Rosenthal raised objections to the second. Bradlee's statement, specifically exempting contacts with news sources initiated by reporters, stipulated a procedure for his staff to follow in briefings held at government initiative:

We instructed our reporters to insist through every means available to them that material offered at these briefings should be on the record and fully attributable.

If ground rules are imposed providing for anything less than full attribution on the record, *Washington Post* reporters will immediately ask that attribution be made direct on the record.

If that request is refused, the reporter will seek attribution specific enough so that no readers can reasonably be confused.

If this request is refused, *The Washington Post* has instructed its reporters to inform the agency or official that the newspaper's handling of the material will be determined by the editor's judgment of their responsibility to inform the public. . . . *The Washington Post* believes that while certain circumstances may make full, on-the-record attribution impractical, the public interest is not served by permitting statements of policy to be made by government officials who are unwilling to be held accountable for their own words.

The decision whether to remain voluntarily in the briefing is one for the reporter's discretion. Under normal conditions he would remain and report under these guidelines.[56]

Essentially Bradlee's statement reaffirmed instructions to *Post* reporters laid down over a decade ago by the then managing editor, Alfred Friendly. Rosenthal's statement, on the other hand, read more like a message to readers than a directive to his staff:

There have been several discussions at the *Times* among editors and reporters on this subject in the past few months. We have laid down no flat rules, because we don't believe in strict regulations on how to cover every story.

But we believe that reporters and editors should be a lot more selective about attending backgrounders called by public officials or politicians, and that the movement should be toward attending them only when the reporters and editors themselves believe there is an important reason beyond the source's convenience for not making the information attributable to the person or government department involved.[57]

The reaction of other newsmen was mixed. David J. Kraslow, bureau chief of the *Los Angeles Times* and part of the press pool on the President's plane, accused the *Post* of "unprofessional, unethical, cheap journalism" in identifying Kissinger as the briefer. When Stanley Karnow of the *Post* walked out of a State Department briefing the following day, only James McCartney of the *Chicago Daily News* joined him. The White House Correspondents Association subsequently rebuked the *Post* for abusing the rules.[58] The reluctance of other newspapers to join in made it difficult for *Post* editors to keep pressure on their reporters. In the end, little changed. Comparable efforts to alter the format of Presidential press conferences have also collapsed.[59] Without some supervision by editors and support from fellow reporters, men on the beat fall back on the routines of newsgathering.

Besides trying to change newsgathering practices, editors may seek to counter the influence of a beat man's sources on news content itself. On April 23, 1962, for instance, the *Times* carried a 6,000-word account of the seventy-two hours during which U.S. Steel announced and then rescinded a price increase. Wallace Carroll, deputy bureau chief to Reston, wrote the story with the aid of nine other *Times* staffers. It told of the meeting at the White House when Roger Blough, president of U.S. Steel, informed President Kennedy of the firm's decision. At the time, the article notes, the President "seems to have kept his temper." How he reacted in the presence of a few aides after Blough's departure became a matter of dispute in the weeks that followed, however. According to the *Times*' version of the events of the 23rd,

He felt he had been double-crossed—deliberately. The office of the Presidency had been affronted. The national interest had been flouted. Bitterly he recalled that: "My father always told me that all businessmen were sons-of-bitches but I never believed it till now."[60]

Earlier, two rather bland accounts of Kennedy's private reaction had appeared in print. Drew Pearson's read, "Father was right. You can't trust the top leaders of banking and industry," and *Newsweek*'s said, "My father told me all about big business. I never really believed him until tonight."[61] Carroll's original draft also had not contained the earthier expression. But national editor Harrison Salisbury learned of the exact words through a photographer who happened to be present to hear Kennedy firsthand.[62] In Gay Talese's account,

Salisbury then called Carroll and asked him to write an insertion that would include this quotation. Carroll objected, saying that *he* had not heard the President use such language. When Salisbury persisted, Carroll snapped back, "The hell with it—you write it in yourself."[63]

The quote caused some stir among businessmen—and still more among newsmen. When the story was trimmed for transmission to the *Times'* news service clients and the quote excised, the paper was chastised by journalists. The Associated Press assigned a reporter to pursue the matter at the White House. A "spokesman" confirmed that the President had said something about big businessmen, but added that he wasn't there and would leave it to history whether Kennedy used the words, "sons-of-bitches."[64] At a subsequent press conference, the President himself sought to modify what he had said by noting that his father had referred only to steel men in those terms. His aide, Arthur Schlesinger, Jr., nevertheless quotes the *Times* version verbatim in his memoirs.[65] What was at issue was the tone of the remark—a tone that, after the price rescission, could prove embarrassing to a man who was of very special concern not only to reporters on the White House beat but also to newsmen throughout Washington and back in the New York home offices, the President of the United States. In retrospect, ironically, Theodore Sorensen has revealed that Kennedy first learned of the price hike from reporter Charles Bartlett—before meeting with Roger Blough. His had not been the foot-stamping petulance of a spoiled child retaliating for not getting his way, but the "angry but contained" reaction of a chief of state calculated to demonstrate *lèse majesté*. But newsmen could not have known that at the time.

The pressure from editors can be a countervailing force against news sources in the reporter's bargaining relations. Even that force is weak. Apart from the infrequency of editors' intervention, occasioned by lack of time and staff resentment, ties between news sources and the editors themselves inhibit their effectiveness. Wooing publishers and editors is one of the methods sources have used to try to keep reporters in line. When they are successful, the home office, far from serving as a bulwark against pressures on the beat, may be a lever for them.

When *The New York Times* undertook to do a series on the Central Intelligence Agency in late 1965, for example, word soon got around the U.S.

government. One day, publisher Arthur Sulzberger received a call from Secretary of State Dean Rusk. Guessing that Rusk wanted to talk about the CIA story, Sulzberger put managing editor Turner Catledge on the line. Rusk, says Catledge, "did not suggest, specifically, that we kill the series. But he did make it clear that he believed publication of the series might upset delicate U.S. intelligence efforts all over the world, might endanger agents, might offend allies, encourage enemies, and otherwise harm the national interest and perhaps the national security. My own feeling was that Rusk was afraid of what *he* might learn if we printed all we could about the CIA. . . ."[66] Clifton Daniel and Harrison Salisbury then suggested calling in John McCone, the former director of the Agency, to go over the series line by line, and the *Times* did. Daniel and Catledge agreed to change details "when we were persuaded we had been in error or that danger to an agent or an operation might result," but they refused to alter the "tone" or the conclusions. As Catledge explained in a memorandum to the publisher, "Every point raised in connection with [the series] by Mr. McCone has been carefully considered and in almost every case the piece has been revised or modified in line with his suggestions. Here and there where he raised points in which nothing but pure value judgments were involved we have preserved our own language."[67]

Officials in the U.S. government, as the most important sources of news in the eyes of the national and foreign staffs at the *Times* and the *Post*, are in a position to exert considerable influence over news content. That content is largely determined by the flow of information between newsmen and their sources. A mapping of social location would show the directions of the flow. Specifically, social relations and political affinity in Washington—in short, party politics—affect the flow somewhat, but the principal sites for exchanging information are beats situated in various government agencies. There, the structure of organizational incentives gives officials the upper hand in bargaining over news content. The need to get news and to get it first, unless countered by pressure from editors, leaves reporters dependent on routine channels for news.

Officials in the U.S. government, as the most important audience for news in the eyes of the national and foreign staffs at the *Times* and the *Post*, also shape news content less directly. News is the product of consensus, which authenticates it, thereby helping newsmen to cope with uncertainty on the job. The exchange of ideas within the news community and between the community and the rest of Washington forges that consensus. The consensus varies from beat to beat and between the beat and the newsroom. Editors back in the newsroom, as well as reporters from other beats, subject the man on the beat to cross-pressures which modify his views and help counteract parochialism. Yet newsmen at the *Times* and the *Post* regard U.S. officials as a significant, if not the most significant, audience they have for their stories. The *Post* may number among its readers "100,000 policy-makers and 100,000 policy players," as its executive editor is fond of putting it,[68] but the *Post*'s own promotional advertising suggests which audience it cares about most:

No rule says that
U.S.I.A. appointees
must read
this newspaper.
(but they all do)

When one newspaper enjoys 100% readership among the key officials of a government department—such as the U.S. Information Agency—you might think reading it was a rule.

It isn't—but reading the Washington Post certainly is the rule throughout official Washington. It is read by 95% of all top appointees, and virtually every Congressman. . . .

The Washington Post—first with the few who have to know—first with the many who want to know.[69]

Notes

1. Quoted in Joseph Goulden, "The Washington Post," THE WASHINGTONIAN 6, 1 (October 1970): 91.

2. Russell Baker, "Fourteen Clues to Washington News," NEW YORK TIMES, April 7, 1963, vi, p. 108. © by the New York Times Company. Reprinted by permission.

3. William L. Rivers, "The Correspondents After 25 Years," COLUMBIA JOURNALISM REVIEW 1, 1 (Spring 1962): 8.

4. Quoted in Fred C. Shapiro, "What's News in New York's Newspapers," COLUMBIA JOURNALISM REVIEW 10, 6 (March/April 1972): 49.

5. NEW YORK TIMES, December 25, 1966, p. 2.

6. WASHINGTON POST, January 1, 1967, p. 1.

7. James Boylan, "A Salisbury Chronicle," COLUMBIA JOURNALISM REVIEW 5, 4 (Winter 1966-67): 14.

8. Quoted in the WASHINGTON POST, December 1, 1969, p. A-10.

9. Ibid. Cf., Seymour M. Hersh, "How I Broke the Mylai 4 Story," SATURDAY REVIEW 52, 28 (July 11, 1970): 46-49, and "Mylai 4," HARPERS 240, 1440 (May 1970): 83-84.

10. Quoted in Talese, THE KINGDOM AND THE POWER, p. 385.

11. David Gelman and Barbara Kempton, "The Trouble with Newspapers: An Interview with Murray Kempton," WASHINGTON MONTHLY 1, 3 (April 1969): 31.

12. Richard Fryklund, "Covering the Defense Establishment," THE PRESS IN WASHINGTON, ed. by Ray E. Hiebert (New York: Dodd, Mead, 1966), p. 179.

13. Robert Cutler, NO TIME FOR REST (Boston: Atlantic-Little, Brown, 1965), pp. 317-18.

14. Roger Hilsman, TO MOVE A NATION (Garden City: Doubleday, 1967), p. 544.

15. George Reedy, THE TWILIGHT OF THE PRESIDENCY (New York: World, 1970), pp. 109-10. Copyright © 1970 by George E. Reedy. Reprinted by arrangement with The New American Library, Inc., New York, New York.

16. Joseph and Stewart Alsop, THE REPORTER'S TRADE (New York: Reynal, 1958), p. 16.

17. Cf. Alfred Friendly, "Attribution of News," REPORTING THE NEWS, ed. by Louis Lyons (Cambridge: The Belknap Press of Harvard University, 1965), pp. 96-97.

18. Stewart Alsop and Charles Bartlett, "In Time of Crisis," SATURDAY EVENING POST 235, 44 (December 8, 1962): 20. Emphasis added.

19. Arthur Schlesinger, Jr., A THOUSAND DAYS (Boston: Houghton Mifflin, 1965), pp. 810-11, 836. Copyright © 1965 by Arthur M. Schlesinger, Jr. Reprinted by permission of Houghton Mifflin Company; Theodore C. Sorensen, KENNEDY (New York: Harper and Row, 1965), p. 714.

20. Baker, "Fourteen Clues to Washington News," p. 110.

21. Harold W. Chase and Allen H. Lerman, KENNEDY AND THE PRESS (New York: Crowell, 1965), pp. 342.

22. Schlesinger, A THOUSAND DAYS, p. 835.

23. "The Big Flap," NEWSWEEK 60, 25 (December 17, 1962): 20.

24. Schlesinger, A THOUSAND DAYS, p. 837.

25. "The Stranger on the Squad," TIME 80, 24 (December 14, 1962): 18. Reprinted by permission from TIME, The Weekly Newsmagazine; Copyright Time Inc.

26. "The Big Flap," p. 20.

27. Karl E. Meyer, "Ordeal by Leak." NEW STATESMAN (London) 64, 1657 (December 14, 1962): 858.

28. Sorensen, KENNEDY, p. 37.

29. Ibid., p. 315.

30. James McCartney, "The Vested Interests of the Reporter," REPORTING THE NEWS, ed. by Louis Lyons, p. 99.

31. The theoretical approach has been derived from the one used to explain relationships between regulatory officials and the industries they are charged with regulating. Cf., Murray Edelman, THE SYMBOLIC USES OF POLITICS (Urbana: University of Illinois Press, 1967), Chapter 3. A comparable finding in a study of local reporting is found in Walter Gieber and Walter Johnson, "The City Hall Beat: A Study of Reporter and Source Roles," JOURNALISM QUARTERLY 38, 3 (Summer 1961): 289-97.

32. Russell Baker, AN AMERICAN IN WASHINGTON (New York: Knopf, 1961), pp. 198-99.

33. Raymond Clapper, WATCHING THE WORLD (New York: McGraw-Hill, 1944), p. 103.

34. James Reston, ARTILLERY OF THE PRESS (New York: Harper and Row, 1967), p. 54.

35. McCartney, "The Vested Interests of the Reporter," p. 99.

36. James A. Skardon, "The Apollo Story," COLUMBIA JOURNALISM REVIEW 6, 4 (Winter 1967-68): 37.

37. McCartney, "The Vested Interests of the Reporter," p. 98.

38. Catledge, MY LIFE AND THE TIMES, p. 188.

39. Talese, THE KINGDOM AND THE POWER, p. 386.

40. Catledge, MY LIFE AND THE TIMES, p. 165.

41. Jeremy Tunstall, THE WESTMINSTER LOBBY CORRESPONDENTS (London: Routledge & Kegan Paul, 1970), Chapters 4, 7, Appendix; Richard Halloran, JAPAN: IMAGES AND REALITY (Tokyo: Charles E. Tuttle, 1970), pp. 181-82.

42. NEW YORK TIMES, November 14, 1971, p. 75.

43. Llewellyn White and Robert D. Leigh, PEOPLES SPEAKING TO PEOPLES, A Report on International Mass Communications from the Commission on Freedom of the Press (Chicago: University of Chicago Press, 1946), p. 68.

44. George E. Reedy, "Speaking for the President," THE VOICE OF GOVERNMENT, ed. by Ray E. Hiebert and Carleton E. Spitzer (New York: John Wiley, 1968), pp. 103, 106.

45. Hilsman, TO MOVE A NATION, p. 514.

46. Adam Yarmolinsky, THE MILITARY ESTABLISHMENT (New York: Harper and Row, 1971), p. 200. Cf., Jules Witcover, "Surliest Crew in Washington," COLUMBIA JOURNALISM REVIEW 4, 1 (Spring 1965): 13-14.

47. Quoted in David Halberstam, THE MAKING OF A QUAGMIRE (New York: Random House, 1965), p. 72; and in John Mecklin, MISSION IN TORMENT (Garden City: Doubleday, 1965), pp. 114-15.

48. Halberstam, THE MAKING OF A QUAGMIRE, p. 268. Cf. Harry S. Truman, MEMOIRS, II: YEARS OF TRIAL AND HOPE (New York: Signet, 1958), pp. 333-34.

49. NEW YORK TIMES, May 14, 1966, p. 30, and May 20, 1972, p. 8; WASHINGTON POST, April 8, 1971, p. A-33, and May 22, 1970, p. B-15; CHICAGO JOURNALISM REVIEW 3, 8 (August 1970): 3-4 ff.

50. NEW YORK TIMES, November 18, 1969, p. 27, and July 2, 1968, p. 6, and December 13, 1972, p. 19; WASHINGTON POST, December 18, 1969, p. A-14; Seymour Hersh, "(But Don't Tell Anyone I Told You)," THE NEW REPUBLIC 157, 24 (December 9, 1967): 13-14; John Rothchild, "The Stories Reporters Don't Write," WASHINGTON MONTHLY 3, 4 (June 1971): 21; Alsop and Alsop, THE REPORTER'S TRADE, pp. 65-68; WASHINGTON POST, November 11, 1971, p. 1.

51. Reedy, THE TWILIGHT OF THE PRESIDENCY, p. 116. Cf., Phil G. Goulding, CONFIRM OR DENY (New York: Harper and Row, 1970), p. 9; Arthur Krock, MEMOIRS (New York: Funk and Wagnalls, 1968), p. 485.

52. "News Under Kennedy," COLUMBIA JOURNALISM REVIEW 1, 1 (Spring 1962): 15.

53. NEW YORK TIMES, December 16, 1971, p. 16.

54. John Osborne, "The Nixon Watch: Toilet Training," THE NEW REPUB-

LIC 166, 1-2 (January 1-8, 1972): 16. Reprinted by permission of the NEW REPUBLIC, © 1972, Harrison-Blaine of New Jersey, Inc.

55. NEW YORK TIMES, December 16, 1971, p. 16.

56. WASHINGTON POST, December 17, 1971, p. A-3.

57. NEW YORK TIMES, December 17, 1971, p. 26.

58. WASHINGTON POST, February 4, 1972, p. A-6.

59. Jules Witcover, "The Presidential Press Conference: Status Report," COLUMBIA JOURNALISM REVIEW 10, 1 (May/June 1971): 52-54.

60. NEW YORK TIMES, April 23, 1962, p. 25.

61. "Quotation of the Year," COLUMBIA JOURNALISM REVIEW 1, 2 (Summer 1962): 37.

62. Grant McConnell, STEEL AND THE PRESIDENCY—1962 (New York: W.W. Norton, 1963), p. 35.

63. Talese, THE KINGDOM AND THE POWER, p. 301.

64. A.P. LOG, quoted in "Quotation of the Year," p. 37.

65. Schlesinger, A THOUSAND DAYS, p. 635; Sorensen, KENNEDY, p. 461; McConnell, STEEL AND THE PRESIDENCY—1962, pp. 34-35.

66. Catledge, MY LIFE AND THE TIMES, p. 289.

67. Ibid., pp. 289-90.

68. Interview with Benjamin Bradlee, May 7, 1970.

69. Reproduced in Ben Bagdikian, "What Makes a Newspaper Nearly Great?" COLUMBIA JOURNALISM REVIEW 6, 3 (Fall 1967): 35.

4   The Journalist's Creed

What, then, is truth? A mobile army of metaphors, metonyms, and anthro-pomorphisms—in short, a sum of human relations which have been enhanced, transposed, and embellished poetically and rhetorically, and which after long use seem firm, canonical, and obligatory to a people: truths are illusions about which one has forgotten that this is what they are; metaphors which are worn out and without sensuous power; coins which have lost their pictures and now matter only as metal, no longer as coins.

Friedrich Nietzsche[1]

Inside the news community the consensus about news takes shape within a framework of shared values, what may be called *the journalist's creed.*

The creed does not consist solely of a formal or codified set of tenets, such as the "Canons of Journalism" of the American Society of Newspaper Editors (ASNE), or of individual and isolated ideas, such as "freedom of the press"; instead, the ideology is the totality of a newsman's beliefs, his world view.[2] This world view does not appear in the writings of any individual newsman, nor is it simply a composite of the public statements of various newsmen. Rather, it is a comprehensive reconstruction of the theoretical underpinnings of the newsman's belief system, an "ideal-type" of the group's ideology.[3] Such an exhaustive analysis of the creed remains beyond the scope of the present study. Instead, it explores three elements of the creed: the conventions, or epistemological premises of newsmaking; the role conceptions, or newsmen's views of their job; and the catch-phrases, or their forensic ideology. Moreover, each element has several variants stemming from differences among the positions newsmen occupy within their organizations, but the analysis concentrates on the elements common to editors, reporters, and columnists.

The 'Conventions' of Newsmaking

Not all information makes the news. More information comes to the reporter on the beat than he can possibly include in his story. More stories flow into the newsroom than editors can possibly fit into the newspaper. What are the newsman's criteria for choosing among information and stories? In his classic work, *Public Opinion*, completed in 1922, Walter Lippmann addressed this question:

Every newspaper, when it reaches the reader, is the result of a whole series of selections as to what items shall be printed, in what position they shall be printed, how much space each shall occupy, what emphasis each shall have. There are no objective standards here. There are conventions.[4]

For the most part, these conventions justify intellectually what the newsman does routinely in processing information. When faced with unstructured, nonroutine occurrences, though, newsmen try to fit them into a pattern congruent with these conventions. As one observer puts it, "Their commodity is not the normal; it is the standardized exceptional."[5] *Conventions*, the customary ways of thinking about news and newsmaking, help to standardize newspaper content. Conventions also form the bases for arguing over news content in the newsroom and on the beat. Information that radically violates these conventions will be subject to greater scrutiny on the desks than information which does not, and reporters may find it harder to justify its newsworthiness. These habits of mind, like the routines of action, seem to reduce the scope of newsmen's uncertainty by providing a set of standards for selecting news and a catalyst for crystallizing consensus. Regardless of their validity, they in effect routinize certitude. Finally, conventions are useful for legitimating the selection made and for deflecting outside criticism.[6] Their very imprecision makes them arcane—secrets, like social science jargon and "legal-ese," understood only by members of the journalism priesthood. "Every profession," as George Bernard Shaw once said, "is a conspiracy against the laity."

'Objective' Reporting

The conventions of "objective" reporting lay out procedures to follow in composing news stories.

One such convention is that of "straight news," setting down information with a minimum of explicit interpretation. Any interpretive material that does appear in the news columns must be attributable to a news source.

Newspapers originated as journals of opinion: "It is a newspaper's duty to print the news and raise hell," was the way Wilbur F. Storey articulated the aims of his fledgling Chicago *Times* in 1861.[7] Straight news did not come into vogue until the turn of the century, when two trends converged to mute the partisan tone of the press in America. First, the drive of publishers to boost circulation and the growth of advertising as a source of revenue made for impartiality in the news columns: promulgating emphatically partisan views which might offend readers or advertisers simply did not pay. Adolph Ochs was among the first publishers to subordinate politics to economics. "To give the news impartially without fear or favor, regardless of any party, sect or interest involved" was the credo he proclaimed in the first issue of the *Times* published after he took over the paper in 1896. Along with the decline of the partisan press came the founding of cooperative newsgathering associations, which supplied stories to clients who were at once vehemently partisan and arrayed on various sides of any issue. To produce copy that would satisfy their diverse clients, wire service men avoided writing anything controversial on their own authority—editorializing, in journalistic parlance. They might smuggle interpretation into their stories by carefully selecting statements from news sources and quoting them verbatim or paraphrasing them without comment, but they tried to avoid inserting their own subjective judgment overtly into the news columns.

The straight news convention reinforces the consequences of newsgathering routines. It permits the publication of stories based on the views of a single news source, so long as he is in a position to issue a press release or call a press conference on a beat regularly covered by reporters. Even more, it guarantees a hearing for a source's views regardless of reporters' personal judgment of their veracity or validity. The ease with which Senator Joseph McCarthy was able to use the press touched off considerable debate about straight news in the journalism community during the 1950s. One critic of the convention contends that

few of the reporters who regularly covered McCarthy believed him. Most came to hate him and fear him as a cynical liar who was willing to wreak untold havoc to satisfy his own power drive. But though they feared him it was not intimidation that caused the press to serve as the instrument for McCarthy's rise. Rather it was the inherent vulnerabilities—the frozen patterns of the press—which McCarthy discovered and played upon with unerring skill. "Straight" news, the absolute commandment of most mass media journalism, had become a strait jacket to crush the initiative and the independence of the reporter.[8]

Newspapers, McCarthy recognized, would publish whatever he said as soon as he said it, while refutations would not run until later, if at all.

To remedy problems such as those caused by McCarthy, newsmen supplemented straight news with another convention, that of "fairness." As codified in the ASNE's "Canons of Journalism," it is the rule of fair play:

A newspaper should not publish unofficial charges affecting reputation or moral character without opportunity given to the accused to be heard; right practice demands the giving of such opportunity in all cases of serious accusation outside judicial proceedings.
... It is the privilege, as it is the duty, of a newspaper to make prompt and complete correction of its own serious mistakes of fact or opinion, whatever their origin.[9]

This convention may provide some recourse to those who feel they have been slandered, but it fails to guarantee equity since charge and rebuttal need not appear in the same story nor receive the same play in subsequent editions.

From the convention of straight news it follows that newsmen distinguish between "hard news" and "soft news"—between stories based on information directly perceptible to human senses, eyewitness reporting of events and recording of statements, which properly belong in the news columns; and stories based on the reporter's subjective interpretation of the meaning of events, which both the *Times* and *Post* usually designate as "news analysis."[a] In making this distinction they reject, at least by implication, an alternative epistemological premise that all seeing is theory-laden.

Notwithstanding the validity of newsmen's conventions of taking their news straight and hard, the scope of their uncertainty was bounded as long as they could adhere steadfastly to these conventions. Accepting these conventions as given, they might manage the task of authenticating news: it was one of setting down the "who, what, where, and when" accurately, faithfully transcribing their sources' statements, and correcting errors in subsequent editions. "If we have a standard of truth," says Max Frankel, "it is the avoidance of cumulative inaccuracy."[10]

These conventions, though, did not incline reporters to widen their search for news beyond routine channels and official sources. Journalists found themselves under attack for concentrating on spot news at the expenses of underlying trends in the society, like the migration of blacks northward in the 1950s and 1960s and the suburbanization of the white middle class. Meanwhile, television, with its rapid transmission and graphic portrayal, touched off a round of self-criticism at newspapers like the *Times* and the *Post*. If newspapermen could not match the speed and vividness of the rival medium, they at least felt capable of providing their audience with more depth and detail.[11] The product of the rethinking, in Frankel's words, was "an exploded concept of what is news." To the "who, what, where, and when" newsmen added an explicit concern with the "why" of news. They had to give greater emphasis to interpretive reporting, to soft news.

Once they did so, however, they exposed themselves to all the uncertainties that they had previously assumed away. It was no longer as simple to draw a line between what was news and what wasn't. The epistemological consensus in journalism began to break down. "Avoidance of cumulative inaccuracy" was no longer enough; newsmen have had to face squarely the difficulty of what information to publish. To the convention of straight news, newsmen have added one of "balance"—making news columns accessible to various sides in a political controversy. Stories are supposed to present the views first of one side, then of another—"writing it down the middle," reporters call it. When stories with discrepant views come in from different bureaus or beats, they can be integrated into a single composite story or, more often, run side-by-side.[12] It is in keeping with the change in convention, too, that *Times* and *Post* reporters who are covering a Presidential race switch candidates in mid-campaign.

---

[a]Traditionalists have slowed the introduction of news analysis into the news columns: the desks subject news analysis to far greater scrutiny than other articles and the TIMES has a rule limiting the number of news analysis pieces, or "Q-headers" as they are called there, to one per desk each day.

Balance is an important ground rule in bargaining between news sources and reporters. Dissidents from the prevailing view in Washington, for instance, can invoke this convention to obtain publicity for their opinions. Even if it does result in the airing of some dissent, though, balance ensures that those backing administration policy always get a hearing: they are usually in a better position than their opponents to air accusations of imbalance against newspapers.

In a broader sense newsmen may find balance a much more difficult standard to comply with than straight news, for it raises more directly the question of who qualifies as a news source.

'Authoritative Sources'

The conventions of objective reporting are inextricably bound up with conventions on news sources. The reporter, like the historian and the social scientist, is not in a position to witness many occurrences in person. Some are not directly visible—economic trends, shifts in public opinion, changes in official thinking. Sometimes he must rely on the observations of others. Yet he, even more than the historian or the social scientist, relies on second-hand information. Even when he is in a position to observe an event directly, he remains reluctant to offer interpretations of his own overtly, preferring instead to rely on his news sources. For the reporter, in short, most news is not what has happened, but what someone says has happened, thus making the choice of sources crucial.

As late as the 1920s, individuals such as Charles Lindbergh, Charlie Chaplin, Albert Einstein, and Babe Ruth qualified as authoritative sources. Their opinions on all sorts of topics were deemed worth quoting, and by implication, worth believing. Gradually, though, authoritativeness as a news source became synonymous with authority in important institutions. Presidents and governors, the J.P. Morgans and the Henry Fords qualified as news sources. According to Walter Lippmann,

The established leaders of any organization have great natural advantages. They are believed to have better sources of information. The books and papers are in their offices. They took part in the important conferences. They met the important people. They have responsibility. It is, therefore, easier for them to secure attention and to speak in a convincing tone.[13]

As the press increasingly organized its newsgathering around governmental institutions, authoritativeness began to vary with distance from positions of formal responsibility for public policy. Today, the higher up in government a man is, the better his prospects to make news. This convention enjoins reporters on beats in the U.S. government to cover the senior officials in their agency. On the White House beat it means "covering the body," following the President's every movement.

By virtue of his responsibility for public policy, the man in the White House has no peer as an authoritative source. "The papers frankly put a very high estimation on the news value of official utterances by the government, at least by the President," says a former managing editor of the *Post*. "I would say that the major newspapers feel a strong compulsion to convey the essence of what the President says on almost any occasion. . . ."[14] This "compulsion" is accentuated at a "newspaper of record" like the *Times*: the man most responsible for public policy is preeminently entitled to have his views recorded. The convention can be useful to the President. In George Reedy's experience,

Presidents have considerable leverage with which to manipulate part of the press and all try to do so with varying degrees of success. The principal source of the leverage is the unusual position of the President as one of the very few figures in public life who has in his exclusive possession a type of news virtually indispensable to the social and economic security of any reporter assigned to cover the White House full time. This category of newsworthy material consists of the President himself—his thoughts, his relationships with his friends and employees, his routine habits, his personal likes and dislikes, his intimate moments with his family and his associates. The fact that these things constitute "news" of a front-page variety gives the President a trading power with individual newsmen of such magnitude that it must be seen at close quarters to be credited.[15]

By virtue of their influence on events, whatever office-holders say may be significant, whether or not it is true. Of necessity, any evaluation of sources is largely reputational, and holding formal office is not a self-evidently inadequate measure of reliability or even veracity. When strictly adhered to, this convention does help to protect the news media from some charlatans and hucksters who compete for coverage. Yet it disposes reporters to rely primarily on men in authority for information. The disposition is the same whether they are covering a student demonstration at Columbia University or a riot in a ghetto.[16] If a man holds no office in a recognized organization, he usually has no claim to publicity. Partly as a result of this convention, information from officials and the conventional wisdom prevailing in official circles dominate press coverage of events.

'News Pegs'

The shift away from hard news weakens the link between news and discrete events. Not only the sources of news but also its timing becomes problematical. As long as reporters can stick to covering events, even those staged precisely for the purpose of receiving coverage, timing poses relatively few difficulties. They either meet their deadlines or they do not. Events are pretexts for running information, and the less recent an event, the worse its prospects for making the news. Analyses of long-run trends, in-depth interpretation, and feature stories, however, are usually not anchored to a particular point in time. Just when is such news newsworthy?

To help resolve this question, there is a convention of "news pegs." Information has a much greater probability of making the news if it is "pegged"—if newsmen can relate it to a discrete event, one that is both determinate in time and recent. Some stories that fail to satisfy the convention meet untimely death at the hands of editors. Others are held up pending events: in the case of its five-part series on the Central Intelligence Agency, the *Times* delayed publication until news broke that the Agency had planted agents among a group of Michigan State scholars studying Vietnam.[17]

Not all events occur autonomously. Congressional committee hearings and speeches can be scheduled to exploit newsmen's need for an event to which they can peg news. News sources also learn to time the release of information to take advantage of the convention. Long-buried reports have a way of surfacing just after the occurrence of related events. Reporters, by asking a question at a Presidential news conference, can give a story the peg that will justify its inclusion in tomorrow's news.

Yet this convention gives news an episodic character: issues surface suddenly and disappear just as suddenly, only to resurface when a new event takes place. News also tends to have a foreshortened time perspective. Undue emphasis on timeliness, coupled with the need for production deadlines, imposes constraints on reportorial enterprise as well: today's events must make tomorrow's news, even if all the evidence is not yet in. Still, the convention persists. The explanation may be in the uncertainty of the newsman's world. Time pressure forces action amid uncertainty. News pegs also give him familiar criteria for selecting the information that makes the news. What other criteria can he substitute for timeliness?

In an earlier period of American journalism, when circulation was the major component of revenues and newsstand sales were the principal source of circulation, timeliness of news mattered more than it does today. Now that the broadcast media supply most Americans with the latest news, extra editions are part of history. For newspapers, the continued emphasis on timeliness is hardly a function of economic competition in the industry. In present-day journalism, the convention on timeliness is just that—a convention.

'Exclusives'

Another legacy from the earlier days is the "exclusive," or "scoop"—information that one reporter or news organization publishes ahead of rivals in the business. Under the highly competitive conditions of news markets at the turn of the century, exclusives may have boosted circulation in the short run—although the

effect of *political* news on circulation even then has probably been overesti-
mated. For most newspapers in most cities in the United States, and especially
those with sizable bureaus in Washington, any rise in circulation because of
exclusives in political news is probably negligible. Strong brand loyalty characterizes consumer demand for newspapers. Only major events such as the
outbreak of war, lunar landings, and assassinations have immediate, measurable
effects on newsstand sales. Political coverage has an appreciable effect on
circulation only over the long run, and even that may be due more to changes in
political tastes and the gradual increase in the size of the politically attentive
segment of the population than to speed of coverage.

If the exclusive is now only remotely related to the market for news, what
accounts for its persistence and importance in the minds of reporters, editors,
and publishers? The answer, again, is rooted in the uncertainty underlying news.
Uncertainty makes measures of the quality of reporting elusive. As one former
Times reporter, Gay Talese writes,

A politician must win elections, a star actor must make money at the box office,
a network-television commentator must maintain ratings, but a titled *Times* man
may go on for decades on the momentum of the institution, facing no singular
test, gaining no confidence from individual accomplishment; and yet he is
personally catered to by statesmen, dictators, bankers, Presidents of the United
States, people who believe that he possesses persuasive powers within the
institution—but they cannot be sure; *he* cannot be sure.[18]

Just as there are no intrinsic standards of success, so it is hard to specify criteria
for hiring and promotion.

The difficulty of agreeing to standards for judging the quality of a reporter's
stories means that editors and publishers and consequently reporters themselves
tend to fall back on an older index of reporting skill: who gets stories first. Some
alternative indices are used—facility with writing, ease of conversation, sharpness
and persistence of questioning, intellectual ability—but they are not as readily
measurable, nor do they unfailingly differentiate the star from the journeyman.
Exclusives win the Pulitzer Prizes and promotions in the profession.

The ability to get exclusives, however, may only reflect the breadth and
importance of a reporter's contacts and their estimations of his "reliability" in
transcribing the information they give him without revealing their identity. The
need for exclusives disposes a reporter to curry favor among key sources on his
beat, especially senior officials in the government. Since an exclusive is
information that he alone receives, he and his editors are tempted to print it
before its source dispenses it to their rivals as well. They have little time and
perhaps less inclination to check the story with other sources. The importance
newsmen attach to exclusives thus tends to reinforce beat parochialism.

'Inverted Pyramids,' Short 'Leads,'
Headlines, and Conventional Explanations

Newsmen traditionally arrange the information in news stories in an "inverted pyramid" style, the most newsworthy bits first, followed in descending order by details of lesser significance. This convention makes it easier to cut stories that do not fit in their allotted space. Men in the composing room, faced with a last-minute need to eliminate some material, with no time to consult an editor, can simply drop the last few paragraphs.

Another convention designs opening paragraphs for the busy reader. A catchy "lead" on a feature arrests his attention. An abbreviated lead on a news story gives him the gist of it without forcing him to wade through columns of print. Headlines abbreviate a story even more.

The shortage of news space and the conventions for arranging information within it—the inverted pyramid, the short lead, the headline—force newsmen to simplify complexity. One way they do so is by repeating slogans, like New Deal, War on Poverty, and Vietnamization. News sources learn to exploit the journalistic need for simplification. As one who is not above advertising himself, Norman Mailer describes his talent for making the news:

"Nuances were forever being munched like peanuts. . . . If the ears of the reporters were geared to capture accurately the mediocre remarks of mediocre men, then one had to look for simple salient statements, so poetically bare, but so irreducible, that they would stick in the reporter's mind like a thorn. It was the only way to talk to a reporter."[19]

Franklin Roosevelt mastered the same technique for sending messages through the press. "F.D.R.," writes Arthur Schlesinger, Jr., "had never hesitated to cast elementary statement or homely metaphor—lend-lease and the neighbor's fire-hose—before the sophisticates of the Washington press corps, knowing that the key phrases would filter through to the people who needed them."[20]

The expository style of journalism allows newsmen to avoid explicit theorizing. They need not put a hypothesis in the lead and marshal evidence pro and con behind it. They simply line information up—implicitly in order of importance—and allow it to march off in whatever direction the reader wants it to go. Yet to capsulate a complex story in the lead requires at least an implicit theory. Leads have been shrinking over time, and the shorter the lead, the greater the need for simplification.[21]

But newsmen lack a body of theory. "Unburdened by excess intellectual baggage" is the way Joseph Kraft describes James Reston: "Indifferent to creed, he is dedicated to the news."[22] Many newsmen are ardently anti-theoretical. Better read than expert is the watchword around the journalism community. Yet, however anti-theoretical their approach to politics and society, newsmen do have an identifiable set of conventional explanations, which influence both their own versions of events and the interpretations they accept from their sources.

First, they look for "rational policy" explanations for events. Their crucial premise is that actions in Washington take place the way they do because someone intended them to. In any controversy, all the major actors have policy preferences, or intentions. The reporter tries to infer from their past acts and statements the intentions officials have and from the actions of the government, what man's aims seem to have prevailed or who had power. In looking for the intentional, he may miss the routine and haphazard. Where he sees personal motivations there may be bureaucratic objectives. This mode of interpreting outcomes in Washington has drawn comment from Emmet John Hughes, a journalist who also served as a speechwriter for President Eisenhower:

The daily press, radio and television *has* to make an intelligible report on national affairs, even though the matters reported may have been handled in a most unintelligible way. Journalistically, it is most difficult to report the details of confusion in an unconfused manner. Thus, at the end of a day of administrative disorder in the White House or State Department, there was an almost tonic effect in reading, in the evening's news columns, a most tidily organized account of all that had happened. And it was a particularly reassuring experience, for example, to scan a thoughtful commentator's analysis of the subtle reasons why the Administration shrewdly avoided or deferred certain action—when anyone within the government might have been naive enough to have thought it a simple case of someone failing to finish his work.[23]

Another set of conventional interpretations of reporters comes out of the muckraking tradition—the constant search for evidence of impropriety and illegality, often at the expense of analysis of other issues. In the words of Roger Starr, Executive Director of New York's Housing and Planning Council, "*The Shame of the Cities* continues to haunt the city rooms of the country's major newspapers."[24] It is no less applicable to their Washington bureaus. The emphasis on corruption resonates with a widely shared liberal ethic that "power corrupts." Even more important, this emphasis shows the effect of uncertainty on reporters. Compared to social and economic analysis of the impact of urban renewal or welfare or other issues, illegality is rather well-defined and clear-cut. It is usually easier to feel "objective" in discussing violations of the law and impropriety.

Sources use this convention in obvious ways. Any policy they oppose is more vulnerable to attack on grounds of corruption than on its merits because of the play which the attack will get in the news. Thus, Supreme Court Justices, police departments, and Saigon regimes, Agency for International Development (AID) projects overseas and poverty programs in Harlem, each opposed for a variety of policy reasons, come under attack primarily for corruption.

'Coins Which Matter As Metal'

The maintenance of established conventions among newsmen is often unrelated to the origin of those patterns of thought. Although most conventions are rooted in earlier economic organization of the newspaper industry, some persist long after that organization has changed. They may not have outlived their usefulness: they remain the tools for newsmen to reduce uncertainty about news. Unsure about the validity of the information they receive, they tend to fall back on long-standing conventions of what news is. Nor is it self-evident that alternative criteria for news provide better guarantees of validity. The more widely the old conventions are shared, moreover, the greater the consensus in the journalism community on what news should be; and the more newsmen publish the same information, the more assured they feel about the validity of that information.

News sources have adjusted their thinking to newsmen's conventions. They talk the same language. They use the conventions to get information disseminated in the press.

How Newsmen View Their Roles

The role of the reporter can be analyzed in terms of his interactions with his editors, his colleagues, and his sources, and the expectations of his behavior that he shares with them. How he himself views his role, his *role conceptions*, form part of the newsman's creed.[25] Like his conventions, these role conceptions may marginally affect his performance on the job. In work situations less structured by organizational incentives, he may seize opportunities to act in conformity with the picture he has of himself.

The Newsman As Neutral Observer

The dominant role conception held in the news community is that of newsman as neutral observer, detached from events and reluctant to pronounce explicit personal judgments on them in print. By this conception, his job is to report the news and inform his audience. His impact on the outcomes of political controversy, it assumes, is nonexistent.

The Newsman As Participant

Newsmen, of course, have their political preferences. Some also yearn for the sense of involvement. Gay Talese expresses this feeling in describing his managing editor at the *Times*. "Men like Daniel," he remarks, "go off to new names, new places, never getting *involved*, although sometimes they worry about the impermanence of their work and wonder where it will lead them."[26] In a similar vein, Joseph and Stewart Alsop wonder "why it is worth devoting so much legwork and so much headwork to a trade that is not notably highly paid." Material gain is not the key, they conclude:

Reporting, in compensation, offers larger intangible rewards. Above all reporting offers the sense of being *engagé* in the political process of one's own time. The reporter who is not consciously *engagé* is in fact likely to be a very bad and unsuccessful reporter.[27]

Douglass Cater likewise argues that the pay scale, "the thrill in chasing after the news," and the ego gratification of getting a front-page byline "do not constitute the basic incentives of a substantial group of correspondents in Washington." Instead, these individuals

... have an acute sense of involvement in the churning process that is government in America. The reporter is the recorder of government but he is also a participant. He operates in a system in which power is divided. He, as much as anyone, and more than a great many, helps to shape the course of government.[28]

To newsmen like Cater, the press is "the fourth branch of government."

Although most journalists see themselves as neutral observers, quite a few of those in Washington have at the same time an alternative—and antithetical—conception of themselves as participants in the governmental process. This role conception has two facets: one as governmental insider, the other as outside critic. The adherents of both seek consciously to influence policy outcomes through their reporting of news, and even through active involvement in policy-making. Joseph Alsop's reminiscences about the halcyon days of World War II, when "a bold reporter could easily play a certain role in national policy decisions," are typical:

Being bold, or perhaps one should say presumptuous, he [Alsop] played such a role in more than one fairly significant decision, like the decision to make the first big loan to the Chinese Nationalist Government. Hence he became an insider as well as a reporter. He was accepted as an adviser by T.V. Soong [Chiang Kai-shek's personal representative in Washington]. He was in frequent touch with all the American governmental experts on China. He was involved, in one way or another, in most of the arguments and intrigues from which our wartime China policy (or pseudo-policy) rather haphazardly evolved.[29]

Alsop even recounts drafting a telegram to Washington from Chiang demanding the recall of General Joseph Stilwell.[30] His involvement, he concludes, enabled him to write "about these problems, and about America's proper approach to them, with lordly self-confidence throughout 1940 and the first months of 1941."[31] Maybe so, but he could hardly have avoided writing about them as an advocate of particular policies. "I always believed," says Robert Kintner, a one-time partner of Alsop's, "that a reporter should report the facts and stay the hell out of the decision-making process. But not Joe. Joe has always wanted to *make* things happen."[32] It is this desire to make things happen that makes many newsmen aspire to be columnists and, beyond that, participants.

Another side of this conception is that of the newsman as an outside critic, willing, even eager, to take a stand. The British version is that of reporter as spectator, in the mold of Addison and Steele. As depicted by a British journalist, his is no crusading zeal, but a curiosity about social and political anomalies and willingness to expose them: "His instinct, when faced with any situation is not to think, 'This situation is wrong. I think this should be changed. I will try to enlist public support for my view. . . . ' " Instead, he feels,

Here is a *queer* situation. This is something inconsistent with the prevailing public assumptions of the community into which I was born and in which I live and work. I do not think the public are aware of the existence of this situation. I shall lay the facts before them. They can do what they jolly well like about it.[33]

The American version, that of muckraker, barely conceals the sense of moral outrage: "Rather naively I yearned for the days of Lincoln Steffens," recalls investigative reporter Clark Mollenhoff, who read the muckraker's autobiography in college, "and rather naively I believed that the journalistic forays of Lincoln Steffens and the political thrusts of Teddy Roosevelt had eliminated most of the corruption in America. I must admit I was more than just a little elated to discover that there were still a few dishonest public officials left to chase." When Mollenhoff got around to writing a book of his own, *Despoilers of Democracy,* it had as its theme, "Fraud and favoritism are sapping the strength of America's democracy. Politics and plunder are wasting billions of tax dollars."[34] Seen this way, the reporter is not just a spectator, but tribune of the people; journalism is not just a job, but a calling.

The participant conception is deeply rooted in the history of the American newspaper. Tocqueville describes the "class spirit" of the American journalist in the 1840s as consisting of "an open and coarse appeal to the passions of his readers; he abandons principles to assail the characters of individuals, to track them into private life and disclose all their weaknesses and vices."[35] For the first hundred years of nationhood, patronage appointments and government printing contracts tied some publishers to those in high public office. With the establishment of the Government Printing Office in 1860 came the disestablishment of the press, but partisanship perpetuated the close ties between journalism and officialdom long afterward.

The journalist's conception of himself as participant disposes him to take a more active part in shaping the content of news than the neutral observer conception does. He follows his own lead in choosing stories as newsworthy. He may rely less heavily on the formal channels of information than the neutral observer, preferring instead to develop stories on his own through his network of sources. He actively makes news, not just reports it. Whereas the journalist's view of his role as neutral observer renders him susceptible to use by his sources, the participant may be more consciously either willing to be used or not. "Why couldn't you get along with me?" James Reston asked Dean Acheson just before the Secretary of State's retirement from public office. "Didn't you realize how useful I could be?"[36]

The journalist's choice of sources may differ depending on whether he sees himself as an insider or an outsider, but the more he sees himself as participant, the more likely he is to absorb the perspectives of men he is assigned to cover on the beat. Covering the government, he writes to influence officials, to gain their acceptance. To hear the Alsop brothers tell it, that acceptance is what makes reporting worthwhile:

[A] reporter can have no more satisfying moment than the moment when a man in high position says, "I don't really mind talking to *you*, because you know what I'm talking about." That really happened to one of us once, and the speaker was a man of extreme brilliance, carrying a staggering load of national responsibility, with a ferocious reputation for hostility to newspapermen.[37]

The participant conception also inspires newsmen to seek out and exploit opportunities for overt involvement in the policy process. A frequent activity is speechwriting. For a 1961 address by President Kennedy on arms control, Sorensen writes, two columnists "who regarded each other as 'hard' and 'soft,' respectively, were asked unbeknownst to each other to contribute drafts, which were then blended. . . ."[38] Another activity is contributing ideas for policy. Besides helping to sell the Marshall Plan in 1947, Walter Lippmann stimulated some substantive changes in the program for European recovery.[39] He later inspired President Johnson to propose a Marshall Plan for Southeast Asia in 1965. Shown a draft of a Vietnam speech prepared for delivery in Baltimore on April 7, Lippmann complained to Johnson that while swinging a stick, it dangled no carrot. By the time it was given, the speech included offers of "unconditional discussions" and construction of a "T.V.A." for the Mekong Delta.[40] A third activity is intelligence-gathering. Foreign correspondents for American papers have been known to submit to "debriefing" upon their return to the United States, occasionally for a fee.[41]

In the course of exchanging information among officials, reporters serve as intermediaries, particularly in situations when formal channels for transmitting information are disrupted or otherwise unusable. During the steel controversy of 1962, first word of an impending price rise by U.S. Steel reached the President through columnist Charles Bartlett. Later on, Bartlett served as a go-between in working out a resolution.[42]

Reporters have also been instrumental in establishing informal contact between, as well as within governments, such as the part John Scali played as an intermediary in the Cuban missile crisis. Scali, then State Department correspondent for ABC, had cultivated numerous contacts in foreign embassies, in addition to the American government. Early Friday afternoon in the second week of the crisis, Scali got an urgent call from Aleksander Fomin, a counselor at the Soviet embassy with whom he had dined on past occasions. Fomin asked Scali's opinion of a proposal to remove Soviet missiles in Cuba under U.N. inspection and to renounce any future installation, in return for a public pledge by President Kennedy not to invade the island. Receiving a noncommittal reply, Fomin begged Scali to solicit opinions from his associates in the State Department, and assured him of the "vital importance" of a response. Scali transmitted the message to Roger Hilsman, State's Director of Intelligence and Research, who relayed it to Secretary of State Rusk. Following discussions within Ex-Com, Rusk asked Scali to tell the Russian that there were "real possibilities" for negotiation, but to emphasize that only forty-eight hours remained to the American ultimatum. The following day, when messages from Premier Khrushchev arrived, contradicting the earlier proposal and raising fears that hard-liners had seized the initiative within the Kremlin, Rusk asked Scali to meet Fomin and get any additional information he could. The Russian reported that there must have been a cable delay and that "the Embassy was waiting word from Khrushchev at any moment."[43] Scali brought this message directly to the President.

Although more direct lines of communication between Moscow and Washington were also in use at that time, it is unclear who in the Kremlin—but presumably officials in high positions—had chosen this channel, and why. It is clear from accounts of the American deliberations, however, that information received through Scali helped shape the actions chosen by Ex-Com.

Ironically, Scali was not the first reporter to disclose his own part in the crisis. The President, wanting to keep open the Scali-Fomin channel and especially anxious not to undermine either Khrushchev's or Fomin's position, asked Scali to refrain from reporting anything of his activities and offered to give him a personal letter of appreciation. Scali replied that the letter would do him about as much good as a reporter as being "renominated by the Democratic National Convention in secret" would do for the President.[44] Kennedy chuckled but got Scali to withhold the story until after he had left office. After Kennedy's death, Scali received State Department permission to break the story, but Robert Donovan of the *Los Angeles Times* learned of the incident first and scooped him. The Scali affair is by no means the only one in which a reporter's desire for involvement in the policy process has impeded the discharge of his journalistic responsibilities.

Newsman As 'Good Citizen'

In the course of newsmaking, newsmen experience a number of conflicts between their obligations as citizens and their obligations as newsmen. In matters of national security, says CBS State Department correspondent Marvin Kalb, "They are pulled from all sides. Their loyalties are divided. One source gives them some information, while a second source asks them to kill it."[45] Many times, both sources invoke "national security" in behalf of their objectives. Other times, reporters are called upon to pass along information of dubious validity. Kalb cites the case of an April 1965 background briefing by Defense Secretary Robert McNamara, who told reporters that the possibility of using nuclear weapons in Vietnam was always open. His views were published and attributed to a "high Administration official."[46] At a press conference the next day, the Secretary drew back somewhat: "There is no military requirement for the use of nuclear weapons in the current situation, and no useful purpose can be served by speculation on remote contingencies."[47]

According to Kalb, "His underlying purpose, of course, was twofold: to frighten the Chinese Communists by unofficially letting them know that the United States might use nuclear weapons, but at the same time to calm the American people by officially denying this policy." How did Kalb decide whether or not to use such information? His answer:

You have to go by your instincts most of the time. For example, on the nuclear weapons leak from McNamara, you knew he was doing this to frighten the Chinese and you said so. Lying is a legitimate part of the defense mechanism of the administration, and the reporter goes along with it when in his opinion it is in the national interest.[48]

Where does a reporter like Kalb get "his opinion" of what is "in the national interest"? In practice, he tends to defer to the judgment of the official who discloses information to him.

Reporters must weigh whether nondisclosure is in the nation's interest or just in the official's. Their relations with the particular officials involved may tip the scales. On March 19, 1959, *The New York Times* ran a lead story by defense correspondent Hanson Baldwin making public the information that the United States had conducted secret nuclear tests in the upper atmosphere the previous September. One newsweekly called the story the year's biggest scoop. Baldwin, however, had first learned of the plan long before the detonations and even had some of the details, says *Times* science editor Walter Sullivan, "but he did not feel the story should be published prior to the tests."[49] Sullivan consulted a friend of his, "a key figure in the space program," who told him that premature publicity might force cancellation of the tests. Later the same day he received a call from the security chief of the Advanced Research Projects Agency in the Defense Department, who repeated the warning and suggested that he would come to New York immediately to discuss the matter further. "I told him this wasn't necessary," says Sullivan. "Hanson and I had already agreed to sit on the story."[50]

Upon the conclusion of the tests, Baldwin and Sullivan, worried that rivals would break the Project Argus story first, pressed Defense officials to approve publication, but they again refused on the grounds "that even though the Russians knew, in theory, the effect demonstrated by Argus, it was better not to draw their attention to it until we had reaped, for the longest possible time, the benefit of carrying out the first experiment."[51] Scientists prominent in the International Geophysical Year program urged full disclosure of the effects of the test. So did their co-workers outside the program, who argued that, given the information already publicly available on closely related scientific phenomena, continued secrecy on Argus was unjustifiable and that "the only reason for withholding the story was political—to avoid embarrassment to the government."[52]

In January, Sullivan met with Dr. Herbert York, the Pentagon's Director of Research and Engineering, to ask him "what was important to conceal, should we decide to publish." Details on the location, size, and height of the explosion, was the reply. Finally, in the second week in March, Baldwin learned that the Pentagon was moving to release some information on Argus. At a meeting with Arthur Hays Sulzberger, Orville Dryfoos, and Turner Catledge, he and Sullivan recommended publication. Publisher Sulzberger made plain his reluctance: "I do not want to do anything that is going to harm the country," he told the others.[53] After questioning the reporters closely, he relented—but not before notifying the White House and the Pentagon.

Situations like these pose not just an abstract question of the social costs and benefits of disclosures, but a very concrete question of risk, both personal and institutional. This risk was a consideration in the *Times'* coverage of the Bay of Pigs. The first public hint that the United States was training Cuban exiles in preparation for an invasion to topple Fidel Castro appeared in the November 19, 1960, edition of *The Nation*. The *Times* dispatched its Central American correspondent to Guatemala to investigate. His findings were published on January 10, 1961:

Retalheleu, Guatemala, Jan. 9—This area is the focal point of Guatemala's military preparations for what Guatemalans consider will be an almost inevitable clash with Cuba. . . .
    The United States is assisting this effort not only in personnel but in material and the construction of ground and air facilities.[54]

By the end of March, when rumors of impending invasion were circulating Washington, Tad Szulc, the *Times'* Latin American correspondent, happened to stop in Miami en route to Washington and got wind of some of the preparations. On April 6, he filed a dispatch detailing CIA recruitment of an invasion force and predicting an imminent invasion. It was scheduled to run as the right-hand lead for Friday, April 7, under a four-column headline. According to Clifton Daniel,

While the front-page dummy was being drawn up by the assistant managing editor, the news editor, and assistant news editor, Orvil Dryfoos, then the publisher of *The New York Times*, came down from the fourteenth floor to the office of Turner Catledge, the managing editor. He was gravely troubled by the security implications of Szulc's story. He could envision failure for the invasion, and he could see *The New York Times* being blamed for a bloody fiasco.[55]

Catledge had qualms of his own:

First, Szulc declared the invasion was "imminent." This bothered me because it was a prediction. If we made the prediction, we ran the risk of being wrong, or at least of enabling the government to make us wrong by changing its plans. I felt we would be safer—we would stay within the facts—if we said the Cuban exiles were massed, they had been trained for an invasion, and they were anxious to launch the invasion—but not to say the invasion was "imminent."

. . . My second concern was his specific reference to CIA sponsorship. I didn't doubt that our cloak-and-dagger men were deeply involved, but the government has quite a few intelligence agencies, more than most people realize, and I was hesitant to specify the CIA when we might not be able to document the charge. I thought it best to use more general terms, like "U.S. officials" and "U.S. experts" in the story.[56]

Dryfoos telephoned James Reston, then Washington bureau chief. "I told them not to run it," says Reston.[57] Catledge corroborates this recollection: "The difference between Reston and me was one of degree. I was willing to say that an invasion was planned but not that it was imminent; Reston would have preferred no reference to an invasion at that point."[58] Yet their reasons were somewhat different. "[I] n some instances, including this one," says Catledge, "Scotty is impressed by pleas that printing certain stories might go against the national interest. . . . I think Scotty allowed his news judgment to be influenced by his patriotism." As to his own stand, Catledge explains, "I was not worried so much about protecting the government as about protecting the *Times*. When people talk about newspapers serving the public interest, I am sometimes forced to admit that I'm never sure what the public interest is, beyond its needs for accurate information."[59]

Dryfoos backed Catledge. Once the text had been emended to satisfy his objections, Catledge ordered the headline size reduced from four columns to one and the story dropped to a lower slot on page one. Theodore Bernstein, the assistant managing editor, and Lewis Jordan, the news editor, went into Catledge's office to protest the changes. They demanded to hear an explanation from the publisher himself. Angered at their insistence on appealing over his head, Catledge nonetheless called Dryfoos, who came down to the newsroom and gave them his reasons—"those of national security, national interest, and, above all, concern for the safety of the men who were preparing to offer their lives on the beaches of Cuba."[60] Yet underlying these considerations was an institutional concern: avoiding blame for a "bloody fiasco." In the event of cancellation or failure of the invasion plans, it would have been the CIA's definition of the national interest, not the *Times*', that most of Washington and the rest of the nation accepted. Szulc shrugged off what happened to his story with the comment that "after all, it takes courage for a newspaper to call its government a liar."[61]

The dilemmas of the citizen-newsman are not confined to national security. Reporters covering labor-management relations are accustomed to hearing pleas from mediators to withhold information that might disrupt ongoing negotiations and damage "the public interest." Yet the pressures are hardest to bear when public officials can call a newsman's patriotism into doubt. From Dean Rusk—"There gets to be a point when the question is, whose side are you on? Now, I'm Secretary of State of the United States, and I'm on our side"—to Supreme Court Justice Harry Blackmun—"I strongly urge, and sincerely hope, that these two newspapers will be fully aware of their ultimate responsibility to the United States of America . . . "—the sentiment of officials, however different their positions and the situation, bear a marked similarity.[62] It was put most forcefully by President Kennedy just a few days after the Bay of Pigs:

In time of war, the government and the press have customarily joined in an effort, based largely on self-discipline, to prevent unauthorized disclosures to the enemy. In times of clear and present danger, the courts have held that even the privileged rights of the First Amendment must yield to the public's need for national security.

Today no war has been declared—and however fierce the struggle may be, it may never be declared in the traditional fashion. Our way of life is under attack. Those who make themselves our enemy are advancing around the globe. . . .

If the press is awaiting a declaration of war before it imposes the self-discipline of combat conditions, then I can only say that no war ever posed a greater threat to our security. If you are awaiting a finding of "clear and present danger," then I can only say that the danger has never been more clear and its presence has never been more imminent.

. . . I am asking the members of the newspaper profession and the industry in this country to reexamine their own responsibilities—to consider the degree and the nature of the present danger—and to heed the duty of self-restraint which that danger imposes upon us all.

Every newspaper now asks itself with respect to every story: "Is it news?" All I suggest is that you ask the question: "Is it in the interest of national security?"[63]

The patriotic fervor of the press during World War I inspired Walter Lippmann to complain, "The work of reporters has thus become confused with the work of preachers, revivalists, prophets, and agitators." He elaborated,

To Archbishop Whately's dictum that it matters greatly whether you put truth in the first place or the second, the candid exponent of modern journalism would reply that he put truth second to what he conceived to be the national interest. Judged simply by their product, men like Mr. Ochs or Viscount

Northcliffe believe that their respective nations will perish and civilization decay unless their idea of what is patriotic is permitted to temper the curiosity of their readers.[64]

The reporter's conception of himself as patriot still inclines him to put considerations of national interest ahead of those of news. "We are, we believe, good citizens as well as good journalists," says the Washington bureau chief of *Time* magazine, John L. Steele. "There are some things you happen on that you simply don't report."[65] What these things are newsmen often let officials determine. The moral that Clifton Daniel drew from retelling the *Times'* decision to tone down the Bay of Pigs story is instructive:

Information is essential to people who propose to govern themselves. It is the responsibility of serious journalists to supply that information. . . .
    Still, the primary responsibility for safeguarding our national interest must rest always with our government. . . .[66]

The Newsman As Adversary of the Government

An antithesis of the participant and citizen conceptions is that of the newsman as adversary of the government. It received its classic expression in an 1852 editorial by Robert Lowe in *The Times* of London on February 6, 1852, lecturing the Palmerston Government on the role of the press:

. . . [W]e cannot admit that its purpose is to share the labours of statesmanship, or that it is bound by the same limitations, the same duties, the same liabilities as that of the Ministers of the Crown. The purposes and duties of the two powers are constantly separate, generally independent, sometimes diametrically opposite. The dignity and freedom of the Press are trammelled from the moment it accepts an ancillary position. To perform its duties with entire independence, and consequently with the utmost public advantage, the press can enter into no close and binding alliances with the statesmen of the day, nor can it surrender its permanent interests to the convenience of the ephemeral power of any government.
    The first duty of the Press is to obtain the earliest and most correct intelligence of the events of the time, and instantly, by disclosing them, to make them the common property of the nation. . . .[67]

William Jennings Bryan had his own version. Announcing his retirement as Secretary of State, he told reporters, "I have been like an old hen. My secrets have been my chickens which I was seeking to protect with my wings while you were trying to get them out from under me."[68]

    In practice, there is a mixture of conflict and cooperation on the beat. If the press "lives by disclosures," as *The Times* leader went on to assert, then reporters and officials must be at once allies and adversaries. Yet both the reporter and the official tend to cast their relationship in terms of this antinomy and to stress either one side or the other. The rhetoric may enable them to maintain trust in each other while reassuring onlookers that both are fulfilling the obligations of their offices as the theory of democracy has so ambiguously specified them.

Newsman As Novelist

The participant, citizen, and adversary conceptions have all challenged the newsman's view of himself as neutral observer, but only recently has this conception come under frontal assault. The assault has been mounted by exponents of what columnist Pete Hamill christened "the new journalism." Gone was the reporter as neutral observer; in his place was the reporter as "Novelist!!" Many a "new journalist" began as a feature writer. According to Tom Wolfe, an early convert,

What they had in common was that they all regarded the newspaper as a motel you checked into overnight on the road to the final triumph. The idea was to get a job on a newspaper, keep body and soul together, pay the rent, get to know "the world," accumulate "experience," perhaps work some of the fat off your style—then, at some point, quit cold, say goodbye to journalism, move into a shack somewhere, work night and day for six months, and light up the sky with the final triumph. The final triumph was known as The Novel.[69]

While the new journalists are a diverse group, at a minimum, the new role conception that most of them supported called for new content and a new style of reporting. "When one moves from newspaper reporting to this new form of journalism," Wolfe relates, ". . . one discovers that the basic reporting unit is no longer the datum, the piece of information, but the scene, since most of the sophisticated strategies of prose depend upon scenes. Therefore, your main problem as a reporter is, simply, managing to stay with whomever you are writing about long enough for the scenes to take place before your own eyes."[70] Remaining on the scene long enough, the new journalist may become part of the scene, an interested party, openly injecting a personal point of view into the story, involving himself in the events he is covering to the point of—like Norman Mailer at the Pentagon—getting arrested.

The reaction may have appeared disproportionate to the threat, but the howls of anguish that the traditionalists have emitted suggest how sensitive a nerve the new journalism had touched. Its content and style were so sharply at variance with those of objective reporting that the new journalism seemed to call the old into question. The complaint of Lester Markel, former Sunday editor of the *Times*, was typical of the reaction: "[M]ost ardently, editors should repulse those among the New-J's who would apparently substitute for who, what, where, how, and why—for all these eternal and absolute basics—a large IF."[71]

The Catch-Phrases of Journalism

In politics, as in literature and religion, language can serve as a cue for emotion as well as a tool for analysis. Catch-phrases may connote reassurance or threat for some audiences while merely denoting phenomena for others. Two such phrases are "credibility gap" and "freedom of the press."

'Credibility Gap'

Partisan argument may be unexceptional; mistakes and half-truths, expected; but outright lies violate the rules of the game between newsmen and their sources. A President, though, by virtue of the routines and conventions of journalism, is almost automatically entitled to coverage. When he lies, newsmen still feel compelled to pass along what he says. But they raise charges of a "credibility gap," perhaps first in editorial columns, and then by picking up similar charges made elsewhere in the political arena. Speaking of credibility gaps may resemble the Victorians' referring to limbs rather than legs, to paraphrase Walter Lippmann, but stirring up this issue is perhaps the only defense the journalist has against the abuse of his newsgathering practices.

The link between lying and the credibility gap is apparent in Hugh Sidey's discussion of an incident that occurred when he was covering President Johnson for *Time* magazine:

It is a singular experience to be told by the President of the United States—the most powerful man in the world—that something you know to be true is not so. Yet this is what happened repeatedly when Johnson first entered the White House. It is the essence of the credibility gap.[72]

Yet other forms of news management would have been less objectionable to Sidey:

Reporters were baffled from the start as to why the President did not simply refuse to talk about things which he felt should not be in the public domain rather than stage elaborate dramas to present false impressions which inevitably were found out. Even a direct request to a reporter not to print something would have been accepted with more understanding than the sleight-of-hand which Johnson tried to practice.[73]

The timing of the emergence of the credibility issue in the press during any administration's tenure may also constitute evidence of its link to lying. Newsmen did not make the charge against Johnson until December 1965, and even then it was not over Vietnam or the Dominican Republic intervention, but instead in response to what they took to be lies by the President on rather trivial occasions. Among the techniques of news management, only lying may be sufficient to trigger charges of a credibility gap because it alone clearly falls outside the bounds of objective reporting.

Press reactions to the post-Cuban crisis speech of Arthur Sylvester, the Assistant Secretary of Defense for Public Affairs and hence the Defense Department's official spokesman, exhibited the same hostility reporters show toward lying. On December 6, 1962, Sylvester, addressed the Deadline Club of New York. He spoke openly to assembled newsmen about news as a "weapon" in the hands of the government. He then justified this characterization by referring to "the government's right, if necessary, to lie to save itself when it's going up toward a nuclear war," and reiterated his stand in the questioning that followed.[74] Until then, press references to news management during the crisis were infrequent and often elliptical; but upon hearing such an assertion from a former reporter whom they assumed was well aware of their conventions and the nuances of official justifications for news management, newsmen were outraged. They counter-attacked with allegations of a credibility gap. James Reston's observations at the time are interesting: "As long as officials merely didn't tell the whole truth, very few of us complained; but as soon as Sylvester told the truth, the editors fell on him like a fumble."[75] Both his implicit attack on the objectivity of reporters' stories dealing with the crisis and his express challenge to existing conventions on validity transformed Sylvester, like Spiro T. Agnew, into a symbolic target of the press. The reactions of newsmen to direct attacks on their objectivity are not unlike those to lying, and perhaps for the same reason: their identity and their self-respect rest heavily on their audience's acceptance of that objectivity.

'Freedom of the Press'

Perhaps the most familiar element in the reporter's creed is "freedom of the press." As a catch-phrase, freedom of the press is an empty vessel into which newspapermen pour much meaning. The slogan embraces a number of assertions of rights by the press: at a minimum, the right of access to government information, the right to publish without prior restraint, and the right to maintain confidentiality of sources. Publishers have extended the doctrine to cover demands for low second-class mailing rates, for exclusion from those provisions of the antitrust laws that would prohibit joint operating agreements and price-fixing among ostensibly competitive newspaper enterprises, and even for double parking privileges for newspaper delivery vans.

Over the years, freedom of the press or freedom of information has acquired an aura of favorable sentiment, or pathos, surrounding it and cloaking it from critical scrutiny.[76] "A subject as dear to the press as theoretical argument is to Talmudic scholars, and often with about the same relevance to reality," Joseph Kraft calls it.[77] A faith in the power of reason has sustained its pathos over the years, even as the metaphors changed from the feudal battlefield of Thomas

Jefferson—"Truth . . . will prevail if left to herself. . . . She is the proper and sufficient antagonist to error, and has nothing to fear from the contest unless by human interposition disarmed of her natural weapons, free from argument and debate"[78]—to the bourgeois marketplace of Oliver Wendell Holmes—"the best test of truth is the power of thought to get itself accepted in the competition of the market. . . ."[79]

As the rationalist faith began to lose its hold, the doctrine of freedom of the press came under challenge from those who saw it as a smokescreen behind which publishers pursued their self-interest, and a new doctrine gradually gained acceptance—"the responsibility of the press." It was expounded by men like Joseph Pulitzer:

Nothing less than the highest ideals, the most scrupulous anxiety to do right, the most accurate knowledge of the problems it has to meet, and a sincere sense of moral responsibility will save journalism from a subservience to business interests, seeking selfish ends, antagonistic to public welfare.[80]

It was a reformation that some publishers took for apostasy. One who did was William Peter Hamilton of *The Wall Street Journal:*

A newspaper is a private enterprise owing nothing whatever to the public, which grants it no franchise. It is therefore affected with no public interest. It is emphatically the property of the owner, who is selling a manufactured product at his own risk. . . ."[81]

Like the two strands of the American business creed, a classical one emphasizing the profit motive and a managerial one emphasizing service to stockholders, employees, customers, and the general public,[82] freedom of the press and responsibility of the press remain in uneasy tandem. Reporters, editors, and some publishers use the doctrine of the responsibility of the press against the exponents of the older doctrine in arguing for changes in the organization of newsgathering.

Ideology and Organization in Newsmaking

Too often, ideological analysis follows the line of reasoning: "I have a social philosophy; you have political opinions; he has an ideology."[83] Use of the concept of ideology here carries with it no necessary implication about the validity of the content of the journalist's creed, only the premise that thought, in general, is related to the position of the thinker in the social structure. Newsmen do not differ from other social groups, whether businessmen, manual laborers, or intellectuals: their specific life situations exert a very strong influence on their view of the world. Ideological analysis, or the sociology of knowledge, following the path staked out by Karl Marx, has stressed the importance of class and generational groupings as the major influence on thought patterns. Yet Marx did not argue that thought was simply a reflection of economic relations in a society, but of all social relations, of which the technological base of the economy was the main determinant. He makes this clear in *The Poverty of Philosophy* when he writes,

Social relations are closely bound up with productive forces. In acquiring new productive forces men change their mode of production; and in changing their mode of production, in changing the way of earning their living, they change all their social relations. . . . The same men who establish their social relations in conformity with their material productivity, produce also principles, ideas, and categories, in conformity with their social relations.[84]

As a more cohesive social grouping than a class, an occupational group such as newsmen, having similar work experiences and sharing many cultural premises and personal qualities as a result of recruitment patterns, might be expected to have a common ideology.

Some parts of the journalist's creed originate in the organization of the news industry at the turn of the century or earlier. Others are legacies of the liberal tradition in America. Apart from the question of the formation of the creed and its development, though, what accounts for its persistence? The brief survey of the creed suggests that many of its tenets are not just atavisms, but continue to serve various functions for journalists who espouse them.

One explanation for the persistence of an ideology and for the linkage between its content and the social structure is that the creed contains rationalizations of the economic self-interest of men in the industry. Freedom of the press has doubtless served such a purpose in some situations, as have various conceptions that newsmen have of their role. The creed as a whole may foster the image of newspapers as a special sort of private enterprise, to be left free from some legal restrictions imposed on other business firms. Yet the economic interests of a publisher are not the same as those of editors or reporters, and they, even more than he, believe in the creed. Moreover, to infer a group's interests from its ideology and then to assume that these interests produced the ideology is to construct an elaborate tautology, unless it is possible to show that adherence to the tenets of the creed is manifestly in the interest of all classes of newsmen, which seems implausible.

Another explanation is that the creed helps enhance the professional autonomy of newsmen by deflecting criticism from outsiders. This explanation, too, accounts for the use of the creed on many public occasions to legitimate the behavior of newsmen, but it is insufficient in that it ignores the private espousal of the creed by newsmen, who invoke its tenets in arguments over newsmaking and come to think about their work in terms of the categories set out in the creed.

A third explanation seems more appropriate in many instances. In his field work on the Trobriand Islanders, anthropologist Bronislaw Malinowski found that they employed myths to sanction moral authority, to justify an otherwise anomalous status in society, or to reduce anxiety over an event by rendering that authority, status or event seemingly comprehensible in everyday terms. "It is clear," he concluded, "that myth functions especially where there is a sociological strain, such as in matters of great difference in rank and power, matters of precedence and subordination, and unquestionably where profound historical changes have taken place."[85] Closer to home, in their study of "the American business creed," Francis X. Sutton and his colleagues analyze ideology as "a patterned reaction to the patterned strains of a social role."[86] These role strains include incompatible demands imposed upon a man by his job, the discrepancy between the demands of his role and his inner needs or personal abilities, and the conflict between his work role and other roles he seeks to play in society.

The precise causal connection between a particular role strain and a particular ideological tenet is unclear: the tenet may provide a guideline for restoring consistency, it may obscure the existence of inconsistency, or it may "redefine" one or more of his roles to resolve a conflict.[87] Thus, a reporter may not perceive any inconsistency between speed and accuracy on the job because he is just too busy to think about this problem under the pressure of deadlines, and even if his story does have a minor inaccuracy or two, he may correct it the next day. But if he does experience a strain, the scoop comes first and the procedures of objective reporting may seem to him sufficient to ensure the validity of his story. Since beliefs about scoops and objective reporting are widely shared in the news community, there exists some social reinforcement for avoiding the strain produced by the incompatibility of making his deadline and reporting the news accurately.

Even if the causal link is unclear, however, the ideological richness of the journalist's creed is strongly associated with the existence of role strains which the creed might ease.

A number of tenets of the creed seem to be associated with a strain resulting from the newsman's involvement and intimate knowledge of the policy-making process in Washington without the status and power that accrues to officials who are as deeply involved. That newsmen experience anxiety over the ambiguity of their status recurs in the discussions of their work. Turner Catledge writes of his early years as assistant managing editor and of the toll that the job took on his marriage: "Throughout these years, given my personal difficulties and my professional frustrations, I kept asking myself, 'Where in hell does all this lead?' "[88] Added to worries about career are the frustrations of watching from the sidelines while others can step into the arena or exhibit their partisanship from the box seats. "Reporters, like lawyers, have opinions," writes Anthony Lewis of the *Times*. "They are naturally interested in public affairs. They are not eunuchs. Almost inevitably they find themselves rooting for one side or another."[89] Some, like Lewis, get to write a column or contribute to magazines where they are freer to express their opinions; others want to jump into the fray. The desire comes out in the ambivalence they feel about going to work for the government. A reporter who took a job in the Public Affairs Division of a federal agency says,

As a rule public information officers are former members of the press; frequently they have worked longer as members of the press than they have as information officers. So between them and the members of the working press there is always the question: "Why did you go to work for the government?" The question has the same nagging quality as that devilish advertising slogan we've all seen: "Is it true blondes have more fun?" Some reporters regard their craft as I once did, as a "calling"–in the old puritanical sense of an ordained occupation. They regard those who have left the craft for other pursuits as somehow akin to fallen priests. And they wonder not only why they did it, but whether they might also find it tempting.[90]

The belief that he has influence, that he and his colleagues comprise a "fourth branch of government" may help a newsman bear this strain. Yet the conception of participation raises new inconsistencies. As J.R. Wiggins, managing editor of the *Post*, once told his staff,

I think the ideal journalist, the ideal newspaperman, is a man who never forgets which side of the footlights he's on, who never forgets that he is a reporter, a recounter, a narrator, and not an actor, who never forgets that he is an observer and not a mover and shaker. We claim, informally and by our attitudes, if not by formal assertion, the privileges of the fourth estate, apart from the other estates. It is inconsistent with this role for any of us to make public statements or to exhibit in our private capacities and in our personal conduct violent and decisive partisan attitudes toward men or measures, so strong as to preclude, in the mind of the ordinary listener, the possibility of unbiased reporting.[91]

If the strain becomes intolerable, a newsman may follow Wiggins' lead: three months after making this statement, he resigned from the *Post* to accept President Johnson's offer of a United Nations ambassadorship.

Another source of strain is the newsman's dependence on officials for their livelihood. For many reporters on the beat and editors in the newsroom, officials are the principal sources of news and its constant critics. Yet officials expect newsmen to know more than they tell in covering them. The journalist's creed expresses this strain in several ways. One is the role conception of an adversary relationship between the press and the government. While the identification of a class enemy may enhance solidarity among reporters, it ignores the extent of their collaboration with that enemy. There is also the image of the hard-bitten reporter.[92] Under the conditions of covering a beat, skepticism soon turns to cynicism, which may help a reporter bear his dependence while obscuring the extent to which he must take what his sources hand him. Finally, the strain may relate to the emphasis on corruption in journalists' explanations of the workings of government.

Of all the strains that newsmen experience on the job, none is as poignant as their uncertainty about what news is and what it means. This uncertainty, and fear of major mistakes that it can induce, are reflected in an episode in David Halberstam's career. His first assignment overseas for the *Times* was to cover the turmoil in the Belgian Congo in 1962, at the time that a plane carrying U.N. Secretary-General Dag Hammarskjöld crashed, killing everyone on board. Halberstam was unable to join several colleagues at the airport in Ndola, the plane's destination. At the moment the Secretary-General was due in, they saw a plane taxi off the runway and a man who bore some resemblance to Hammarskjöld emerge. An airport guard and a Rhodesian Information Ministry official sought out by the reporters both confirmed the identity of the passenger, and so they cabled word that Hammarskjöld was in Ndola. Halberstam speculates about his career had he been among those at the airport who cabled home the false report:

I doubt that I would have gotten the prized Vietnam assignment; more importantly, had I been sent to Vietnam nevertheless, I would have been writing under a terrific cloud. I would probably have been under considerable pressure to be extra cautious not to stray from the official version of events there; I would have been forced to play the story much closer to the vest. And I would have been a marvelous target for all those opposed to realistic coverage of Vietnam; instead of repeating incessantly, as they did, that I and my colleagues were too young, they could have used my mistake as a weapon.[93]

Uncertainty also permits readers to question the choice of content at every turn. Newsmen need protection from audience dissatisfaction, and the techniques of objective reporting may provide the requisite protection. In a foreword to a collection of essays by reporters who describe how they obtained particular stories, Turner Catledge expresses his desire to have his staff keep stories about their newsgathering exploits out of the newspaper: "It is simply that I think shop talk is just that—talk for the shop." His reason for this stand "has to do with something called objectivity":

There are techniques that make for objectivity and there are techniques and habits of thought that work against it. And among these last perhaps the most dangerous is the injection of the reporter into the newspaper story. It is dangerous because the reader begins to think of a reporter as a participant rather than an observer and is likely to lose trust in him. The reader's trust is the only real stock in trade any reporter has. It is even more dangerous because the reporter who injects himself into a story begins thinking of himself as a participant, a shaper, and pretty soon he is writing about himself for himself.[94]

Yet the conventions of objective reporting, more than defenses for the newsman's autonomy, provide standards that satisfy his own doubts, even while failing to solve the insoluble. They permit him to make news without worrying about what it is or what it means. The newsman's dilemma is not unlike Hamlet's, who, before taking his revenge, wanted to be certain about the identity of his father's slayer. Gradually realizing that Claudius might die of old age before he attained the requisite certainty, Hamlet sees a vision of his dead father which impels him to act. Ideologies are the ghosts, coupling a simplification of reality with an emotional stimulus to action, that force men to act in uncertainty. So it is with the journalist's creed.

Ideology and the News

The newsmen's creed has some bearing on the content of news. The treatment newspapers give to stories involving freedom of the press and the ways role conceptions inspire newsmen to shape news content are rather straightforward. The effects of the conventions on news may be somewhat harder to document. Partly, they support and reinforce the organizational routines of newsgathering. Partly, too, they are the theoretical lenses through which newsmen peer at events. During the 1970 Congressional election, for example, when President Richard Nixon made a campaign stop in San Jose, Robert B. Semple, Jr., the *Times'* White House correspondent, filed a dispatch which appeared on page one on October 30 under the headline, "Eggs and Rocks/Thrown at Nixon/After Coast Talk":

Demonstrators threw eggs, rocks and placards at President Nixon's limousine tonight as he left the San Jose Municipal Auditorium following a political speech.

According to eyewitness accounts, Mr. Nixon narrowly escaped being struck by four or five eggs thrown in his direction from a crowd about 25 yards away as he emerged.

The President had seen the antiwar protestors, estimated at more than 1,000, before he entered the hall and branded them the "violent radical few" in his speech.

After his talk, the President jumped onto the top of his car and waved. He drew cheers from his partisans and jeers from the demonstrators.

He then climbed into his glass-topped limousine and his motorcade left the parking lot at high speed. According to Ronald L. Ziegler, the President's press secretary, and reporters in a car near the Presidential limousine, Mr. Nixon's car was hit by several eggs. Placards and other missiles were also hurled in his direction.

"This is just like Caracas," Rose Mary Woods, Mr. Nixon's personal secretary, was quoted as having said. She was referring to an episode in which Mr. Nixon was the target of stones thrown by demonstrators in Venezuela during a trip there in 1958 when he was Vice President.

Three windows in one of the press buses were broken by stones thrown by hecklers tonight.

The Secret Service reported that a number of antennas on official cars were broken and that the automobiles behind the President's car were spat on.

The President was reported to have said later in the evening, before his plane departed for the Western White House in San Clemente, that he knew that some objects were hitting his car as he drove through the crowd.

According to Mr. Ziegler, the press secretary, Mr. Nixon reported feeling something fly by his head before he entered his car. A Secret Service agent was said to have told the President that it was a small stone.

At no time, however, was the president struck, and the motorcade was not delayed.[95]

The story went on to report the President's speech.

There are some noteworthy aspects to the dispatch. It is punctilious in detail, more careful than most that were filed that hectic evening. It is sparing in adjectives and virtually devoid of overt interpretation with the exception of a quote attributed to Rose Mary Woods added by the desk in New York from a wire service story. Semple himself did not witness the attack, only the aftermath, but he attributes almost every detail to a specific source.

The next evening, President Nixon made a speech in Anaheim, which was retelecast nationwide an hour later in a half-hour spot purchased by the Republican National Committee. The *Times* covered the speech in a right-hand lead written again by Semple under the headline, "Nixon Bids Voters/'Draw the Line'/At Violent Youth ... Speaks Day After His Car/Is Pelted With Eggs and/Stones on Coast." Seven paragraphs down in the story, Semple added some material to his coverage of the San Jose incident. It was a marked contrast to his narrative of the previous day:

Judging from the press secretary's comments, Mr. Nixon had suffered no emotional after-effects from the incident, in which he narrowly missed being hit by a thrown object. The angry antiwar demonstrators later pelted his car with eggs, spat upon Secret Service men and threw stones at cars and buses in the Presidential motorcade.

The Presidential staff, though, was shaken by the most serious physical attack on the Presidential entourage in Mr. Nixon's 21 months in office.

The episode may have important political implications. It has already raised several questions here about the security precautions taken to protect the President. Some newsmen had advance warning that there would be trouble, so presumably the Secret Service, which was said to have plainclothes operatives circulating in the crowd, had similar information.

The White House was unable to explain why the demonstrators had been allowed to mass so close to the motorcade; usually, they are kept behind barricades erected in advance some distance away from the motorcade route.

Politically, some Republican strategists here believe that the incident has given a lift to the campaigns of Senator [George] Murphy and Governor [Ronald] Reagan. Both men were in the Presidential limousine when it was struck. They have been running on tough law-and-order platforms aimed at youthful "permissiveness," and both issued tough statements deploring the violence shortly after the episode.

As reconstructed here today, the stage was set for the incident when the demonstrators—estimated by the Secret Service to number 900 in all and by some reporters at twice that figure—massed in two lines on either side of the roadway leading to the entrance of the San Jose Municipal Auditorium about an hour before the President's arrival.

They did not throw any objects when he arrived but waved their peace signs and taunted him with chants that, at least to the ears of those in the press buses following behind, were uniformly obscene. . . .

When the ceremonies in the auditorium finished, about 30 minutes later, Mr. Nixon emerged and started to walk toward his limousine. Four eggs were hurled in his direction but did not touch him. Mr. Ziegler later said that a small stone had narrowly missed the President.

At this point, Mr. Nixon climbed on top of the hood of his limousine and gave his familiar campaign gesture, a "V" sign with both hands. According to a later account by Marty Schramm, White House correspondent for *Newsday*, who was standing below the President, Mr. Nixon smiled and said to no one in particular: "That's what they hate to see."

Mr. Ziegler said last night, however, that the President had not intended to taunt or defy the demonstrators but thought he had seen a "friendly face" and simply wanted to wave to them.[96]

This account contains considerably more interpretive material than the first. Much of the reconstruction bears no attribution. Unlike the first account, it lends itself to an inference that the danger that the President had been exposed to was exaggerated and that Republicans might benefit from playing up the incident while ignoring the President's part in, perhaps, inciting it.

Semple, who had been inside the auditorium filing his story on the President's speech in order to make the late city edition, had to rely on a pool report for his first account. In compiling his updated story for the late city edition, he followed the procedures of objective reporting, citing authoritative sources and incorporating the latest news. But the pool report, and hence Semple's story, relied heavily on the comments of press secretary Ziegler and another briefing given by White House aide H.R. Haldeman before the President's departure for San Clemente. The only interpretive material came from the President's personal secretary, a long-time Nixon associate. Semple was the *Times'* White House correspondent, a job which entailed accompanying the President, and so he did not remain in San Jose to piece together details. Even so, a rethinking of the incident and a canvass of other reporters present led him to balance their accounts against those of White House personnel, producing considerable change in his story the next day. The difference between the two depends quite a bit on the conventions of reporting in the journalist's creed.

Men explain the unfamiliar in terms of the familiar. It would thus be both out of place and anachronistic in the United States of the 1970s to describe a Presidential directive as "the will of God" and to justify it by "the divine right of kings." The fourth estate in the United States has been more fortunate in this respect than the third estate in France in having doctrines like freedom of the press available in the political culture to put to use in its own ideology. Other tenets are the legacy of earlier forms of organization in the newsmaking industry.

But the older tenets now attract fewer believers. Their decline is partly a reflection of the ideological unravelling of the society at large, but even more, the reaction to challenges within the news community itself. The alternatives proposed as replacements seem to raise more problems than they solve, which enables the older creed to linger on, resisting change through a combination of mental inertia and social reinforcement. The persistence of the old creed slows adoption of organizational changes altering the content of news. In particular, it encourages reporters' continued adherence to traditional patterns of newsgathering.

Notes

1. Friedrich Neitzsche, "On Truth and Lie in an Extra-Moral Sense," THE PORTABLE NIETZSCHE, tr. by Walter Kaufman (New York: Viking Press, 1968), pp. 46-47.

2. A distinction between "particular" and "total" and between "specific" and "general" is made by Karl Mannheim, IDEOLOGY AND UTOPIA (New York: Harcourt, Brace, 1936), p. 77.

3. Mannheim, IDEOLOGY AND UTOPIA, p. 59. In addition to Mannheim, other contributions to the sociology of knowledge have formed the theoretical perspective of this chapter: Karl Marx, THE GERMAN IDEOLOGY (New York: International, 1970); Peter L. Berger and Thomas Luckmann, THE SOCIAL CONSTRUCTION OF REALITY (New York: Doubleday, 1966); Francis X. Sutton, et al., THE AMERICAN BUSINESS CREED (New York: Schocken, 1962); and Robert Lane, POLITICAL IDEOLOGY (Glencoe: Free Press, 1962).

4. Walter Lippmann, PUBLIC OPINION (New York: Free Press, 1965), p. 223. Reprinted by permission of Macmillan Publishing Co., Inc.

5. Silas Bent, "Two Kinds of News," YALE REVIEW 16, 4 (July 1927): 696.

6. Cf. Merton, "Bureaucratic Structure and Personality," p. 368; and Gaye Tuchman, "Objectivity As a Strategic Ritual: An Examination of Newsmen's Notions of Objectivity," AMERICAN JOURNAL OF SOCIOLOGY 77, 4 (January 1972): 660-79.

7. Quoted in William Rivers, THE ADVERSARIES (Boston: Beacon Press, 1970), p. 204.

8. Cater, THE FOURTH BRANCH OF GOVERNMENT, pp. 72-73.

9. American Society of Newspaper Editors, "Canons of Journalism," MASS COMMUNICATION, ed. by Wilbur Schramm (Urbana: University of Illinois Press, 1949), p. 237.

10. Interview with Max Frankel, Washington bureau chief of the TIMES, September 18, 1970.

11. For example, Catledge, MY LIFE AND THE TIMES, pp. 210-11; Talese, THE KINGDOM AND THE POWER, p. 208.

12. Cf. Halberstam, THE MAKING OF A QUAGMIRE, pp. 238-39.

13. Lippmann, PUBLIC OPINION, pp. 157-58.

14. J. Russell Wiggins, transcript of Voice of America feature broadcast February 7, 1966, in U.S. Congress, Senate, Committee on Foreign Relations, HEARINGS: NEWS POLICIES IN VIETNAM, 89th Cong., 2nd Sess., August 17, 1966, p. 120.

15. Reedy, THE TWILIGHT OF THE PRESIDENCY, p. 100-101.

16. Paul Weaver, "How the Times Is Slanted Down the Middle," NEW YORK 1, 13 (July 1, 1968), pp. 32-36; 36; REPORT OF THE NATIONAL ADVISORY COMMISSION ON CIVIL DISORDERS (New York: Bantam, 1968), pp. 364-65.

17. Catledge, MY LIFE AND THE TIMES, p. 290.

18. Talese, THE KINGDOM AND THE POWER, p. 121.

19. Norman Mailer, THE ARMIES OF THE NIGHT (New York: New American Library, 1968), p. 66.

20. Schlesinger, A THOUSAND DAYS, p. 717.

21. Max Hall, "Leads Grow Shorter," NIEMAN REPORTS 15, 4 (October 1961): 18-19.

22. Joseph Kraft, PROFILES IN POWER (New York: New American Library, 1966), p. 85.

23. Emmet John Hughes, THE ORDEAL OF POWER (New York: Atheneum, 1963), pp. 78-79. Reprinted by permission of Atheneum Publishers. Copyright © 1962, 1963 by Emmet John Hughes.

24. Roger Starr, executive director of New York's Housing and Planning Council, quoted in Irving Kristol, "The Underdeveloped Profession," PUBLIC INTEREST 6 (Winter 1967), p. 47.

25. The distinctions made here resemble those of Bernard Cohen, THE PRESS AND FOREIGN POLICY (Princeton: Princeton Univ. Press, 1963), Chapter 2, but with some key differences.

26. Talese, THE KINGDOM AND THE POWER, p. 68.

27. Alsop and Alsop, THE REPORTER'S TRADE, p. 9.

28. Cater, THE FOURTH BRANCH OF GOVERNMENT, p. 7.

29. Alsop and Alsop, THE REPORTER'S TRADE, p. 41.

30. Ibid., p. 168.

31. Ibid.

32. Robert Kintner, quoted in Bernard Law Collier, "The Joe Alsop Story," NEW YORK TIMES, May 23, 1971, VI, p. 73.

33. Robert Sinclair, THE BRITISH PRESS: THE JOURNALIST AND HIS CONSCIENCE (London: Home and Van Thal, 1949), p. 86. Emphasis added.

34. NEW YORK TIMES, June 1, 1970, p. 28. A comparable portrait of Jack Anderson appears in the WASHINGTON POST, January 16, 1972, p. G-1.

35. Alexis de Tocqueville, DEMOCRACY IN AMERICA, tr. by Henry Reeve, Part I, Chapter 11. Cf., Mott, AMERICAN JOURNALISM, p. 128; James Young, THE WASHINGTON COMMUNITY (New York: Columbia University Press, 1966), pp. 173-74; Doris A. Graber, PUBLIC OPINION, THE PRESI-

DENT, AND FOREIGN POLICY (Chicago: Holt, Rinehart and Winston, 1968), p. 122; and Kenneth M. Stampp, AND THE WAR CAME (Baton Rouge: Louisiana State University Press, 1950), p. 183, for examples of newsmen's ties to government.

36. Quoted in Kraft, PROFILES IN POWER, p. 86.

37. Alsop and Alsop, THE REPORTER'S TRADE, p. 9.

38. Sorensen, KENNEDY, p. 512n.

39. Joseph Marion Jones, THE FIFTEEN WEEKS (New York: Harcourt, Brace and World, 1964), pp. 181-82, 226-32.

40. Henry Brandon, ANATOMY OF ERROR (Boston: Gambit, 1969), p. 53. © 1969 by Times Newspapers Ltd. Published in the United Stated by Gambit Incorporated.

41. Under pledge of anonymity, reporters have acknowledged the practice in interviews. Cf., William Worthy, "Debriefing the Press: 'Exclusive to the C.I.A.,'" THE VILLAGE VOICE (December 7, 1972), p. 1; Kim Philby, MY SILENT WAR (London: Panther, 1969), pp. 50-51.

42. Sorensen, KENNEDY, pp. 447, 457.

43. Schlesinger, A THOUSAND DAYS, p. 828.

44. Quoted in William Rivers, THE OPINIONMAKERS (Boston: Beacon Press, 1964), p. 161.

45. Marvin Kalb, "Covering the State Department," THE PRESS IN WASHINGTON, ed. by Ray E. Hiebert, p. 162.

46. NEW YORK TIMES, April 25, 1965, pp. 1, 3.

47. U.S., Department of State, BULLETIN 52, 1351 (May 17, 1965): 752.

48. Kalb, "Covering the State Department," pp. 161-62.

49. Walter Sullivan, "Two Times Reporters Share a Troublesome Secret," THE WORKING PRESS, ed. by Ruth D. Adler (New York: G.P. Putnam's, 1966), p. 88. Copyright © 1961, 1966 by The New York Times Company.

50. Ibid.

51. Ibid., p. 89.

52. Ibid., p. 90.

53. Ibid., p. 91

54. NEW YORK TIMES, January 10, 1961, p. 1.

55. Clifton Daniel, Address to the World Press Institute, excerpted in THE NEW YORK TIMES, June 2, 1966, p. 14.

56. Catledge, MY LIFE AND THE TIMES, p. 261.

57. Quoted in Daniel, Address to the World Press Institute.

58. Catledge, MY LIFE AND THE TIMES, p. 262, Cf., Tad Szulc, "THE NEW YORK TIMES and the Bay of Pigs," HOW I GOT THAT STORY, ed. by David Brown and W. Richard Bruner (New York: Dutton, 1967), p. 322.

59. Catledge, MY LIFE AND THE TIMES, p. 261.

60. Quoted in Daniel, Address to the World Press Institute. Cf., Catledge, MY LIFE AND THE TIMES, pp. 262-63.

61. Szulc, "THE NEW YORK TIMES and the Bay of Pigs," pp. 325-26.

62. Don Oberdorfer, TET! (Garden City: Doubleday, 1971), p. 366; and THE NEW YORK TIMES v. U.S., 403 U.S. 713 (1971). Cf., Mecklin, MISSION IN TORMENT, pp. 114-15; and I.F. Stone, THE HIDDEN HISTORY OF THE KOREAN WAR (New York: Monthly Review Press, 1952), p. 307.

63. John F. Kennedy, "The President and the Press," Speech to the Bureau of Advertising, American Newspaper Publishers Association, New York City, April 27, 1961, reprinted in VITAL SPEECHES 27, 15 (May 15, 1961): 451.

64. Walter Lippmann, LIBERTY AND THE NEWS (New York: Macmillan, 1920), pp. 8-9.

65. Voice of America broadcast of August 27, 1965, in U.S., Congress, Senate, Committee on Foreign Relations, HEARINGS, NEWS POLITICS IN VIETNAM, p. 128.

66. Daniel, Address to the World Press Institute.

67. TIMES (London), February 6, 1852, quoted in H. Wickham Steed, THE PRESS (Harmondsworth: Penguin, 1938), pp. 75-76.

68. Quoted in Oswald Garrison Villard, "The Press and the President," CENTURY 89 (December 1925): 198.

69. Tom Wolfe, "The Birth of 'The New Journalism,' " NEW YORK 5, 7 (February 14, 1972): 30.

70. Tom Wolfe, "Why They Aren't Writing the Great American Novel Anymore," ESQUIRE 78, 6 (December 1972): 278.

71. Lester Markel, "So What's New?" A.S.N.E. BULLETIN 556 (January, 1972), p. 9.

72. Hugh Sidey, A VERY PERSONAL PRESIDENCY (New York: Atheneum, 1968), p. 159.

73. Ibid., p. 160.

74. Martin Gershen, "The 'Right to Lie,' " COLUMBIA JOURNALISM REVIEW 5, 4 (Winter 1966-67): 15. Cf., NEW YORK TIMES, December 7, 1962, p. 5.

75. NEW YORK TIMES, November 2, 1962, p. 30.

76. "Pathos" is a concept used by William G. Sumner, FOLKWAYS (New York: Blaisdell, 1965), p. 180. Cf., Alfred McClung Lee, "Freedom of the Press: Sources of a Catch Phrase," STUDIES IN THE SCIENCE OF SOCIETY, ed. by George P. Murdock (New Haven: Yale University Press, 1937), p. 355, for a somewhat similar analysis of the doctrine.

77. Kraft, PROFILES IN POWER, p. 112.

78. THE WRITINGS OF THOMAS JEFFERSON, ed. by Paul L. Ford (New York: Putnam's, 1894), v.II, p. 441.

79. ABRAMS v. U.S., 250 U.S. 616 (1919).

80. Joseph Pulitzer, "The College of Journalism," NORTH AMERICAN REVIEW, 178 (May 1904): 658.

81. Quoted in Theodore Peterson, "The Social Responsibility of the Press,"

FOUR THEORIES OF THE PRESS, ed. by Fred S. Siebert, Theodore Peterson, and Wilbur Schramm (Urbana: University of Illinois Press, 1963), p. 73.

82. Francis X. Sutton et al., THE AMERICAN BUSINESS CREED (Cambridge: Harvard University Press, 1956), pp. 356-57.

83. Clifford Geertz, "Ideology As a Cultural System," IDEOLOGY AND DISCONTENT, ed. by David Aptor (New York: Free Press of Glencoe, 1964), p. 47.

84. Karl Marx, THE POVERTY OF PHILOSOPHY (New York: New World, 1963), p. 109.

85. Bronislaw Malinowski, "Myth in Primitive Societies," MAGIC, SCIENCE AND RELIGION AND OTHER ESSAYS (Garden City: Doubleday, 1954), p. 126.

86. Sutton, THE AMERICAN BUSINESS CREED, p. 307-308.

87. Robert P. Abelson, "Modes of Resolution of Belief Dilemmas," JOURNAL OF CONFLICT RESOLUTION 3 (1959): 343-52.

88. Catledge, MY LIFE AND THE TIMES, p. 180. Cf., Talese, THE KINGDOM AND THE POWER, p. 270.

89. Anthony Lewis, "Newspapermen and Lawyers," REPORTING THE NEWS, ed. by Louis Lyons, pp. 253-54. Cf., Rosten, THE WASHINGTON CORRESPONDENTS, pp. 244-45.

90. Wayne Phillips, "Information and the Newsman," THE VOICE OF GOVERNMENT, ed. by Ray E. Hiebert and Carlton E. Spitzer, p. 305.

91. NEW YORK TIMES, October 5, 1968, p. 12.

92. Rodney Stark, "Policy and the Pros: An Organizational Analysis of a Metropolitan Newspaper," BERKELEY JOURNAL OF SOCIOLOGY 6 (1962): 29, makes a similar connection.

93. Halberstam, THE MAKING OF A QUAGMIRE, pp. 15-16.

94. Turner Catledge, "Foreword," HOW I GOT THAT STORY, ed. by David Brown and W. Richard Bruner, p. 14.

95. NEW YORK TIMES, October 30, 1970, p. 1, 45.

96. NEW YORK TIMES, October 31, 1970, p. 1, 12.

5 The Routines of Newsgathering

News breaks through definite channels; it cannot do otherwise. Cover those channels and you catch the news—much like casting a net across a salmon stream.

Edwin L. James[1]

Men on the job do not perform tasks de novo. Patterns of action tend to reiterate past patterns. Repeated time after time, these actions become standard operating procedures. Like other organization men, reporters engaged in newsgathering follow established routines. Some routines originated out of a need to coordinate the activity of large numbers of people; others, to restrict the play of individual subjectivity; still others, to economize on staff. Yet these routines, no matter how they were adopted initially, take on a life of their own. Learned during apprenticeship, reinforced in daily experience on the job, they become "the way things are done." News organizations do alter their procedures, and they do make innovative responses to some novel situations. Nevertheless, in an era that puts a premium on change, that experiences the revolutionary as commonplace, it is important to emphasize the regular, the habitual, the routine, that marks newsgathering.[2]

Government officials, for their part, have adapted their practices to the standard operating procedures of newsmen. Doing so facilitates obtaining coverage for what they have to say, as an examination of some of these procedures will indicate.

Some Standard Operating Procedures of Newsgathering

Dailies

One routine, obvious enough to be overlooked, is the regularity with which newspapers are produced. Every day finds a new front page with space to fill. Some days filling it is easier than on others. Theodore Roosevelt used to joke that he "discovered Monday" because Sundays generate little news around Washington, and Roosevelt found that by timing his announcements properly, he could obtain page-one coverage on Monday mornings for items that might on other days get buried inside.[3]

Apart from affecting the timing of public announcements, daily publication underlies many of the other routines of newsgathering. Editors need reporters who can come up with stories day in and day out that merit page-one display; reporters need sources who can provide them with newsworthy information on a regular basis. This need becomes especially compelling when editors have committed considerable resources—news space and staff—to coverage of an event such as a summit conference.

Daily publication also leaves little time for reflection around the newsroom. Newsmen are too busy getting out a newspaper by the deadline to spend a lot of time thinking about it or changing things they don't like.

Deadlines

Putting out a daily newspaper imposes another form of routine on newsmen—the deadline. Stories must be set in type, pages composed, and several editions printed and delivered. Since each stage of production and distribution depends upon completion of an earlier stage, setting and meeting deadlines are essential. For the reporter, deadlines impose an arbitrary cut-off to newsgathering, constraining him to write with the information he has in hand and to hope for more another day.

Rarely are deadlines as oppressive as they are on election night. In the 1960 Presidential race, early returns showed Kennedy far out in front of Nixon, and the *Times* accordingly ran an eight-column headline on its first edition, "Kennedy Elected President." By midnight, returns from the Midwest began to narrow the margin. *Times* managing editor Turner Catledge stopped the presses to await what he felt sure was impending word of a Kennedy victory. The *Chicago Tribune*'s "Dewey Wins" fiasco in 1948 counseled caution, but two hours later, with Kennedy's lead still slimmer and with no more papers for distribution, the *Times* resumed publication and began backing away from its initial story. In its third edition, Kennedy had "piled up such a spectacular lead in the states east of the Mississippi" that "he seemed almost certain to be elected the thirty-fifth President of the United States." The fourth and fifth editions called Kennedy the winner, but by the 7 a.m. "extra" Kennedy "appeared to have won the election."[4] Especially on page one, what makes the news often depends on when the news is made.

Officials have long grown accustomed to timing their statements to the press with an eye toward exploiting newsmen's deadlines. Press briefings in some executive departments take place in two shifts: one at noon for the afternoon papers, another at four for the morning editions. Officials can use reporters' deadlines for more than just ensuring coverage. By timing his charges for release in late afternoon, for example, Senator Joseph McCarthy reduced the chances that a denial would run concurrently with his accusation.

Reading the Papers

National editors at the *Times* and *Post* routinely scan the United Press International (UPI) "daybook," a daily listing of events, hearings, and goings-on around Washington, in order to anticipate the next day's stories and assign a man to cover them. All newsmen, whether reporters or editors, whether a specialist or on general assignment, adhere to a similar routine in coming up with ideas for stories. They all read the newspapers, in particular, *The New York Times* and *The Washington Post*. They supplement this reading by keeping abreast of the flow of news over the wire service teletypes and by scanning other newspapers and magazines.[5] The newsman's first impression of what the news is comes from what newspapers, especially the *Times* and *Post*, cover. This accounts in part for the importance officials attach to the initial version of a story. Officials compete to fashion that first impression and to forestall the attempts of others to do so, for later articles will react to the content of the first.

'Legwork' and 'Contacts'

In the jargon of newsmen the term legwork denotes a set of routines, a program, for newsgathering. It is implied, in the words of Joseph and Stewart Alsop, that "going there is immeasurably better than not going there." Their prescription for foreign correspondence reads:

Go smell the weather in the streets. Go spend no more than a few hours in the midst of a foreign situation you have minutely studied at long range. Suddenly, even before you can consult the local experts, or call on the ambassador, or interview the prime minister, the whole outline of the situation begins to change in your own mind, simply because the weather in the streets has an altogether unexpected smell.[6]

Olfactory perceptions aside, legwork implies interviewing people either in person or by telephone, rather than poring over documents in a library or analyzing statistical data with a computer. Mostly, reporters confine their research to newspapers and periodicals, with occasional forays to the morgue to examine old clippings.

Legwork does not proceed at random. A reporter, whatever his assignments, has a group of contacts, potential information sources developed over the years, with whom he checks on a regular basis. Some he consults only when a particular question arises on which they might have the relevant information. Others he makes a point to look up periodically—"touching base," he calls it.

Beats

The beat is little more than the formal routinizing of periodic checks with a network of contacts. Coverage of the American government, in particular, is structured along beat lines. In addition to making the rounds of officials, the reporter on the beat has the responsibility of maintaining liaison with the senior officials on his beat and also with the "official spokesman"—variously designated public information officer or press secretary. Organizing reporters by beats not only limits the locus of their activity in a city as dispersed as Washington but also identifies them as targets for officials wishing to purvey information to the press.

On the beat reporters adhere to other routines as well. In so doing, they come to rely heavily on facilities provided for their convenience by the officials they are assigned to cover. Travel arrangements are one example. When a senior official goes abroad, news organizations request accommodations for their reporters to go along. Denial of their requests by press officers is rare; but it is tantamount to denial of access, inasmuch as these trips provide reporters with an opportunity to obtain exclusive interviews and informal chats with the men they accompany.

Routine Channels for News
Dissemination and Newsgathering

Of all the facilities that officials routinely provide and reporters routinely rely on, no others compare with the handout and the press conference in their impact on the news. Nongovernmental sources employ these channels, too, but on governmental beats around Washington, these are the two principal *routine channels* through which most information passes from news sources to reporters.

The reporter cannot depend on legwork alone to satisfy his paper's insatiable demand for news. He looks to official channels to provide him with newsworthy material day after day. To the extent that he leans heavily on routine channels for news, he vests the timing of disclosure, and hence the surfacing of news stories, in those who control the channels.

What is routine for the reporter has become standard operating procedure for the official as well. Not only does the disclosure of information through these channels occur regularly but also the process of deciding which information to disclose follows a prescribed route, or action channel. Officials along that route are in a position to intervene in that process; others cannot. In most departments this excludes all but the bureau in charge of public affairs and a few senior officials. Fewer still have the authority to clear information for release. Those who can are in a position to influence the content as well as the timing of news that reporters collect through routine channels. A detailed examination of the routine channels bears this out.

Handouts

Handouts include press releases, communiqués, advance copies of officials' speeches, and records of bureaucratic activity ranging from unemployment statistics to treaty documents. Since these handouts constitute an important part of an administration's public record, details of their release are usually carefully worked out. According to Phil Goulding, a former Assistant Secretary of Defense for Public Affairs, "Our public affairs plan included not only specific approved wording of a great many announcements, but also agreed-upon procedures on which level of government would make which announcements."[7]

Procedures vary slightly from department to department, depending on the substance of the release. The "drill" on a Navy matter starts in the office of the admiral serving as Chief of Information, which prepares a first draft with help from experts on the issue inside the Navy Department. On matters of special importance the office submits the draft to the chief or Vice Chief of Naval Operations, and then to the Secretary of the Navy. Next, it goes to the Defense Department's Public Affairs Office where, as Goulding points out, his aides check it "for accuracy, omissions, language, and tone":

Was the Navy leaving out something important simply because it did not want to acknowledge error? Did the wording suggest that this tragedy never would have happened if the Secretary of Defense had not cut the Navy's budget last year? Was the draft a gentle plug for expanding the bombing of North Vietnam or an indirect sales pitch for a weapon the Secretary of Defense already had disapproved? Was it, in brief, a Navy announcement or a Department of Defense announcement?[8]

In the Pentagon, responsibility for the release of information belongs to the Assistant Secretary of Defense for Public Affairs. The Navy draft represents a recommendation, albeit with the approval of the Chief of Naval Operations or the Secretary of the Navy, just as the naval budget is a recommendation to the Secretary of Defense. The Public Affairs Office then circulates the draft to other Defense Department Offices—to Systems Analysis if it deals with force structures, to International Security Affairs if it relates to other nations, to Research and Engineering if it unveils a new weapon. "Acting first as coordinators and middlemen," writes Goulding, "our office would try to produce a draft satisfactory to the Navy and to all interested elements of OSD [the Office of the Secretary of Defense]." If this proves impossible, then his office redrafts the release. As Assistant Secretary, he usually had the last say:

Relevant Assistant Secretaries of Defense could appeal to me if they were displeased with the final draft, and so could the Secretary of the Navy, but the decision was mine. If any of these officials felt deeply enough, they could, of course, take the issue to the Secretary or Deputy Secretary of Defense, for whom we all worked. Rarely would they win, for if the matter were that important, I probably had already discussed it privately with the Secretary. One of the built-in advantages enjoyed by the Assistant Secretary of Defense for Public Affairs is that he is apt to see the Secretary and Deputy Secretary more often than any other high official in the building.[9]

Whenever a release touches on relations with foreign governments, it then goes to the State Department for review and clearance. "State's contribution," writes Goulding, "would be confined to the international aspects of the release, over which they had the final say."

The pressure of time may short-circuit the procedure. Many clearances can be obtained concurrently. In a crisis, top officials take over as the action officers and draftsmen. At the time of the Pueblo seizure, for example, only four men were involved in the preparation of the initial press release: the Secretary of Defense, a member of the Joint Staff, Goulding, and his deputy. At the State Department only the Secretary of State heard or saw the announcement before its release.[10]

The release of advance texts has also become a standard operating procedure both for officials and for reporters. By distributing a speech or a report slightly before its scheduled release and briefing reporters on its contents or underscoring key points, officials usually can obtain not only fuller coverage but also the desired interpretation. In poring over a long speech or report, sometimes on complex subjects and under pressure of deadlines, reporters come to rely on officials for cues to the most significant passages.

From routine reliance it is but a short step to dependence. It is the folk wisdom of academics that in a lecture words pass from the professor's outline to the student's notebook without passing through either's mind. The same mindlessness sometimes characterizes the transmission of words from press release to news dispatch. When, for example, Winston Churchill delivered a speech in March 1946 that some historians mark as the start of the Cold War, most reporters on hand in Fulton, Missouri, omitted a now famous phrase from their stories. Edward T. Folliard of the *Post* was one. "I heard Churchill use the words, 'iron curtain,' no doubt about it," he recalls, "but in writing my story I muffed the whole passage. Why? How?" His explanation is "that the advance text of Churchill's speech, the text given to newspaper reporters, did not contain the iron curtain passage. Churchill inserted it midway in his speech." Stenotypists did record it. "By the time they had transcribed it, however, all of us White House newsmen had finished our stories and were headed back for the train."[11]

Press Conferences

While continuing to rely on press releases in newsgathering, reporters often express considerable doubts about their reliability. They are less negative about another routine channel, the press conference. Many, though not all, sustain themselves with an image of the British Parliament's Question Period. The analogy may have some merit, but not for the reasons reporters like to cite.

The press conference is more than a Presidential practice. Senior officials throughout the government arrange occasional press conferences, open to all accredited members of the press corps. Departmental press officers hold briefings on a more regular basis. The State Department, for one, has for years had a daily briefing at noon. While these rarely attain the degree of formality that characterize the President's, their procedures are roughly the same.

Even the President's press conference acquired its present form only gradually. Theodore Roosevelt, while he was in the White House, met with correspondents sporadically. The President spoke to a small select group, recalls one correspondent of the time: "Newspapermen who were more or less friendly to his program could manage to see him alone, more frequently in small groups of five or six." The "seances," as one reporter dubbed them, were casual affairs, often conducted while the President was getting a shave:

"Teddy" in an ordinary armchair would be lathered and, as the razor would descend toward his face, someone would ask a question. The President would wave both arms, jump up, speak excitedly, and then drop again into the chair and grin at the barber, who would begin all over. Sometimes these explosions interrupted a shave ten or a dozen times.[12]

Woodrow Wilson, not surprisingly, introduced a modicum of formality into relations with the press, meeting correspondents as a group twice a week initially, often with a stenographer present to take down a shorthand transcript against which reporters could check the accuracy of their own notes.[13] Warren Harding added to the formality by insisting that reporters submit all questions in writing prior to his press conferences. Calvin Coolidge introduced the shadowy figure of the "White House spokesman," to whom his comments had to be attributed.[14] Herbert Hoover, while maintaining Harding's practice, abandoned Coolidge's.

It was left to Franklin Roosevelt and his press secretary Stephen Early to elaborate the full range of options, short of direct quotation of all that transpires. In his first meeting with the White House press corps, Roosevelt spelled out the ground rules that would govern press conferences for the duration of his and his successor's tenure. He dispensed with the practice of written questions. Instead, he announced, "Steve and I thought it would be best that straight news for us from this office should always be without direct quotation. In other words, I do not want to be directly quoted unless direct quotations are given out by Steve in writing." He distinguished two other categories of announcements. One was "background information," or "material which can be used by all of you on your own authority and responsibility." The other was "off-the-record" information, which was "confidential" and available "only to those who attend the conference."[15]

Ultimate formalization came with the introduction of television cameras. Televised press conferences, according to former White House press secretary George Reedy, became performances "as spontaneous as a Javanese temple dance but without the grace which makes the latter such a deeply moving experience."[16]

The more formal the Presidential conferences with the press grew, the more elaborate became preparations for them. Woodrow Wilson has been quoted as claiming that he "prepared for the conferences as carefully as for a Cabinet meeting."[17] Truman's press secretary, Charles Ross, instituted a briefing beforehand as a precaution against Presidential misstatements. According to one White House aide, "We had a hell of a time during the first few months because the old man had a habit of shooting from the hip whether he was sure of his answers or not. After some pretty embarrassing bobbles, Charles Ross ... hit on the idea of having a pre-conference briefing."[18] Eisenhower's press secretary, James Hagerty, carried the procedure one step further by soliciting lists of possible questions and recommended responses from various departments for the President's information. By the time John Kennedy had taken office, the press conference was serving as a deadline for bureaucrats around Washington, one nearly as compelling as the Question Period was for their counterparts in London. Questions had to be anticipated, responses prepared." "[D]epartments concerned with that subject," notes Theodore Sorensen, "however laggard they have been up to then, will make certain that their views are crystallized and forcefully presented."[19]

Departmental officials have copied Presidential practice. The standard operating procedure followed in the State Department to prepare for its noon briefing is illustrative. The State Department spokesman who conducts the briefings has, in the Nixon Administration, served in the dual capacity of Deputy Assistant Secretary of State for Public Affairs and Special Assistant to the Secretary of State. His subordinates in the news division are organized along geographic lines corresponding to the five regional bureaus in the Department. From about 6:30 to 8:30 each morning they go over the available morning newspapers and wire service files that have accumulated overnight and compile a list of matters that might provoke questions at noon. They then meet with the Deputy Assistant Secretary and draw up a rough list of potential questions. These are circulated to the regional bureaus and sometimes to the functional offices in the Department. Their responses come back usually in the form of a restatement of the question, a summary of pertinent information, and recommendations on which information to make public, how to answer the question, and what pitfalls to avoid in the reply. When desk officers incline toward reticence in their dealings with the press, the Deputy Assistant Secretary may occasionally challenge their recommendations. His bureaucratic position in the Secretary's office gives him an advantage. Often he will have cleared important issues in advance, but if not, he can carry his appeal up to the Secretary.[20]

Reporters, like the men they confront, do not enter press conferences totally unprepared. In the newsroom and on the beat they engage in a neverending exchange of ideas with editors and fellow reporters that helps them to formulate the lines of questioning for the next press conference. On occasion, their sources inside the government may pass along a question or two. Before major Presidential press conferences, such as President Nixon's after the 1970 Cambodian invasion, editors at both the *Post* and the *Times* may convene small staff meetings to map their strategy for coverage. They carve up tentative areas of substantive responsibility for the eight or nine stories to be written. The half dozen reporters who attend the press conference solicit questions from others who will watch it on television. They then draw up a list of critical questions that need asking and discuss possible follow-ups to them. Even on these occasions, though, newsmen shy away from mapping out detailed strategies for confronting officials or for gauging reactions to what they say. Overt collusion between news organizations is even rarer.

Extensive preparations precede the Question Period in Parliament, too, for the same reason. Both are tests of skill. If an official does not perform well, his professional reputation may suffer. In either performance, though, this is hardly a risk. The man up front is in a position to run the show, and he usually does. George Reedy has described the Presidential encounter:

The President dominates the scene completely. The lead questions are easily predictable. The "follow-up" questions—the kind that narrow down generalizations or pinpoint evasions—are nearly impossible in a situation where 200 to 400 correspondents are clamoring for recognition and where time is limited. Any President who has done his homework will emerge unscathed, with a generality for the "tough" questions and rebuff for the "impertinent" questions. It is a breeze. . . . Rarely does the off-beat question bear upon important issues that are giving a President trouble. If he is witty, he can pick up some mileage with a quick response. If he is not, he can be noncommittal and no one will be hurt.[21]

Briefings in the departments may be more intimate, but the results hardly differ. The portrait of these encounters sketched by reporters is one emphasizing the penetrating question that elicits the reluctant but truthful response. This occurrence is a rarity. More often the experienced and well-briefed official can turn a question to his own use, give a partial reply, or evade it entirely. In the words of Reedy's predecessor, Bill Moyers, "Yeah, they pull it out of me until there's nothing more I want to tell them."[22]

Officials have an assortment of techniques for maintaining control. Finessing the awkward probe is one. FDR once offered this lesson in the finer points of public relations in a talk with a group of agency heads:

A reporter had asked him to comment on a statement by Ambassador Bingham in London urging closer relations between the United States and Britain. If he had done the natural thing of backing up Bingham, the newspapers would have made headlines of the President's statement, with likely ill effect on naval conversations then under way with Japan. If he had said "no comment," he would have sounded critical of Bingham's statement. So he simply said he had not seen it—although in fact he had.[23]

When the questioning gets rough, officials can filibuster or simply avoid calling on those reporters who might prove troublesome, a gambit President Nixon resorted to at his press conference after the Cambodian invasion, when he systematically ignored *Times* and *Post* correspondents, even those seated in the front row.

Another technique, employed in parliamentary Question Periods, too, is the "planted" question.[24] Usually all this requires is some indication from an official to a reporter that he can get newsworthy information by raising a particular matter.

Sometimes it takes more than a hint. President Johnson's announcement of the appointment of Nicholas Katzenbach to be Under Secretary of State came in response to a question from *St. Louis Post Dispatch* correspondent Marquis Childs, whom State Department aides had primed. As the press conference dragged on without the question from Childs, Assistant Press Secretary Robert Fleming jotted it down on a pad and was ready to pass it to another reporter, but his thoughtfulness proved unnecessary.[25] Not all "plants" elicit newsworthy responses, however. Some are little more than invitations for officials to score debating points or polish their images.[26] The official attitude, it seems, is that a press conference is too important a matter to be left to reporters. Yet, as Bill Moyers once responded to a reporter who accused the White House of planting questions, "It takes two to tango."[27] The presence of television cameras can add the necessary inducement to take to the floor.[28]

A technique available to senior officials, if not to those who run the daily briefings, involves exploiting their control over the timing of their meetings with the press. The Washington press corps includes a number of specialists covering other beats who are likely to probe deeper than the men regularly assigned to the White House. Knowing this, Lyndon Johnson simply stopped announcing his press conferences in advance.[29] Richard Nixon has tried to circumvent the Washington press corps entirely by holding briefings with groups of editors from around the country or by opening press conferences only to local newsmen on his travels. In the words of Herbert G. Klein, the Administration's director of communications, "We are also trying to look beyond Washington, and to provide the background information available to Washington reporters to those who must analyze it in other parts of the country."[30]

It is at this point that the press conference diverges from the path of the Question Period. In the United States a senior official's control of timing has no limits: he can simply dispense with the bother altogether. Unlike the Question Period, the press conference has not been institutionalized—become an unavoidable feature of a President's or any senior official's job. Woodrow Wilson found that he could withstand the heat from the press about his Administration's lack of "openness." By his third year in office, he had let his semi-weekly press conference lapse, leaving liaison with the press to one of his aides. The lesson has not been lost on his successors. Bill Moyers once pointedly reminded reporters of the impermanence of the "institution" while he was press secretary in the Johnson White House: "It's to serve the convenience of the President, not the convenience of the press, that Presidential press conferences are held."[31]

What has become thoroughly institutionalized over time is the briefing by press officers. They take place regularly in many departments and employ a fairly substantial administrative apparatus. They are part of the standard operating procedure of the press as well. There is widespread expectation both in and out of Washington that they will take place.

The Background Briefing:
An Informal Channel

Press conferences by senior officials have been on the decline in the past two administrations. In their place has emerged a hybrid resembling the Presidential press conferences of bygone days—the background briefing. The backgrounder is a quasi-routine or *informal channel* for newsgathering. The news source does not necessarily initiate the exchange. Often no transcript is kept, leaving the reporter with greater flexibility as to the substance and format of his story. Coverage is not automatic, less of a reflex action of reporter and editor alike. The backgrounder also is less of a formality on the official side. It does not necessarily invoke the elaborate preparations, the clearance procedures, and the commitments of formal authority that routine channels do. It is often a means of avoiding these very preparations, procedures, and commitments.

Backgrounders can take several distinct forms. Press officers, often accompanied by senior officials, can conduct all or part of their daily briefings on a background basis. On other occasions, an official will call in a select group of beat reporters, either en masse or in single file, for a backgrounder. During the Johnson Administration, Secretary of Defense McNamara and Secretary of State Rusk held such sessions on a regular basis, McNamara's on Thursday in the Secretary's dining room at the Pentagon and Rusk's Friday afternoons over drinks on the eighth floor of Foggy Bottom. Attendance was restricted to a few regulars covering these beats for American newspapers, but transcripts were kept on file in the press offices, available to all accredited correspondents regardless of their beats. Finally, reporters themselves have formed groups that regularly invite officials to dine with them and sing for their supper—or breakfast—on a background basis. The best known is the so-called "Sperling group," formed in 1966 by Godfrey Sperling, Jr., bureau chief of the *Christian Science Monitor* and currently the author of the TRB column in the *New Republic*. The group, which meets over breakfast sometimes as often as twice a week, includes some eighteen regulars, among them Warren Weaver of the *Times*, columnists Roland Evans, David Broder, and Bruce Biosset, and several Washington bureau chiefs or their stand-ins. Attendance varies with the guest. As a response to its size and diversity, this group has spawned another one, a more intimate supper club composed of men primarily interested in American politics. Like college secret societies, these groups and others coalesce and dissolve beneath the surface of Washington journalism. The *Times* and the *Post*, too, host luncheons with senior government officials, usually on a background basis.

Whenever a backgrounder takes place at the instigation of officials, the choice of participants is theirs as well. It is usually quite deliberate. Two days before Defense Secretary Robert McNamara's September 1967 speech supporting limited deployment of an anti-ballistic missile (ABM) system, a dozen newsmen were called in one at a time, handed an advance text, and briefed about its contents. "On this occasion," Phil Goulding recalls, "we had chosen each participant with a specific purpose in mind." In talking to managing editor Benjamin Bradlee and editorial editor Philip Geyelin of the *Post*, he explains, he and McNamara sought "a reasonably rational editorial" and, "more important to us, to spark their interest in the speech so that the *Post* might run a full text." From bureau chief Tom Wicker of the *Times*, they wanted "an intelligent column, input into his New York office for an editorial, and a recommendation to the *Times* in New York that consideration be given to printing the text." They did not extend invitations to any of the fifty Pentagon regulars, and even delayed distribution of the advance text to them until the morning of the speech. "The risk of the ABM decision's leaking out, possibly in a garbled version, was too great," argues Goulding.[32] So was the likelihood that they could uncover dissident views elsewhere in the department.

No matter who initiates these sessions, however regularly they meet, backgrounders have one element in common: a set of conventions governing the quotation and attribution of information disclosed. Although the conventions are long-standing and widely known in Washington and abroad, no agreement has ever been reached on the terminology employed to denote the various rules. This lack of agreement has caused considerable friction between reporters and officials, only some of it unintentional.

Back in 1958 when he was managing editor of *The Washington Post*, Alfred Friendly distributed a memorandum to his staff seeking to clarify these conventions. While it urged reporters to resist the efforts of officials to avoid putting their words on the record, its effect was to codify rules of the game previously adhered to informally:

These methods, because they lack the virtue of complete candor and do not have the advantage of straightforward processes, get newspaper people into a great many misunderstandings. They are, in many cases, a means by which officials seek to evade responsibility for knowledge and information for which they should be willing to assume responsibility. In many cases, citizens have a right to know not only the information, but also the source of it.

Still, we do not make the circumstances under which some information is available. They exist. We have to live with them. It is the purpose of this memorandum to make it more convenient to live with them and to minimize the possibilities of misunderstanding between the newspapers and our colleagues and our sources.[33]

"Off the record," in Friendly's glossary, means that the reporter may not publish the information disclosed in any form. "He may not use it in anything he writes," Friendly stipulates, "even without attribution to the source, however guarded. A violation of a confidence of this kind is considered, and properly, a cardinal newspaper sin."[34] Strict adherence to this allows an official to trap a reporter into silence. "If the source persists in speaking off the record and the reporter does not accede," warns Friendly, "he must leave the gathering, for if he dissents and yet remains, he places himself in a challengeable position with respect to later independent discovery of the information." Friendly does leave a way out, however: "He may, unless forbidden by the original source, seek out the same information from another source, but without in any way indicating that he has already heard the news, or is in possession of it, from someone else."[35]

No rule, however explicit, is free of loopholes for the determined evader. Whenever the information or the identity of its source is publicly disclosed elsewhere, the reporter's obligation becomes ambiguous. In these situations, Friendly recommends consultation with the desk. Another point that allows room for maneuver is the applicability of the rules to reporters who did not participate in the session. A common path of transgression reporters take is to pass along off-the-record information to nonparticipants, who publish it or a portion of it, thereby freeing the reporter from any further obligation to remain silent. Consequently, many an official has adopted a practice followed by President Kennedy, "to say comparatively little to a newsman in confidence, even 'off the record,' that he could not afford to have published."[36]

A second convention is "deep background." First spelled out by Ernest K. Lindley of *Newsweek*—and hence sometimes referred to as the "Lindley rule"—it allows the reporter to publish the information he receives, but without any quotation or attribution whatsoever, as if he came to the conclusion on his own.

The convention that usually governs the proceedings at these sessions, "for background only," refers to a variety of forms of attribution other than by name. According to Friendly,

In such cases the reporter may not, of course, identify the source and may not hint at, imply or suggest his identity. In some cases, the source may insist that no attribution be given even to the agency or organization of the source, forbidding the reporter even to divulge in such vague attribution as "State Department sources," or "Internal Revenue Service sources," and the like.[37]

Because of the confusion that exists, experienced officials specify the precise wording of the attribution and the portions of the briefing that may be quoted or must be paraphrased. Sometimes they even insist on an embargo on the information to time its release in phase with other events or to afford them an opportunity to leave town and establish an alibi. These attempts to tamper with the rules sometimes only add to the confusion, as indicated by this exchange between Jerry W. Friedheim, the Principal Deputy Assistant Secretary of Defense for Public Affairs, and Pentagon correspondents during the invasion of Laos in February 1971:

FRIEDHEIM: I would not be saying anything here on anything that General Abrams has embargoed. I would like to point out that General Abrams feels that he has made it very clear that the fact that he had an embargo was embargoed and the announcement that he was withholding some information was embargoed, and he felt that there was good safety reason to do that. And most of you, I think, know that he responded with an advisory to the media in MACV [Military Assistance Command Vietnam] which we tried to get to all of you for information purposes over the weekend that he had embargoed some things and embargoed the fact that he had announced the embargo situation to the media. And, as that advisory indicated, he felt he had done that to deny intelligence information to the enemy which could be detrimental to the safety of his troops. We also here considered it that the fact there is an embargo—is embargoed.
    Q. Well, what you just said, is that embargoed? (*Laughter*)
    FRIEDHEIM: Yes, it is.[38]

The ground rules are open to contravention. A notable example took place in 1954 when then Vice President Richard M. Nixon, just back from Southeast Asia, spoke on a background basis to the American Society of Newspaper Editors. He advocated introduction of American troops to Vietnam if they were needed to prevent a Vietminh victory. News stories attributed his views to a "high Administration official," but the identity of their author soon became known around the capital. A British correspondent, not present at the luncheon, felt no obligation to conceal the source's identity and filed a dispatch naming him.[39] On other occasions, reporters band together and refuse to play by the rules. One such revolt came in the spring of 1967 in response to what they considered abuse of backgrounding by the Johnson Administration.[40] By and large, however, these instances are rare. As *Post* editor Friendly concludes in his memorandum,

In all circumstances, and whatever the conventions stated or implied, remember that a cheap [scoop], won by cutting a corner, by a technicality, or by violating the spirit if not the letter of the understanding of the news source and of other newsmen, is empty, usually worthless, and is followed by penalties and regrets far heavier and longer enduring than any momentary gains that are obtained. Conduct yourself so that you can look your source in the eye the next day.[41]

The basic price that reporters pay for accepting information on a nonattributable basis is one of accountability. If the validity of a story's information rests on anything at all, it rests on the premise that public statements imply a commitment to telling the truth which can be judged against subsequent statements and actions. Without attribution, there is no public commitment. By assuming the responsibility for the validity of his story himself, the reporter frees the official to use him.

Newspaper Routines and Government News

Like other large-scale organizations, newspapers have standard operating procedures that govern much of their employees' activity. Reporters, particularly when they are covering the U.S. government, rely on routine channels—handouts and press conferences—and informal channels—principally, background briefings—to obtain much of their information. They also permit government officials to set the rules governing most disclosures through these channels, thereby giving these officials a measure of control over the information flowing through the channels.

Inside the government, the standard operating procedures for authorizing disclosures put these channels under the control of the senior officials in any department. Senior officials, and senior officials alone, have the authority to issue press releases, hold press conferences, and call background briefings. If they could prevent unauthorized disclosures, they would determine the timing of information release. They might also dominate, though not control, the content of news about government activity.

Notes

1. Edwin L. James, "The Organization of a Newspaper," in THE NEWS-PAPER: ITS MAKING AND ITS MEANING, ed. by THE NEW YORK TIMES (New York: Charles Scribner's Sons, 1945), p. 103.

2. Some of the discussion in this section has been anticipated in the earlier work of Leo Rosten, THE WASHINGTON CORRESPONDENTS (New York: Harcourt, Brace, 1937); Bernard C. Cohen, THE PRESS AND FOREIGN POLICY, Chapter 3; Dan D. Nimmo, NEWSGATHERING IN WASHINGTON (New York: Atherton, 1964), and Ben H. Bagdikian, THE INFORMATION MACHINES (New York: Harper and Row, 1971), Chapter 5.

3. Reston, ARTILLERY OF THE PRESS p. 49. Cf., Mark Sullivan, OUR TIMES (New York: Charles Scribner's Sons, 1930), v. III, p. 74.

4. The only complaint editor Catledge heard from his superiors was publisher Arthur Hays Sulzberger's: "I think we should have gotten out some papers." Catledge, MY LIFE AND THE TIMES, pp. 212-13.

5. The newspapers most frequently cited are THE WALL STREET JOURNAL, the WASHINGTON EVENING STAR, the BALTIMORE SUN, and the CHRISTIAN SCIENCE MONITOR. For the evidence on this, Bernard Cohen, THE PRESS AND FOREIGN POLICY, p. 60, and William L. Rivers, "The Correspondents After 25 Years," COLUMBIA JOURNALISM REVIEW, 1, 1 (Spring 1962); 7-8.

6. Alsop and Alsop, THE REPORTER'S TRADE, pp. 42-43.

7. Goulding, CONFIRM OR DENY, p. 26.

8. Ibid., p. 275.

9. Ibid., p. 276.

10. Ibid., p. 277.

11. WASHINGTON POST, February 16, 1971, pp. B-1,2.

12. Louis Brownlow, A PASSION FOR POLITICS (Chicago: University of Chicago Press, 1955), p. 399.

13. Elmer E. Cornwell, Jr., "The Press Conferences of Woodrow Wilson," JOURNALISM QUARTERLY 39, 3 (Summer 1962): 293.

14. Louis M. Lyons, "Calvin Coolidge and the Press," NIEMAN REPORTS 18, 3 (September 1964): 6-8.

15. Transcript of press conference, March 1933 (Harvard University Library Microfilm). President Truman announced his adherence to Roosevelt's practices at his first press confernece. Cf., Harry S. Truman, MEMOIRS, Vol. I: YEAR OF DECISIONS (Garden City, N.Y.: Doubleday, 1955), pp. 47-48.

16. Reedy, THE TWILIGHT OF THE PRESIDENCY, p. 162.

17. Cornwell, "The Press Conferences of Woodrow Wilson," p. 298.

18. Quoted in Cabell Phillip, "Questions and Answers on the Press Conference," NEW YORK TIMES, February 13, 1955, VI, p. 62-63.

19. Theodore C. Sorensen, DECISION-MAKING IN THE WHITE HOUSE (New York: Columbia University Press, 1963), p. 32.

20. Descriptions of this process appear in John P. Leacocos, FIRES IN THE IN-BASKET (New York: World, 1968), p. 20; in Marvin Kalb, "Covering the State Department," THE PRESS IN WASHINGTON, ed. by Ray E. Hiebert, p. 158; and John Hohenberg, BETWEEN TWO WORLDS (New York: Praeger, 1967), p. 57.

21. Reedy, THE TWILIGHT OF THE PRESIDENCY, pp. 163-64.

22. Quoted in Benjamin C. Bradlee, "Backgrounders: A Conspiracy in Restraint of Truth," WASHINGTON POST, January 2, 1972, p. B-7.

23. James MacGregor Burns, ROOSEVELT: THE LION AND THE FOX (New York: Harcourt, Brace, 1956), p. 189.

24. SUNDAY TIMES (London), December 12, 1971, p. 1, documents a British case.

25. Hugh Sidey, A VERY PERSONALIZED PRESIDENCY, pp. 188-89.

26. A memorandum in the White House files of the Roosevelt Administration even contains the precise wording of at least one planted question: "Mr. President, did you notice the annual report yesterday of the American Civil Liberties Union? What happened to the efforts of the government to protect civil liberties?" Cited in Elmer E. Cornwell, Jr., PRESIDENTIAL LEADERSHIP OF PUBLIC OPINION (Bloomington: University of Indiana Press, 1965), p. 159n. Also, pp. 158-59, 196-97. The tradition has persisted. Cf., Sorensen, KENNEDY, p. 318; and THE BOSTON GLOBE, August 30, 1970, p. A-6.

27. NEW YORK TIMES, January 12, 1966. p. 14.

28. The publicity that it produces for the news organization, even more than the reporter's vanity, may encourage planting. Cf., Ernest K. Lindley, in THE ROLE OF THE MASS MEDIA IN A DEMOCRATIC SOCIETY, ed. by DeWitt C. Reddick (Austin: University of Texas Public Affairs Press, 1961), p. 58; and Robert MacNeil, THE PEOPLE MACHINE (New York: Harper and Row, 1968), p. 299.

29. James Reston, "The Press, the President, and Foreign Policy," FOREIGN AFFAIRS, 44, 4 (July 1966): 563.

30. R. Gordon Hoxie (ed.), THE WHITE HOUSE: ORGANIZATION AND OPERATIONS, Proceedings of the 1970 Montauk Symposium of the Center for the Study of the Presidency, p. 37. Cf., NEW YORK TIMES, August 24, 1970, p. 18.

31. NEW YORK TIMES, January 11, 1966, p. 12.

32. Goulding, CONFIRM OR DENY, pp. 220-21.

33. Alfred Friendly, "Attribution of News," REPORTING THE NEWS, ed. by Louis Lyons, p. 92.

34. Ibid.

35. Ibid., p. 93.

36. Sorensen, KENNEDY, p. 314.

37. Friendly, "Attribution of News," p. 94. A directive offering guidance to all American military advisory personnel in South Vietnam on "Ground Rules for Discussion with the Press, Interviews, Press Conferences, and Press Briefings," issued by the American military command in December, 1962, makes a similar distinction. Cf., U.S., Congress, House, Committee on Government Operations, HEARINGS, GOVERNMENT INFORMATION PLANS AND POLICIES, 88th Cong., 1st Sess. (1963), p. 406.

38. WASHINGTON POST, February 5, 1971, p. A-20.

39. Reston, ARTILLERY OF THE PRESS, p. 3.

40. WALL STREET JOURNAL, April 10, 1968, p. 1.

41. FRIENDLY, "Attribution of News," p. 97.

6 Channels and Sources of News

The American press makes me think of a gigantic, super-modern fish cannery, a hundred floors high, capitalized at eleven billion dollars, and with tens of thousands of workers standing ready at the canning machines, but relying for its raw material on an inadequate number of handline fishermen in leaky rowboats.

A.J. Liebling[1]

Organizational routines and bureaucratic politics have a significant impact on the structure of newsgathering and on the shape of news content. At *The New York Times* and *The Washington Post*, reporters working in bureaus around the United States and overseas as well as those covering beats in Washington seem relatively free of newsroom constraints in gathering news. On the beat, however, efficiency dictates newsgathering through routine channels. Reporters cannot witness many events directly because they are few in number and must locate themselves in places where information is most likely to flow to them and because their access to information is usually barred and control over disclosures centralized. The necessity of locating themselves at key points of information flow and the restriction of access both apply to reporters in Washington, where the two newspapers maintain sizable staffs, but these factors are hardly peculiar to the nation's capital.

The foregoing analysis generates two principal hypotheses that lend themselves to testing by examining the content of newspapers:

First, *most national and foreign news in* The New York Times *and* The Washington Post *comes to reporters through routine channels.*

Second, *most nonlocal news, regardless of subject matter, comes from officials and agencies of the U.S. government.*

Other researchers have found some indications of the importance of routine channels for news content. Two studies of Presidential press conferences, for instance, have concluded that over time, despite variations in the number of such press conferences, the total number of stories based on information from them has remained roughly constant.[2] Surveys of reporters have also turned up evidence for their reliance on routine channels of newsgathering.[3]

Another way to test these hypotheses is to count the channels and sources cited in a sample of stories in the *Times* and the *Post*. This procedure presents two main problems: (1) how to draw a sample that is, at best, unbiased or, at

119

worst, biased against acceptance of the hypotheses; and (2) how to classify channels and sources which the story has only vaguely identified or has deliberately disguised.

Drawing a sample over a period of years permits an assessment of changes over time and differences among administrations. For economy of effort, five-year intervals were chosen: 1949, 1954, 1959, 1964, and 1969. To control as much as possible for variations by season and by day of the week, the same two weeks in each year, selected at random, are used: those beginning with the first Sunday in February and the second Sunday in December. On the assumption that more important stories are less routinely gathered, only stories beginning on page one are examined.[a] Stories less than two inches long are excluded. Since the study focuses on foreign and national news, other stories are eliminated if they meet *all three* of the following conditions: they have no dateline (i.e., *Times* stories written in New York and *Post* stories from Washington); the reporter works for any desk other than foreign or national; and the sources cited in the story are local.[b] This leaves 599 stories from the *Times* and 547 from the *Post* in the sample.

Channels, the paths by which information reached the reporter, are classified into three categories: routine, informal, and enterprise. *Routine* channels include (1) official proceedings such as trials, legislative hearings, and election tabulations; (2) press releases as well as reports monitored over official radio or from TASS; (3) press conferences, including daily briefings by "official spokesmen" and broadcast interviews; and (4) nonspontaneous events, such as speeches, ceremonies, and staged demonstrations. *Informal* channels include (1) background briefings; (2) leaks; (3) nongovernmental proceedings like association meetings or trade union conventions;[c] and (4) news reports from other news organizations, interviews with reporters, and newspaper editorials. *Enterprise* channels include (1) interviews conducted at the reporter's initiative; (2) spontaneous events which a reporter witnesses firsthand, like fires, riots, and natural disasters; (3) independent research involving quotations from books and statistical data; and (4) the reporter's own conclusions or analysis.

In stories that fail to specify the channels used, the critical choice is between enterprise and informal channels. The procedure adopted is to classify as coming

---

[a]The POST uses mutt boxes and headlines on page one which refer to stories on inside pages. Both newspapers occasionally use pictures on page one but run the accompanying story inside. In the fifteen cases where this occurred, the stories are included.

[b]Six stories that satisfied these criteria but dealt with international financial matters were nevertheless included.

[c]Coverage of nongovernmental proceedings can be quasi-routine: the TIMES and the POST cover many labor, agriculture, political party, and academic conventions with beat correspondents just as reporters assigned to Capitol Hill cover the sessions of Congress. Most of the time, however, this is not the case. The decision to include nongovernmental proceedings in the informal rather than the routine category was, in the end, dictated by the need to bias the classification against the routine in order to strengthen the null hypothesis.

from a background briefing the information that has little or no attribution but that appears in more than one paper the same day; thus, backgrounders, by definition, have more than one reporter in attendance. When unattributed information appears in one and only one newspaper on a given day, it is classified as having been obtained through an interview, unless independent evidence from subsequent news articles, historical studies or memoirs, or officials' and reporters' recollections indicates that it was a leak. The restrictiveness of the background briefing and leak categories is designed to bias the choice toward enterprise channels, to favor the null hypothesis.

Those individuals or organizations passing information through a channel, or *sources* as they are known, are classified into one of five categories: (1) U.S. government officials; (2) foreign government officials, including officials of international agencies; (3) officials of state and local governments in the United States; (4) foreigners not in any government; and (5) private citizens of the United States. Even when a source was only vaguely identified, it still proved possible in almost every instance to place him in one of the broad categories.

Channels for News

For all stories at the *Times* and *Post* combined, routine channels outnumber enterprise channels by well over two to one (see Table 6-1). Editors at both newspapers rely on the wire services to cover some routine spot news. They also run occasional stories from Reuters and from other newspapers which their own

Table 6-1
Channels of Information for News in the *Times* and *Post* Combined—All Stories (N=2,850)[1]

Routine	58.2%	Official proceedings	12.0%
		Press releases	17.5
		Press conferences	24.2
		Nonspontaneous events	4.5
Informal	15.7%	Background briefings	7.9%
		Leaks	2.3
		Nongovernmental proceedings	1.5
		News reports, editorials, etc.	4.0
Enterprise	25.8%	Interviews	23.7%
		Spontaneous events	1.2
		Books, research, etc.	–
		Reporter's own analysis	0.9
Not ascertainable	0.3%		

[1] Percent of total channels; stories may have more than one channel.

staff did not obtain. When only stories by the staffs of the two newspapers are included, routine channels still outnumber enterprise channels by about two to one, regardless of the newspaper, as shown in Table 6-2.

A count of channels cited is one indication of the routine in newsgathering. News stories in the sample average between two and three channels per story, so that counting total channels does not discriminate between the story that relies primarily on one channel and the story gathered through numerous channels. About one-third of all stories in the sample cited one channel only. For the stories with more than one channel, a distinction was drawn between the primary channel and secondary channels of information. The *primary* channel is defined as the channel for the information which (1) comprises the lead and/or the major portion of the story as a whole; and (2) accounts for the timing of its appearance in the news. A few stories had no identifiable channel that satisfied both criteria. In these cases, the second criterion was considered sufficient for purposes of classification.[d]

Single-channel stories, based entirely on information received from one channel, account for one-third of the stories sampled. The channels for such stories are predominantly routine. So, too, are the primary channels for multichannel stories (see Table 6-3). The implication of these findings is that

Table 6-2
Channels of Information in the *Times* and the *Post*—Staff Stories Only

	The Times (N=1,398)[1]	The Post (N=822)[1]	Both Papers (N=2,220)[1]
Routine	53.7%	58.9%	55.6%
Informal	18.5	13.0	16.4
Enterprise	27.6	28.1	27.8
Not ascertainable	0.2	–	0.1

[1]Total number of channels.

Table 6-3
Channels of Information in Single- and Multi-Channel Stories

	Single-Channel Stories (N=405)	Primary Channel for Multichannel Stories (N-741)	All Primary Channels (N=1,146)
Routine	74.6%	68.6%	70.7%
Informal	18.7	19.6	19.3
Enterprise	6.6	11.7	9.9

---

[d]One caveat is worth mentioning here. The term *primary* does not necessarily mean that the information passed through that channel is the most important in the story to any reader. Reporters have a way of inserting sentences near the end of their stories which cast doubt on the information in the bulk of the preceding copy. The discerning reader may well consider that the most important part of the story.

stories usually emerge through routine channels. These channels thus determine when most stories happen to surface. In one out of three stories, moreover, newsgathering goes no further than a single channel. In the other two-thirds, the reporter subsequently follows up his initial information through other channels, frequently involving his own enterprise. Thus, the breakdown among secondary channels is 49.7 percent routine, 13.3 percent informal, and 36.5 percent enterprise.

Newsgathering in Washington, even with the larger staffs that both the *Times* and *Post* devote to it, relies as heavily on routine channels as newsgathering elsewhere, as Table 6-4 shows. The small bureaus in foreign capitals and around the United States, many of them one-man operations, might be expected to cover spot news routinely, just as undermanned bureaus covering Washington for regional and foreign newspapers do, monitoring other newspapers and following the most important story in their locale. A look at only those stories written by staff members supports this finding. *Times* and *Post* correspondents in London, for example, made greater use of news reports in other newspapers and background briefings for both primary and nonprimary channels of newsgathering, but did about as much interviewing in following up a story as did their Washington colleagues. The same applies to those stationed in the Paris and Bonn bureaus. The predominant use of routine channels in Washington newsgathering seems to reflect efforts of official news sources everywhere to confine the dissemination of news to routine channels, as well as reporters' reliance on them.

Defining the categories of channels in the way the study has done and counting each channel without weighting it according to the space or placement of the information from it may yield an overrepresentation of the importance of enterprise channels. Nevertheless, the evidence supports the proposition that most page-one news in both the *Times* and the *Post* derives from routine channels.

News Sources

Numerically, the most important sources of information are officials of the U.S. government. They account for nearly one-half of all the sources cited in the

Table 6-4
Channels of Information in Washington and Elsewhere

| | Washington Dateline | | Other U.S. Datelines | | Foreign Datelines | |
	Primary Only (N=548)	All Channels (N=1,316)	Primary Only (N=197)	All Channels (N=492)	Primary Only (N=397)	All Channels (N=1,034)
Routine	72.3%	60.2%	68.0%	56.5%	70.3%	56.4%
Informal	20.1	13.3	16.2	8.1	19.9	19.0
Enterprise	7.7	26.2	15.7	35.3	9.8	24.0

sample of *Times* and *Post* page-one stories (see Table 6-5). Although the category "U.S. official" subsumes officials in all three branches of government, officials in the Executive Branch predominate as news sources: the federal judiciary contributes about 2 percent of all sources and the Congress 6 percent, nearly all in the course of judicial and legislative proceedings.

When stories not written by *Times* and *Post* staff correspondents are excluded, American officials are still the dominant sources of information in both newspapers (see Table 6-6). The contrast between the two newspapers seems largely a function of the number of bureaus each has outside Washington. Until the early 1960s, the *Post* staff was heavily concentrated in Washington. During that decade, as the *Post* expanded its network of overseas and domestic bureaus, the differences in news sources between the two newspapers diminished.

The dominance of American official sources is even more pronounced in stories with only one source and among primary sources. American officials were

Table 6-5
Sources of Information in the *Times* and the *Post*—All Stories (N=2,850)

	% of Total Sources
U.S. officials, agencies	46.5
Foreign, international officials, agencies	27.5
American state, local government officials	4.1
Other news organizations	3.2
Nongovernmental foreigners	2.1
Nongovernmental Americans	14.4
Not ascertainable[1]	2.4

[1] Not Ascertainable includes stories in which the channel was a spontaneous event or the reporter's own analysis.

Table 6-6
Sources of Information in the *Times* and the *Post*—Staff Stories Only

	The Times (N=1,398)[1]	The Post (N=822)[1]	Both Papers (N=2,220)[1]
U.S. officials	42.3%	62.8%	49.9%
Foreign, international	31.4	13.5	24.7
State, local government	3.6	3.9	3.7
Other news organizations	3.6	2.2	3.1
Nongovernment foreigners	2.4	1.1	1.9
Nongovernment Americans	14.9	15.2	15.0
Not ascertainable	1.9	1.3	1.7

[1] Total number of sources.

the sole source in 56.3 percent of the 405 single-source stories and were 53.8 percent of all primary sources.

American officials, as expected, contribute the bulk of information for stories datelined Washington, but they also serve as sources for many stories from across the country and around the world (see Table 6-7). American officials, for instance, were 21.2 percent of the sources of news out of London, 24.8 percent out of Paris, 15.9 percent out of Moscow, and 54.0 percent out of Saigon.

The spread of bureaus around the country and overseas nevertheless counter-balances somewhat the dominance of U.S. official sources. Reporters in domestic bureaus, to a much greater extent than those in Washington, get information from individuals and groups who do not work in the Federal government. Reporters in foreign bureaus, to a greater extent than those in Washington, get their stories from officials, but most are officials of foreign governments, with perspectives on the world that might be at variance with those of American officials.

Routine Channels, Official Sources

Whatever the location of their bureaus and their beats, reporters rely mainly on routine channels to get information. The beat system of the *Times* and *Post* concentrates staff at routine channels set up by the U.S. government—channels generally under the control of senior officials. *The routine channels for newsgathering thus constitute the mechanism for official dominance of national and foreign news in the two papers.*

One way to indicate this relationship is to count information "transfers," defining a transfer as the passage of information from a single source through a single channel to a reporter. Of the 2,850 transfers in the sample, American

Table 6-7
Sources of Information in Washington and Elsewhere—Staff Stories Only

	Washington		Other U.S.		Foreign	
	Primary Sources (N=478)	All Sources (N=1,183)	Primary Sources (N=124)	All Sources (N=334)	Primary Sources (N=251)	All Sources (N=696)
U.S. officials	85.1%	71.8%	45.2%	28.7%	18.3%	23.0%
Foreign, international officials	3.6	9.1	1.6	3.6	70.9	61.8
State, local officials	0.4	1.9	11.3	17.4	0.0	0.1
Other news organizations	1.5	2.1	0.0	1.8	2.4	5.3
Nongovernment foreigners	0.4	0.8	0.0	0.3	2.4	4.5
Nongovernment Americans	7.9	13.4	36.3	44.6	2.8	3.0
Not ascertainable	1.0	0.8	5.6	3.6	3.2	2.3

officials using routine channels alone account for 31.4 percent. An additional 17.6 percent of all transfers involve officials in foreign governments and international agencies employing routine channels. By contrast, only 16.5 percent of all transfers comes from nonofficial sources, whatever their channel.

Another way to point up the interdependence of routine channels and official sources in newsgathering is to contrast dominance of routine channels by American officials to the relatively equal accessibility of enterprise channels to foreign officials and nongovernmental sources (see Table 6-8). To the extent that a reporter receives information through routine channels, he has a one-in-two chance of getting it from a source in the American government.

Alternatively, while American officials are three times as likely to pass information to reporters through routine channels as through enterprise channels, nonofficials are more likely to do so through enterprise channels than through the other two types of channels (see Table 6-9).

Official dominance of routine channels is particularly evident in the place where both the *Times* and *Post* concentrate their staffs—on beats in Washington. Of the 794 uses of routine channels sampled there, U.S. officials were the sources of information 80.7 percent of the time—ten times as frequently as either foreign officials or nongovernment sources. Of the 345 uses of enterprise

Table 6-8
Official Dominance of Routine Channels

Sources	Channels			
	Routine (N=1,658)	Informal (N=361)	Enterprise (N=823)	All Channels (N=2,850)
U.S. government officials	53.8%	50.1%	30.5%	46.5%
Foreign, international officials	30.3	28.0	21.3	27.4
Nongovernment sources[1]	11.3	12.5	28.8	16.5

[1] Foreign plus American

Table 6-9
Routine Channels and Official Sources

	Sources				
	U.S. Govt. Official (N=1,365)	For., Intl. Official (N=782)	State, Local Official (N=116)	Nongovt. Foreigner (N=60)	Nongovt. American (N=410)
Channels:					
Routine	67.3%	64.3%	61.1%	35.0%	40.5%
Informal	13.7	12.9	3.5	5.1	10.3
Enterprise	18.9	22.4	35.3	60.0	49.0
Not ascertainable	–	0.4	–	–	0.2

channels, American officials were the sources for 52.5 percent, foreign officials for 7.8 percent, and private citizens 24.9 percent. When only stories by *Times* and *Post* staff members are considered, the relationship still holds.

The combination of the beat system and reporter reliance on routine channels has affected the ability of Members of Congress to make news. As the beat system has expanded over time, relatively fewer correspondents on the *Times* and the *Post* are assigned to the Capitol Hill beat. Legislators in pivotal positions in Congress have become more adept at disseminating information to the press, releasing reports on Saturday for Sunday papers, issuing press releases, and, in general, making themselves available to reporters. Walter Pincus' experience in working for the chairman of the Senate Foreign Relations Committee, J. William Fulbright, is illustrative:

In 1962-63, when I first worked for him, Senator Fulbright avoided private interviews with reporters. He was an infrequent visitor in the Senate television gallery studio for interviews. It was not that he didn't have things to say in those days—he did. But he confined his remarks primarily to statements made on the Senate floor, believing that the press would either hear him or have a chance the next day to read the *Congressional Record*. Advance texts of his speeches were rare, and a press release on his floor statements was rarer still. When I returned to the Committee [in 1970], there had been quite a change. Advance speech texts and press releases were the rule. The senator himself was well aware that in order to make the evening news shows it was wise to do the filming around noon—never after 4 p.m.—to permit the networks to plan for it.[4]

However adept they have become at using the press, Congressmen have not kept pace with the expansion of newsmaking capabilities in the Executive Branch. The consequence has been a decline over time in the proportion of Congressmen among official news sources for page-one stories in the *Times* and the *Post*.

The beat system, in concentrating staff at locations where news emerges through routine channels, underlies the predominance of these channels. Yet there are variations from beat to beat in reporters' reliance on routine channels, which seems due to the centralization of news dissemination rather than to reporters' specialization. Men on a beat have a wider circle of contacts in the agencies they cover than outsiders do. They have built up relations of trust with officials. They know which officials to seek out and what questions to ask them. Men on general assignment or on beats elsewhere in the capital do not have these advantages. They might be expected to rely much more heavily on routine channels than correspondents on the beat, and they do; but they do not do less enterprise reporting. Beat correspondents, while using routine channels less, turn instead to informal channels—backgrounders and leaks—channels less accessible to those who do not cover the beat regularly. Still, the variation from beat to beat is more pronounced than the differences among reportorial types.

On news emanating from the White House, for example, 71.8 percent of all channels were routine, 18.0 percent informal, and 10.4 percent enterprise. These percentages may be considered an *average value* for use of the various channels on that beat. White House correspondents on the *Times* and *Post* staffs used routine channels in 70.0 percent of the transfers, informal channels 26.6 percent, and enterprise channels 3.3 percent. General assignment reporters, gathering news at the White House, used routine channels in 54.0 percent of the transfers, enterprise channels 21.6 percent, and informal channels 24.3 percent, as indicated in Table 6-10. The data should be read with caution because in one out of five cases the reporter's assignment could not be ascertained. While differences among types of reporters do exist, they are slight compared to the differences between beats. News dissemination at the White House is much more centralized through routine channels than at the State Department.

Changes over Time

Despite the expansion of bureau networks and staff size at both the *Times* and the *Post* from 1949 to 1969, most patterns of channel and source use did not change markedly during the period. Over time there was little change in the dominance of American officials as sources for news—if anything, American officials increased overall as sources for news while nongovernment sources showed no change and foreign officials declined. In stories by staff reporters only, the *Times* increased its use of U.S. officials as sources from 38.8 percent in 1949 to 47.9 percent by 1969, while the *Post* decreased its use, from over 80 percent in 1949 down to 53.1 percent by 1969. Foreign officials made page one less and less often in the *Times*, but more and more often at the *Post*, as it

Table 6-10
Variation in Channel by Beat and Reportorial Assignment

	White House			
	Average Value (N=173)	White House Correspondents (N=30)	Men on General Assignment (N=37)	Correspondents from Other Beats (N=62)
Routine	71.8%	70.0%	54.0%	75.7%
Informal	18.0	26.6	21.6	14.9
Enterprise	10.4	3.3	24.3	9.5

	State Department			
	Average Value (N=138)	State Department Correspondents (N=66)	Men on General Assignment (N=12)	Correspondents from Other Beats (N=9)
Routine	50.7%	39.4%	50.0%	33.3%
Informal	29.6	36.4	16.7	44.4
Enterprise	18.8	24.2	33.3	22.2

opened new bureaus abroad. Nongovernment sources registered little change in either paper. American officials increased their dominance of the routine channels of newsgathering over the period and increasingly dominated informal channels as well.

But one significant difference did emerge. Reporters' reliance on routine channels declined throughout the period 1949-1969, and their use of enterprise channels showed a corresponding rise (see Table 6-11). The trend was not nearly as pronounced in primary channels. Over time, then, reporters have increasingly followed up information obtained through routine channels by interviewing other sources. Along with this change has come a slight rise in enterprise stories, stories which the reporter develops on his own initiative.

These conclusions have two major corollaries. First, although the proportion of nonofficial sources showed no significant rise, it did register an increase in absolute terms, particularly in 1969, as the total number of sources and channels rose. Second, although the proportion of U.S. official sources remained steady over the twenty-year period, the relative decline in the use of routine channels may have altered the ratio of stories from senior officials to stories from lower-echelon bureaucrats. The data bearing directly on this question point in this direction, but they are too sketchy to permit any firm generalization. It is nevertheless a reasonable inference that as reporters do more and more interviewing, they will obtain more information from "permanent government" as opposed to "Presidential government" officials. Career bureaucrats may have an institutional inclination to hew less closely to a given administration line than do political appointees. What both the Johnson and the Nixon Administrations perceived as increased hostility in the press, then, may have an explanation other than just a change in newsmen's political attitudes. At the *Times* and the *Post*, at least, it may also be a manifestation of longer-run trends in newsgathering away from channels dominated by senior officials, trends resulting from an expansion of news staffs and a proliferation of news bureaus and beats.

Routine News as 'Certified' News

Imbedded in the words *news medium* is a connotation that aptly defines the function of the press: it mediates between the officialdom and the citizenry of

Table 6-11
Channels of Information in the *Post* and the *Times*, 1949-1969—All Stories

Year	Routine	Informal	Enterprise	N=
1949	65.9%	11.7%	21.4%	(545)
1954	62.2	14.8	22.5	(502)
1959	57.9	11.6	30.5	(556)
1964	57.5	15.6	26.9	(534)
1969	50.1	10.6	39.1	(713)

the United States. Like a pipeline carrying water from a reservoir to a city, it has some effect on what arrives at the end of the line. Not all droplets that enter the pipeline end up in the same destination; some are routed elsewhere, others evaporate en route. Yet the effects of the pipeline are minor compared to the source of the water—the reservoir. Similarly, newsmen, by adhering to routine channels of newsgathering, leave much of the task of selection of news to its sources.

Adherence to routine channels allows newsmen to cope with the uncertain world of journalism. Newsmen cluster around these channels, each gathering much the same information as his colleagues. Uncertainty loves company: the similarity of their stories provides some reassurance that newsmen understand what is going on in their world. For men who do not and cannot know what the "real" news is, the routines of newsgathering produce "certified news"—information that seems valid insofar as it is common knowledge among newsmen and their sources.

Notes

1. A.J. Liebling, "Goodbye, M.B.I.," THE NEW YORKER (February 7, 1948), reprinted in THE PRESS (New York: Ballantine Books, 1964), p. 139.

2. Elmer E. Cornwell, Jr., "The Presidential Press Conference," MIDWEST JOURNAL OF POLITICAL SCIENCE 4, 4 (November 1960): p. 388; Delbert McGuire, "Democracy's Confrontation: The Presidential Press Conference," JOURNALISM QUARTERLY 44, 4 (Winter 1967): 638-44.

3. Nimmo, NEWSGATHERING IN WASHINGTON, passim.

4. Walter Pincus, "Before the Pentagon Papers: Why the Press Failed,". NEW YORK 4, 39 (July 19, 1971): 36.

7

Bureaucratic Objectives and Tactical Use of the Press

You think we lie to you. But we don't lie, really we don't. However, when you discover that, you make an even greater error. You think we tell you the truth.

Lord Tyrrell, Permanent Undersecretary of
the British Foreign Office,
to a reporter

More news emanates from officials than from any other source. Most of it passes routinely through formal channels of public information in the government to reporters on newsbeats around Washington. But not all newsgathering is routine. Some nonroutine news comes from officials who disclose a pertinent piece of information to the press on their own initiative and without specific authorization to do so. The rest reporters piece together by making their rounds, exchanging and cross-checking bits of information with their contacts in the government, and taking educated guesses. In these instances, too, officials are the ones who provide the information that makes the news.

Understanding why officials talk to reporters can help explain what information makes the news and how it gets there, two factors that render the news comprehensible.

Why Officials Talk to Reporters

Why do officials talk to reporters? "We live in a democracy," answer many officials. "The people have a right to know, and we have an obligation to inform them." To others, the explanation lies not in social norms but in ego gratification. "Some people just can't keep a secret," they say knowingly. Yet neither democratic ideology nor personal idiosyncracy accounts very well for the selection of information that officials pass on to the press.

The contrast between the American and British press suggests another explanation. The volume of detailed information on the inner workings of the U.S. government in the press astonishes, and occasionally dismays, foreign observers. "The outsider who takes the trouble," attests David Butler, "can get a great deal nearer to what is really happening in the United States than he can in Britain."[1] The reason for the difference is not so much legal sanction or

131

reportorial aggressiveness as it is bureaucratic need. Getting things done in Washington requires greater use of the press than it does in London.

In both capitals the test of a good policy is its ability to muster and maintain support among officialdom. Changes of policy thus entail coalition-building inside the bureaucracy as well as the legislature. The tools for forging and dismembering policy coalitions are *maneuvers* or, to borrow Morton Halperin's coinage, "the games bureaucrats play."[2] They include statements inserted in Presidential messages, fact-finding trips, reports, and commissions. Officials also exploit the press tactically in order to achieve the governmental outcomes they desire.

Why, then, is the press a more prominent field for maneuvers in Washington than in London? First, policy innovation and career advancement do not occur randomly in any governmental system. Each system tends to have a few characteristic paths, or *strategies*, for changing policy and for ascending to the top echelons of officialdom that distinguish it from other systems. Differences in intrinsic strategies account for systemic variations in tactics.

The United States, in Richard Neustadt's phrase, has "a government of separated institutions sharing powers."[3] Institutional autonomy has social as well as constitutional sanction. The Congress, the Presidency, and the various government bureaus depend upon each other for actions but rely on different constituencies for support. This condition virtually eliminates the possibility that major policy change will percolate up through the bureaucracy rather than drip down from the top. It makes White House involvement in multibureau policy innovation almost mandatory. The dominant strategy for policy innovation is then to get the President "signed on" as a precondition for moving the rest of the government.

Moreover, career patterns in Washington are more strongly related to personal policy preferences than in London. American officials frequently enter government service out of a substantive interest in policy and a desire to play a role, rather than in search of a high-status profession. Once in government service, they often find that the right policy commitments can speed advancement. Policy can make a difference to the careers of permanent officials. Autonomous ladders of promotion nurture departmentalism. The fact that each military service has its own career line, for instance, may strengthen an officer's resolve to defend a service goal against the other services, and helps explain the volume of press maneuvers in interservice rivalries. The ambitious, whether in-and-outer or career bureaucrat, come to have a sizeable stake in outcomes. This puts the cost of unauthorized disclosure at a discount to officials.

Consequently, strategies for career advancement make it feasible for U.S. officials to go over the heads of their department secretaries to achieve their policy goals. Strategies for policy innovation make it necessary to use the press to do so.

A second reason for the extensive use of press maneuvers in Washington is that the network for circulating information inside the American government is inadequate to the task. In this respect, Whitehall presents a striking contrast to the vast size, geographic diffuseness, and insularity of Washington bureaus. In 1968, when the Administrative Grades of the British civil service totaled some 2,700, equivalent grades in the American government had fifty times that number.[4] Scattered throughout the capital, various bureaus tend to interact primarily at rather senior levels. Departments in London, by comparison, link up formally through an extensive network of interdepartmental committees and informally through the "old boy net," the clubs, the luncheon, the weekend in the country. The British Establishment simply has no Washington peer. Under their circumstances, using the press to circulate information is less imperative.

The contrast between Great Britain and the United States suggests that officials give a lot of information to reporters in order to disseminate it in and around Washington, especially to other officials in the Executive Branch and the Congress, in order to affect policy outcomes. Cataloguing the purposes of press maneuvers offers additional evidence for this proposition. It also throws light on the ways in which information is disclosed.

Informational Press Maneuvers

Informational press maneuvers seek to influence the outcome of a decision by changing the information on which it is predicated. The condition which makes possible the success of such maneuvers is the uncertainty endemic to all governmental systems. Uncertainty in the minds of all political men about the nature of the reality they confront permits alternative formulations of the "meaning" of events and issues to coexist. It allows everyone to have within himself "his own special world." Like a Pirandello play, much of politics consists of conflict among actors, each of whom seeks to gain acceptance for his own definition of reality, his own version of the facts. From the ideologue at the barricades of eighteenth century Paris to the bureaucrat in the corridors of present-day Washington, all political actors have sought to shape each others' perceptions of events and issues as a means of achieving their goals.

Conflict over the meaning of reality implies disagreement on the criteria for evaluating specific bits of information. Much information, then, is unknowable, in the sense that there is no agreement on its meaning. The extent of the unknowable puts a premium on the unknown—information whose significance would be clear to all if it became available. If such a piece of information were common knowledge, moreover, it might favor one side or another in a policy debate. That side has a stake in planting it in the news, giving it currency throughout Washington, and focusing the attention of other officials on it in order to make it the basis of their actions.

Officials monitor the press for information about their external environment, particularly about the world and public opinion. Their reliance on the press gives other officials a stake in manipulating what information they get through the news.

Information About the World

A classic illustration of officials' use of the press to disseminate information that implied acceptance of their policy preferences occurred during the Formosa Straits crisis of 1954-55. Gradual redefinition of the Eisenhower Administration's China policy produced a spate of stories with contradictory assessments of Chinese intentions. *The New York Times* of March 26, 1955, ran a three-column right-hand lead headlined, "U.S. Expects Chinese Reds to Attack Isles in April; Weighs All-Out Defense." Under it defense correspondent Anthony Leviero reported a "significant change" in American planning, grounded "in the belief Red China will begin its campaign to capture Quemoy and Matsu about the middle of April."[5] Leviero pictured military advisers as urging the President to intervene on an "all-out" basis in the event of attack. Three days later in the same position on page one the *Times* ran another three-column headline, "Eisenhower Sees No War Now Over Chinese Isles." Again failing to identify his source by name, White House reporter Bill Lawrence wrote,

The President did not like stories published over the weekend that said his military advisers were satisfied that such attacks might begin by mid-April. . . . The White House believes it is aware of the source of these stories and treats them as "parochial," representing the view of only one man or one service. . . . One statement published last weekend was that the President was being urged to use atomic weapons, if necessary, to destroy Red China's industrial potential and thus end its expansionist tendencies. This view did not please the President either.[6]

What Chinese leaders could have taken for a veiled threat turned out to be a figment of a split developing within the Joint Chiefs of Staff over employment of tactical nuclear weapons in defense of the offshore islands. The first story originated from a background dinner addressed by Chief of Naval Operations Robert B. Carney, who was pushing his analysis of Chinese intentions. At that time the United States had no means other than nuclear for blunting a potential invasion. If his definition of the situation were to prevail, then Admiral Carney might succeed in committing the Administration to the use of tactical nuclears in the present situation—a policy precedent that would be difficult to overturn in any future confrontation. White House press secretary James Hagerty was the source of the second briefing. President Eisenhower makes its purpose plain in his notes:

Lately there has been a very definite feeling among the members of the Cabinet, often openly expressed, that within a month we will actually be fighting in the

Formosa Straits. It is, of course, entirely possible that this is true, because the Red Chinese appear to be completely reckless, arrogant, possibly overconfident, and completely indifferent as to human losses.

Nevertheless, I believe hostilities are not so imminent as is indicated by the forebodings of a number of my associates. It is clear that this gloomy outlook has been communicated to others because a number of articles in the papers state that the Administration is rather expecting hostilities within a month.[7]

The need to pass information via the press becomes particularly acute in the field. As John Kenneth Galbraith, one-time Ambassador to India, attests in the affadavit filed in U.S. v. Ellsberg, "I found it easier to bring my views to bear on the President of the United States by way of *The Washington Post* and its New Delhi correspondent than by way of the State Department."[8]

Information About Public Opinion

Especially important among the imponderables in the official's calculus is the state of public opinion. What the public—or some key segment of it—wants is the subject of considerable argument in most official debates. Molding other officials' perceptions of public opinion in order to affect governmental outcomes can involve several different uses of the news. The news itself may influence public opinion and, thus indirectly, the perceptions that officials have of it. Moreover, what news stories say about public opinion can directly affect officials' perceptions. Finally, because of the difficulty of ascertaining public opinion on any given issue, officials rely on the opinions of commentators and editorial writers for a "quick reading of the public mind." As a consequence, the press not only shapes and represents public opinion but also *is* public opinion in the eyes of officials. Stimulating public reaction, disclosing poll results, and trying to persuade opinion-makers in the press are all commonplace in an effort to impress other officials that the public favors a particular course of action during the formative states of policy development.

Senior officials float trial balloons for the purpose of testing public and Congressional sentiment on a policy issue before committing themselves overtly to a stand. While the Kennedy Administration was drafting the Civil Rights Act of 1965, for instance, a Justice Department aide recalls that "Administration spokesmen—though generally careful not to be identified by name or even by agency—kept key reporters rather fully advised on Administration thinking." In particular, Deputy Attorney General Nicholas Katzenbach served as a major source for stories by *New York Times* reporter Anthony Lewis during the period.[9]

Inside Dope

Given their uncertainty about the world outside, officials inside the government often take their cues on what policy stand to adopt from other officials around them. Their need to adjust themselves in relation to other officials often indicates their analyses of the external environment, not the reverse. Even when their policy preferences do rest on their understanding of the world outside, translating these preferences into governmental action requires a thorough grasp of the world inside the government. In particular, officials need to know what their boss wants, who has power, and "who's got the action."

What the Boss Wants. Officials at all levels of government depend to some extent upon their immediate superiors for career advancement. Giving the boss what he wants, or at least avoiding the appearance of insubordination, is a bureaucratic way of life. Conversely, the boss has an interest in letting subordinates know what he wants.

Because of his constitutional authority, if not his power, the President is the senior official whose preferences matter most to bureaucrats. Not many bureaucrats work for the President, but many have to pay attention to him. The importance of the President's preferences gives rise to a variety of maneuvers.

1. *Issuing a 'Hunting License.'* To obtain the outcome he desires from the policy process, a President first must find subordinates who want to do what he wants and then enable them to begin work. What they require of him is a "hunting license," a mandate to act in his behalf, to invoke his name in order to persuade reluctant colleagues to go along. Publicity implies commitment. It means alerting outsiders with a stake in having that commitment kept. It means putting his reputation on the line.

But public commitments run the risk of premature opposition, of foreclosing options, and sometimes even of successful defiance from below. A prudent President may prefer to avoid locking himself in. Harry Truman, in defending his ban on direct quotation of Presidential press conferences, stated it this way:

The idea of a press conference is to find out what the President thinks about pending matters, but it must be obvious that he should not be quoted directly on every question. That could often change an answer from an expression of opinion to a final commitment. This would serve no useful purpose, for in order to avoid commitment on matters still pending, the President would be reluctant to answer or even suggest a clue that might reveal his line of thought.[10]

To the extent that he dare not offer formal commitment to a course of action, a President must resort to veiled indications, which, while making commitment more ambiguous and hence subject to avoidance, provide minimal license for action to those who want to act. When Lyndon Johnson, for example, wanted to curb State Department promotion of the multilateral force (MLF) in December 1964, he not only had a memorandum to that effect drafted for circulation within the government, but also showed a copy of it to James Reston of the *Times*, who published selections practically verbatim in a right-hand lead on December 21.[11] Unlike an internal memorandum with limited circulation inside the Executive Branch, a press clipping could be cited as proof of the President's wishes by opponents of the MLF on both sides of the Potomac and the Atlantic.

2. *Eliciting Commitment from Above.* Mirroring the need of a senior official to demonstrate commitment in order for subordinates to act is the desire of the subordinate to elicit that commitment. The news thus serves as a means of communicating upward instead of down. Thus, the "theologians" in the State Department, pressing for the MLF, succeeded in inserting a line into a speech President Kennedy delivered to the Canadian parliament in May 1961 that the United States was looking toward "the possibility of eventually establishing a NATO seaborne force which would be truly multilateral in ownership and control, if this should be desired and found feasible by our allies..."[12] In briefings for the press, they saw to it that this line was not ignored, thereby giving themselves a go-ahead to sell their plans abroad.

Subordinates can also prod their boss by making information public which makes it harder for him not to act. In the months prior to Diem's overthrow, for instance, many "inspired" stories emanating from Saigon signified the outbreak of a long-simmering attempt to reform the South Vietnamese regime. Upon taking over as ambassador in Saigon, Henry Cabot Lodge began feeding stories to American correspondents there, among them David Halberstam of the *Times* and Neil Sheehan of Associated Press, in part to push Diem into instituting reforms and in part to prod Washington into withholding support from the regime if Diem remained unmoved. "The leak," argued Lodge, "is the prerogative of the ambassador. It is one of my weapons for doing this job."[13] It is also in the arsenal of staff members on Capitol Hill trying to get reluctant Congressmen or committees to take action.[14]

3. *Announcing a Decision.* Announcing a decision can influence subordinates' behavior even more than publicizing a tentative policy preference. Publicity may not guarantee their compliance, but it greatly enhances the prospects. A President often finds it effective to tell the press what he has decided in order to ensure that officials get the word quickly, and to tell them openly through press conferences and press releases in order to demonstrate that his mind is made up. Such disclosures are quite often part of a formal governmental decision.

Because publicity makes execution more likely, officials whose policy goals are advanced have an incentive to put Presidential decisions on the record. They sometimes plant questions at press conferences to that end, as in the case of President Johnson's appointment of Nicholas Katzenbach to be Under Secretary of State in 1966.[15]

4. *Promulgating a Policy Preference As If It Were a Decision.* Issuing hunting licenses and announcing decisions to get subordinates moving are maneuvers available to senior officials other than the President. Some actions, however, he and he alone can authorize. The need for Presidential authorization gives rise to a maneuver which a politically independent senior official may attempt, which is

to promulgate policy on his own initiative as if it were the product of Presidential decision in the hope that he won't be reversed. General Douglas MacArthur frequently indulged in such tactics. On one occasion, when he became impatient with Washington's hesitancy in getting negotiations on a peace treaty underway with Japan, he called a press conference in Tokyo and, to the dismay of officials back home, simply announced, "The time has now approached that we must talk peace with Japan."[16] On another, he publicly called for enemy surrender in Korea at the very time the Truman Administration was seeking to negotiate a ceasefire.[17] It was this act that precipitated the General's dismissal.

Enjoying the President's support can facilitate such maneuvers. As Ambassador to India, John Kenneth Galbraith was in this position:

I had a huge press conference at which I announced the changes which I am hoping to put into effect in our technical assistance program—concentration on fewer fields, on fewer agricultural institutions, with fewer people in New Delhi. I needed some news and one of the best ways of getting the policy is to proclaim it. Washington will be surprised and may wonder which part of the bureaucracy there authorized the change. However, no one will challenge it.[18]

When the President's stand is unclear, interpreting his words for reporters on a not-for-attribution basis may accomplish similar ends. After President Johnson's speech of March 31, 1968 announcing that he would not seek reelection, Defense Secretary Clark Clifford did just that in imposing limits on American involvement in Vietnam and trying to reverse the policy of escalation. Justifying his actions in the President's own words and implying that they represented Administration policy, Clifford unilaterally set a ceiling of 549,500 on U.S. forces in South Vietnam. He publicly refuted arguments for a resumption of the bombing in North Vietnam north of the Twentieth Parallel. Again and again he sounded optimistic notes about the peace talks being conducted in Paris. "[W]hile scrupulously refraining from burrowing under the ground on which the President presently stood," writes an aide, "Clark Clifford consistently and skillfully moved in public to occupy the ground the President had not yet reached."[19] Like the young women who send premature wedding announcements to society editors, officials can sometimes use the news successfully to create a fait accompli.

Who Has Power. Power, like beauty, is in the eye of the beholder. Presidential power, as Neustadt employs this concept, depends crucially on the perceptions of other players in the political system.[20] It rests ultimately on the expectations of those upon whom he must rely for execution of his decisions that unacceptable costs will accrue to them if they fail to comply with his wishes. Estimations of his will and skill in getting others to do what he wants them to do, his "professional reputation," are important to any official, not just the President. Officials' assertions to reporters about their success in having their way, their intimations about their closeness to the President, and their revelations to show they are in the know involve more than egomania; they are the building blocks of reputation.

In 1934, for instance, President Franklin Roosevelt appointed Donald Richberg to chair both the Executive Council and the National Emergency Council, two Cabinet-level committees dealing with domestic affairs. When the two bodies were consolidated in October, *The New York Times* carried a story describing Richberg as the Assistant President and bearing the headline, "Richberg Put Over Cabinet in New Emergency Council . . . Now No. 1 Man."[21] According to Interior Secretary Harold Ickes, many attributed the *Times* piece to Richberg's staff.[22] The President sought to allay Cabinet pique by dismissing Richberg as no more than "an exalted messenger boy." He had his press secretary get in touch with *Times* correspondent Arthur Krock and tell him "that this kind of thing is not only a lie but that it is a deception and a fraud on the public."[23]

Palace politics can be endlessly intriguing. As George Reedy, who worked in the Johnson White House, writes,

The inexperienced courtier may make the mistake of using his press contacts . . . to secure favorable mention of his name in public. But the wilier practitioners of the art of palace knife-fighting take a different tack. They seek to feature their competitors' names in a context which will displease the man who holds the real power. The reverse-thrust technique is somewhat more complex than it appears at first glance. It is not inconceivable, for example, that a newspaper story speculating on the promotion of an assistant to higher office may be the death knell of that assistant's government career.[24]

Presidents can conspire, too. While assuming public responsibility for the Bay of Pigs debacle, for instance, President Kennedy privately put the blame on the Joint Chiefs of Staff, who had given *pro forma* endorsement to the CIA plan. *Times* columnist Arthur Krock recalls, "The President said he had 'lost confidence' in the Chiefs of Staff. When I asked him if I could publish that on my own responsibility, he agreed."[25]

'Who's Got the Action.' Decisions within the government do not occur at random. Constitutional and legal authority and custom all structure who may take action, attend meetings, even read internal documents. Often, where officials look for clear lines of responsibility they find only ambiguity. Charters are then a matter of choice. This is frequently the case inside the White House. Whenever an issue comes up for decision, the President delegates to one of his staff the task of channeling information and options to him. Knowing "who's got the action" is a prerequisite for exerting influence over a President's decision.

If they want to solicit information and options—and it is not always the case—those who have got the action must publicize the fact. They may do so through the press. In announcing his appointment of McGeorge Bundy as Special

Assistant for National Security Affairs, for example, President-elect Kennedy simply issued a press release detailing the responsibilities of the new post.[26] Promulgating job description by press release has its limitations, however. A companion press release abolishing the Operations Control Board of the National Security Council did not delegate to the Secretary of State the legal authority he required in order to control operations. The press release did not supersede a standing executive order, and could be ignored by other agencies.[27]

Other Maneuvers in the Press

There is more to politics than persuasion. Besides manipulating the information upon which decisions are premised, officials use the press to alter the ways in which decisions are made.

1. *Getting other officials involved.* On many issues, law and custom mandate who must become involved in a policy dispute. On most issues for most officials, however, involvement is a matter of choice. Fighting losing battles does not enhance a bureaucrat's reputation. Even fighting winning battles depletes time and energy, resources not without limit. Press maneuvers can be employed to get officials into the game, or to keep them on the sidelines. What observers may mistake for a trial balloon is frequently a premature disclosure of a policy option—or a deliberately distorted version of it—designed to kill it off by arousing opponents before the arguments in its favor are fully articulated or its potential supporters mobilized.

A 1958 attempt to transfer a team of rocket experts led by Wernher von Braun from the Army to the newly chartered National Aeronautics and Space Administration prompted just such a disclosure. Under the terms of the chartering legislation no Congressional assent would be required if the transfer took place before January 1. Anticipating that White House approval for the shift would come the next morning and aware of the protective attitudes that Congressional committees adopt towards agencies in their purview, the director of the Army program, General John B. Medaris, plotted his strategy. He ruled out a direct appeal to the President over the heads of immediate superiors: "If we had done so, discipline would have demanded that the offender be sacrificed, regardless of the justice of his cause." Instead, he reasoned,

I had one particular friend in the press, whom I had found over the years to be honest, reliable, objective, patriotic, and thoroughly dependable. He was Mark Watson of *The Baltimore Sun*. ... I laid the whole situation before Mark and asked his opinion. If he had told me it should be let alone, I would have heeded his advice. However, he too recognized the gravity and essential unfairness of the situation, and agreed that the only proper thing to do was to make sure that the President knew that this was a highly controversial matter.[28]

Medaris describes the results of Watson's story:

Almost immediately press representatives began to call the White House for comment. In other places, the press sought out important members of Congress and asked their views. Some of these Congressmen sent messages to the White House and at least one prominent Senator dispatched a telegram. Our point was made.[29]

2. *Obtaining a change of venue.* Instead of holding a hearing in order to influence a decision to be made elsewhere, the Committee could have gone further and introduced legislation to bar the transfer. Such action entails more than merely getting other officials involved. It moves the locus of decision-making out of the Executive Branch up to Capitol Hill, where it is susceptible to an entirely different array of procedures, pressures, and personalities. More generally, officials losing a fight in one decision-making arena, say, inside their own department, attempt to shift it to another, most often the White House or Capitol Hill, by publicizing their plight. This maneuver is especially prevalent during budget preparation at the Defense Department when cutbacks in procurement are at issue. Whenever agreement is unattainable within the Defense Department, the Office of Secretary of Defense may raise the issue in the White House, whereupon the military service may seek to reinstate the cut before a Congressional committee. The Navy adopted this maneuver in 1949 after President Truman backed Defense Secretary Louis Johnson's rejection of a new aircraft carrier requested in its 1950 budget submission. Once the hearings began, the Navy launched a campaign of disclosures, the so-called "revolt of the admirals" inspired by Admiral Arleigh Burke, to win approval for its program.[30]

3. *Changing the rules of the game.* Many procedures followed in the policy process are not codified and hence are subject to alteration. But changes in the rules of the game can stimulate intense opposition among officials normally not inclined to talk to reporters. The internal deliberations of the Supreme Court, for instance, are almost never made public. Traditionally, too, the Chief Justice assigns the task of writing the opinion of the Court only in cases when he votes with the majority. When his view is in the minority, he routinely allows the senior Justice on the majority to make the assignment. When Chief Justice Warren Burger reversed this tradition in 1972, a law clerk disclosed the change to a *Washington Post* reporter covering the Court.[31] The breach of silence seemed symbolically equivalent both as a break with the Court's past rules of the game and a threat to the traditional process of obtaining an internal consensus.

4. *Triggering outside intervention.* Many agencies have constituencies vitally interested in a narrow range of issues which officials can mobilize in a policy fight. To trigger intervention by those outside the U.S. government, officials pass the word to reporters, particularly those in the trade press and on specialized journals.

In the foreign policy area, officials of foreign governments are important outsiders capable of intervening in behalf of their allies inside Washington. When foreigners are the target, officials must be circumspect in disclosing information, lest they leave themselves open to the charge of damaging national security. In March 1961, for example, a task force headed by former Secretary of State Dean Acheson proposed strengthening NATO's conventional forces to meet a conventional attack in Europe with a purely conventional response, a shift away from reliance on U.S. Air Force bombers. When Secretary of State Rusk sent a memorandum to Secretary of Defense McNamara discussing changes in NATO deployments, Air Force officers disclosed a distorted version of the memorandum, one calculated to upset already uneasy Europeans.[32]

5. *Wooing allies for the future.* The readiness of allies outside the government to intervene is a negotiable asset in policy disputes. Publicizing who won and who lost and assessing blame by letting onlookers know that he has "fought the good fight" and his opponents have not helps an official to woo allies for the future and alienate the affections of rivals' constituencies. A spate of self-serving disclosures after the Cuban missile crisis in 1963 came from a variety of insiders claiming responsibility for the outcome and trying to show the proper mix of toughness and restraint. During the crisis preparations for the aftermath had proceeded *pari passu* with debate on the options. Even after the President had decided on a blockade, the Joint Chiefs of Staff continued to push for either an air strike or an invasion. "It was clear," says Roger Hilsman, "that some of the memoranda being written were not so much to present this or that case to the President—since he had already heard them all—but to build a record. If something went wrong, many of these papers would obviously begin to leak."[33]

6. *Keeping reporters obligated.* Reporters are themselves important allies. Their favorable treatment of information can aid an official's cause at some future date. Dispensing "exclusives" to a reporter increases the likelihood of such treatment because the exclusive, or "scoop," the story he and only he obtains, enhances a reporter's reputation among his colleagues. One man's leak is the other's exclusive. Keeping reporters in their debt is a subsidiary motivation in most officials' disclosures.

How Information Makes the News

Instrumental concerns dominate the relations of the men who govern with the men who write about them. These relations are a reflection of operating need. That need is not idiosyncratic but organizational in origin. It is intrinsic to the policy process in Washington and elsewhere. Officials have incentives to tell reporters what they want them to know and nothing more.

From the array of purposes elaborated above, it is clear that the incentives are more varied and more compelling in Washington than in London. The American governmental system gives greater scope to the tactical use of the press than does the British system.

Another inference from the catalogue of press maneuvers is that the way information gets to reporters is a function of its purpose. News management encompasses more than just keeping secrets a secret. Officials want to disclose the information they want, when they want, and in the way they want. Getting out the message they want to deliver to the audience they want to reach poses two choices: where to put the message and how to get it there.

The Medium for the Message

The target audience for many press maneuvers is not the general public, but attentive elites in and around Washington, especially bureaucrats and Congressmen. That audience pays more attention to newspapers than to other media. The evening news shows on network television may provide the general public with the latest word on public affairs, but work schedules effectively impose a blackout for officials. A handful of them receive news summaries prepared by their staffs, more listen to the radio while driving to and from work, but the vast majority get their news from newspapers. In Washington, as mentioned earlier, nearly everybody reads the *Post* and the *Times*.

Two other characteristics of newspapers as a medium, permanence and precision, make them more effective than television for transmitting intra-governmental messages. The words are there on paper to be shown to others, filed away and retrieved. As for precision, reportorial inaccuracy may matter less than audience misperception.

Most important of all in favor of using newspapers over television is the accessibility of newspapermen to many officials. Not all the news media position their reporters where officials can get at them. Television newsmen cover few beats around Washington. They tend to operate like general assignment reporters, responding to news initially reported by the wire services or other news organizations. Moreover, the "newshole," the time or space available for news stories, imposes far greater restriction on television than on newspapers. Only a handful of senior officials can get coverage for what they have to say; lesser functionaries must get to a newspaperman if they are to make the news.

Alternative Channels to the Press:
To Leak or Not to Leak

How the official gets word to reporters also depends on who he, the official, is. Three routine channels exist: the press release, the press conference, and the background briefing. Use of these channels, though, is virtually the exclusive prerogative of senior officials and public information officers. Lesser officials can issue their own press release or hold their own press conference and get reporters to pay attention to them only if they intend to quit, and doing so may well be tantamount to retirement. Instead, they must resort to a fourth channel, the leak.

A leak, as used here, differs in three respects from a background briefing. First, the official deals with reporters as individuals, never in a group. Most often, he discloses his information on an exclusive basis. Secondly, the contact is nonroutine and initiated by the official. Some background briefings are held on a regular basis at the instigation of the reporters themselves, meeting as a group over breakfast or dinner. Above all, cloaking the identity of the source of the information and even obscuring the fact that it became available through a leak are critical to tactical success. This is not always the case with backgrounders, as evidenced by many of Henry Kissinger's sessions in the Nixon Administration or the weekly backgrounders by Secretaries McNamara and Rusk in the Johnson Administration. Officials will adopt the expedients of embargoing what they say until they can establish an alibi by leaving town or employing an intermediary such as a friendly Congressman or a Ralph Nader to reach reporters discreetly.

Senior officials, too, find it essential to leak information to the press. When they are at odds with the Administration, few care to risk open insubordination. From Douglas MacArthur to Walter Hickel, the precedents are all too clear. The fear of reprisal forces official opposition underground. Dissenters must leak; they dare not do otherwise.

Even when he is hewing to the Administration line, a senior official can see advantages in using a covert channel to get information to reporters. In informational press maneuvers, he faces three operating dilemmas.

First is his desire to shape the context in which other officials and the public view an issue without revealing that he is doing so and thereby prejudicing his audience against the effort. What might smack of partisan arguments coming from an official's own lips may seem like disinterested observations in a newsman's story.

Second is the dilemma inherent in having to address a multiplicity of audiences simultaneously—wanting to tell one audience what he knows the other will not like to hear him say.

Third is the dilemma of policy innovation: the incompatibility between providing firm commitments to subordinates as a stimulus to change and avoiding such commitments lest they foreclose his options.

The frequency with which these dilemmas recur in policy-making explains the heavy traffic in covert channels by senior officials acting in accordance with Administration policy. As a consequence, most unattributed disclosures in the news are not leaks from below deck, but semaphore signals from the bridge.

The Struggle to Control Disclosures

The threat of leaks invites retaliation. Every recent President has tried to shut off the flow of disclosures. But as one aide to President Johnson puts it, "Of course, the people at 1600 Pennsylvania Avenue are not really worried about all leaks—only those that originate outside the White House."[34] In a broader sense, officials at the top of every government agency try to centralize control over the disclosure of information as a means of determining policy outcomes. It is through the efforts of most senior officials to exercise this control—and of subordinates to circumvent it—that newsmaking has its most profound impact on the policy process.

Superiors have introduced a variety of tactics in order to seal leaks.

They have tried jawboning. President Eisenhower once confided in a Congressman the steps he intended to take to achieve a no-leak administration. Word quickly passed to columnist Arthur Krock, who commented, "The fact that this report of the President's attitude is in itself a leak suggests how difficult of attainment the goal will be."[35] They also have taken reprisals against reporters who accept information from dissident subordinates. They have withheld favors ranging from exclusives to admittance to briefings. They have criticized offenders and complained to their editors. They have harassed them with FBI investigations.[36]

They have sought to monitor contacts by requiring subordinates either to obtain prior permission to talk to newsmen or to report all conversations at which public information personnel are not present.[37] They have circulated memoranda warning dissidents to keep their expressions of opposition within proper channels, with the usual result of having their own memoranda leak to the press.[38] They have required advance clearance for texts of any public statements.[39]

They have singled out offenders as object lessons for their colleagues. Prosecuting them for violation of criminal statutes or imposing administrative sanction is unnecessary. A simple notation in personnel files can suffice to retard advancement. This seems to have occurred in the case of two Air Force officers suspected of leaking the Rusk-McNamara memorandum on NATO deployments.[40] Dismissals are rare but not unknown. General Douglas MacArthur and Dean Acheson are among those fired for unauthorized disclosures.[41]

But more subtle pressures are the rule. Calling in the FBI to track down the source of a leak, sometimes by means of lie detectors, can have a quieting effect.[42] A "persistent if less visible source of restraint" is described by ex-ambassador John Kenneth Galbraith:

Anything that comes in over the press wires is scrutinized by the score or more people in Washington who are concerned in one capacity or other with that country. There is not much that will not strike someone as out of line even when the location of the line is known only to God. . . . This alert officer then tucks the clipping or tape in his pocket and at the next meeting with his Assistant Secretary, says, "Did you see, sir, what came out of Phnom Penh yesterday? Going a little far I think. . . ." In all organizations the cultivation of executive vanity is a considerable industry. The State Department is up to average. Officals are rather easily persuaded that their prerogatives are being prejudiced. Out goes a telegram of warning, "We note with some concern. . . ."[43]

Admonitions have little force without the threat of harsher reprisal to come, and in some circumstances that threat is not compelling. Sometimes commitment to a cause can overcome fear of the consequences. In 1934 a fight raged within the Agricultural Adjustment Administration over whether or not to permit collusion among firms in order to raise farm prices. The A.A.A.'s legal staff opposed the codes on antitrust grounds. One attorney explains his decision to disclose an economist's report critical of a meat-packing code which was awaiting final approval:

I went right over to talk to Justice Brandeis about it and he said that if I thought it was worth my job to stop the code, why, go right ahead. He pointed out that if I did it, I would then automatically have to expect to be fired. But if I was willing to let the job go, why then, I might just as well do it if the code was that important. Well, at that time I didn't have to worry about the job so I went back to the department and gave [the Associated Press] the report.[44]

Even the risk of dismissal fails to hold a man like this in thrall. Strong beliefs brace weak knees. For the in-and-outer with a constituency back in the corporate or academic world, moreover, losing a job may mean gaining a reputation for taking righteous stands.

Other times, immediate superiors can shield career officials against reprisals from above. It was not until a year after the dropping of the code that the attorney lost his job. By then, the pro-code faction had gained the upper hand inside the A.A.A., and this disclosure along with others served as the pretext for purging the legal staff. Sympathetic superiors can provide protection from lesser sanctions as well. A few years after they were reprimanded, the two Air Force officers accused of leaking the Rusk-McNamara memorandum were publicly cleared by Air Force General Nathan F. Twining, then chairman of the Joint Chiefs of Staff.[45] Even when formal charges are brought, a plea of overzealousness can mitigate punishment if the right man makes the appeal. In 1957 the Army courtmartialed Colonel John C. Nickerson, Jr., for disclosing classified information about the Jupiter missile. The man in charge of the Army missile program, Dr. Wernher von Braun, testified in his behalf,

The Jupiter involves several hundred million dollars of the taxpayer's money. One hundred percent security would mean no information for the public, no money for the Army, no Jupiter. . . . The ideal thing would be 100 percent security and all the money you want. But the world is not built that way. The Army has got to play the same game as the Air Force and the Navy.[46]

Despite a guilty plea, Nickerson got off lightly. As these cases suggest, being on the right side in a policy dispute affords protection from retaliation to subordinates.

It is the threat to restrict access to the "inner councils" that most inhibits talkative subordinates, particularly those most ardently committed to their policy preferences. Other sanctions have little demonstrable effect on officials, whether in-and-outers or career bureaucrats, so long as the danger to their careers seems remote. Exclusion, however, is a penalty at once easy for superiors to impose and hard for subordinates to bear. It is thus a common practice.

Among those excluded from Nixon Administration councils is the State Department. Secretary of State William P. Rogers himself had to pay a steep price for admission. "I had to pledge to the President personally that there would be no leaks from our department on the Peking and Moscow trips and the shift in monetary policy," Rogers acknowledges. "We had favored all these actions, but it would have been difficult to keep the secret if it had been known by more than a few. After the announcements were made, many of the people here were, of course, disappointed that they didn't know of them in advance. . . . But I breathed a sigh of relief when we passed the test of silence. That was what really counted."[47]

There is nothing unique about the Nixon Administration's attempts to exclude dissidents. Under President Johnson, the arena for many key decisions on the Vietnam War was a weekly luncheon attended by a handful of senior officials. "The Tuesday luncheons were where the really important issues regarding Vietnam were discussed in great detail," recalls Secretary of State Dean Rusk. "We were always talking about ways and things to do with the bombing. This was where the real decisions were made. And everyone there knew how to keep his mouth shut."[48] Among those kept out for most of 1965 was Vice President Hubert Humphrey.[49] In the Kennedy Administration, the barring of staff subordinates from the deliberations of ExCom during the first week of the Cuban missile crisis was aimed at sealing off potential leaks.[50]

The workings of the classification system can best be understood in terms of the bureaucratic politics of public disclosure. What began as a way of keeping information out of the hands of enemies abroad has become primarily a way of keeping it away from rivals at home. The apparatus for circulating information internally to those subordinates with a need to know can readily be used to cut off those whom senior officials feel a need to exclude. By routing documents around them, by barring them from crucial meetings, and by avoiding substantive discussions in their presence, senior officials can keep troublesome subordinates in the dark. Decision-making is moved out of the back room into the closet.

Both the quest for secrecy and the need for disclosure are intrinsic to a governmental process in which the test of a good policy is the support it can muster and maintain in and out of Washington. Disclosures are essential to win policy fights. The basic issue is who should control them. Any system that allocates this control to a small number of high officials gives those officials substantial influence over the outcomes of the policy process, influence which others in the government are bound to resist.

Notes

1. David E. Butler, "Political Reporting in Britain," STUDIES IN BRITISH POLITICS, ed. by Richard Rose (New York: St. Martin's Press, 1968), p. 171.

2. Morton H. Halperin, "Why Bureaucrats Play Games," FOREIGN POLICY 1, 2 (Spring 1971): 70-90.

3. Richard E. Neustadt, PRESIDENTIAL POWER (New York: Wiley, 1960), p. 33.

4. Great Britain, Parliamentary Papers, REPORTS, Cmnd. 3638, June 1968, "The Civil Service," I, p. 97, 147.

5. NEW YORK TIMES, March 26, 1955, p. 1.

6. NEW YORK TIMES, March 29, 1955, pp. 1-2.

7. Dwight D. Eisenhower, MANDATE FOR CHANGE (New York: Doubleday, 1963), pp. 478-79. Further details are in Sherman Adams, FIRSTHAND REPORT (New York: Harper, 1961), p. 133.

8. John Kenneth Galbraith, affadavit filed in U.S. v. ELLSBERG, quoted in THE WASHINGTON POST, June 26, 1972, p. A-15.

9. David Filvaroff, "Origins of the Civil Rights Act," (Mimeographed), Institute of Politics, Kennedy School of Government, Harvard University, pp. 16-17.

10. Truman, MEMOIRS, I: YEAR OF DECISIONS (New York: Signet, 1955), p. 61.

11. NEW YORK TIMES, December 21, 1964, p. 1. Further details are in Philip Geyelin, LYNDON B. JOHNSON AND THE WORLD (New York: Praeger, 1966), pp. 174-76.

12. U.S., Department of State, BULLETIN 44, 1145 (June 5, 1961): 841.

13. Mecklin, MISSION IN TORMENT, p. 223. Cf., Hilsman, TO MOVE A NATION, p. 514.

14. Clark Mollenhoff, WASHINGTON COVER-UP (New York: Doubleday, 1962), pp. 116-19.

15. Sidey, A VERY PERSONAL PRESIDENCY, pp. 188-89.

16. Martin E. Weinstein, JAPAN'S POSTWAR DEFENSE POLICY, 1947-1968 (New York: Columbia University Press, 1971), p. 14.

17. Neustadt, PRESIDENTIAL POWER, p. 20.

18. John Kenneth Galbraith, AMBASSADOR'S JOURNAL (Boston: Houghton Mifflin, 1969), p. 206-207. Copyright © 1969 by John Kenneth Galbraith. Reprinted by permission of Houghton Mifflin Company. Cf., p. 328-51.

19. Goulding, CONFIRM OR DENY, p. 329.

20. Neustadt, PRESIDENTIAL POWER, Chapter 4.

21. Arthur Schlesinger, Jr., THE COMING OF THE NEW DEAL (Boston: Houghton Mifflin, 1958), p. 546.

22. THE SECRET DIARY OF HAROLD L. ICKES (New York: Simon and Schuster, 1954), I, pp. 220-21.

23. Schlesinger, THE COMING OF THE NEW DEAL, p. 546.

24. Reedy, THE TWILIGHT OF THE PRESIDENCY, pp. 90-91.

25. Arthur Krock, MEMOIRS (New York: Funk and Wagnalls, 1968), p. 371.

26. Henry Jackson (ed.), THE NATIONAL SECURITY COUNCIL (New York: Praeger, 1965), pp. 302-303.

27. Ibid., pp. 304-305.

28. John B. Medaris, COUNTDOWN FOR DECISION (New York: G.P. Putnam's Sons, 1960), p. 246.

29. Ibid., p. 247.

30. Walter Millis, ARMS AND THE STATE (New York: The Twentieth Century Fund, 1958), pp. 241-42. Cf., Jack Raymond, POWER AT THE PENTAGON (New York: Harper and Row, 1964), pp. 198-201.

31. WASHINGTON POST, July 4, 1972, p. 1.

32. NEW YORK TIMES, March 24, 1968, p. 9. Cf., Hilsman, TO MOVE A NATION, p. 8.

33. Hilsman, TO MOVE A NATION, p. 205.

34. George E. Reedy, "Moynihan's Scholarly Tantrum," MORE 1, 1 (September 1971): 6.

35. Arthur Krock, IN THE NATION (New York: McGraw-Hill, 1966), p. 219.

36. Hanson W. Baldwin, "Managed News: Our Peacetime Censorship," ATLANTIC MONTHLY, 211, 4 (April 1963): 54. Cf., Alsop and Alsop, THE REPORTER'S TRADE, pp. 64-68; WASHINGTON POST, July 9, 1971, p. A-1.

37. U.S., Congress, House, Committee on Government Operations, HEARINGS, GOVERNMENT INFORMATION PLANS AND POLICIES, 88th Cong., 1st Sess., 1963, pp. 105-107, 122-24. Cf., WASHINGTON POST, November 5, 1971, p. A-2.

38. NEW YORK TIMES, November 22, 1971, p. 1. Cf., Samuel P. Huntington, THE COMMON DEFENSE (New York: Columbia University Press, 1961), p. 305.

39. Truman, MEMOIRS, II: YEARS OF TRIAL AND HOPE, p. 167, 383. Cf., Raymond, POWER AT THE PENTAGON, pp. 176-81.

40. NEW YORK TIMES, March 24, 1968, p. 9.

41. Neustadt, PRESIDENTIAL POWER, p. 20n. Schlesinger, THE COMING OF THE NEW DEAL, p. 242.

42. Sorensen, KENNEDY, p. 314. Cf., NEW YORK TIMES, September 3-4, 1971, p. 1.

43. John Kenneth Galbraith, "Why Diplomats Clam Up," REPORTING THE NEWS, ed. by Louis Lyons, p. 377.

44. William H. Riker, "The Firing of Pat Jackson," Inter-University Case Program No. 1 (Mimeographed), pp. 7-8.

45. NEW YORK TIMES, March 24, 1968, p. 9.

46. NEW YORK TIMES, June 27, 1957, p. 8. Cf., Michael H. Armacost, THE POLITICS OF WEAPONS INNOVATION (New York: Columbia University Press, 1969), pp. 125-28; and Medaris, COUNTDOWN FOR DECISION, pp. 124-33.

47. Milton Viorst, "William Rogers Thinks Like Richard Nixon," NEW YORK TIMES, February 27, 1972, VI, p. 30.

48. John B. Henry, II, "March 1968: Continuity Or Change?" (Senior thesis, Harvard University, Department of Government, April 1971).

49. NEW YORK TIMES, April 17, 1966, IV, p. 3.

50. Schlesinger, A THOUSAND DAYS, p. 802. Also, the Kennedy, Johnson, and Nixon Administrations have all excluded intelligence panels like the Office of National Estimates from advance knowledge of sensitive options under consideration by the President for fear of leaks. [Chester L. Cooper, "The C.I.A. and Decision-Making," FOREIGN AFFAIRS 50, 2 (January 1972): 225.]

The International Politics of Newsmaking: The Skybolt Controversy

The Skybolt crisis was a phony crisis which ought never have been allowed to happen, but it did create a difficult position for the British Government and it did create an ugly atmosphere of anti-American feeling in London last week.

Leader in *The Sunday Times* (London),
December 23, 1962

International politics complicates the tactical use of the press. Gauging what another government will do, which is to say, trying to predict the outcomes of its policy process, is an endeavor fraught with uncertainty. Even for senior officials, reading dispatches from newspaper correspondents abroad can provide a useful corrective to the intelligence reports and diplomatic cables that cross their desks each day; indeed, a good many of those reports and cables are themselves based on analyses of stories in the foreign press. For lesser officials and for legislators not privy to the full flow of internal documents, the press is often the main source of up-to-date information on goings-on in other capitals.

If officials in one government rely on foreign correspondence as a source of information, then officials in another government have some incentive to use the news to transmit information to them. And if the press transmits information from government to government, it is also usable as a medium for "disinformation," for dissemination of material which is relevant but misleading, or even untrue. Inevitably, too, information in the news aimed at the home front gets entangled in international politics just as information targeted for foreign officials becomes accessible to domestic audiences in various capitals.

To highlight some of the complexities, it may be of some use to examine a case in detail, focusing on the question, how, if at all, did the ways in which news was gathered and transmitted contribute to its outcomes? The case chosen was the controversy over the Skybolt missile that embroiled the United States and Great Britain in late 1962. A number of accounts of what happened within the two governments at the time are now available.[1] Setting these accounts side by side with the stories that the news media carried during the controversy may illustrate a number of key aspects of the international politics of newsmaking as well as illuminate some previously obscured details of the events and news coverage of them.

Skybolt and the News

On November 7, 1962, shortly after the Cuban missile crisis and before the Soviet Union had completed the dismantling of its missile sites in Cuba, four senior administration officials were ushered into the Oval Office for a long-postponed meeting with President John F. Kennedy. One was Secretary of Defense Robert S. McNamara, who was about to inform his colleagues that studies by civilians in the Pentagon had persuaded him to terminate further work on an air-to-surface ballistic missile, the Skybolt. Another, on hand to second his chief, was Paul Nitze, Assistant Secretary of Defense for International Security Affairs and author of one of the studies. The presence of two others, Secretary of State Dean Rusk and the President's Special Assistant for National Security Affairs McGeorge Bundy, signified that cancellation of the project had consequences overseas as well as across the Potomac. Even though Skybolt had prompted the gathering, other concerns would dominate the agenda, in particular, the clashes along the Sino-Indian border and the Soviet bombers still on Cuban soil.

Skybolt, then under development by Douglas Aircraft, had been designed for launching from beneath the wing of a bomber in flight and delivering nuclear bombs on enemy targets on the ground. Appropriately styled "the Polaris of the skies," the missile was the Air Force's answer to threatened loss of its strategic mission to the Navy's missile-carrying submarines as its bombers became obsolescent. Skybolt's proponents claimed for it a capacity to contribute to deterrence and defense in three ways certain to "keep the boys flying." One was counterforce strikes against enemy air bases and missile installations. Another was countercity attacks on enemy population centers. The third, and most important to the Air Force, was "defense suppression," knocking out enemy air defenses so that its parent bomber could penetrate enemy territory and "mop up" targets remaining after a nuclear exchange. This last function required an aircraft guidance system precise enough to direct a bomber to a predetermined point in mid-air and a missile guidance system capable of programming the flight of a Skybolt fired from a launch pad moving at 600 miles an hour while pinpointing an enemy target as small as a missile site as far away as 800 miles.[2]

The reason for American diplomatic concern lay in an understanding reached with British Prime Minister Harold Macmillan by Dwight Eisenhower, Kennedy's predecessor in the White House. The pair had met at the Presidential retreat at Camp David, Maryland, in March 1960, when Skybolt was not even off the drawing boards. In response to Macmillan's expressions of interest in the weapon, Eisenhower agreed informally that *if* Skybolt proved technically feasible and came into production, the British might purchase a few, paying only the costs of producing the number they ordered plus whatever research and development costs were necessary to adapt the missile for use by Vulcan bombers of the Royal Air Force (RAF). At the same time, Macmillan made available port facilities at Holy Loch, Scotland, as a base for America's Polaris submarines. Though never expressly linked, Holy Loch became in Macmillan's mind a quid pro quo for Skybolt, an interpretation that coincidence argued for and Eisenhower never publicly argued against.[3]

From its inception Skybolt's development had run into considerable difficulty. Eisenhower's Defense Secretary, Thomas Gates, on advice from his civilian staff, had gone as far as to eliminate development funds from the fiscal year 1962 budget upon leaving office in January 1961. With echoes of Democratic campaign charges of a "missile gap" still in the air, McNamara restored the cuts and even requested $50 million in new obligational authority above the $80 million already sought. Later that spring, however, the research efforts of a national security task force under Paul Nitze turned up little evidence of any gap. In budget season that fall, a committee composed of Budget Director David Bell, Presidential science adviser Jerome Wiesner, and the Director of Defense Research and Engineering Dr. Harold Brown nearly persuaded McNamara to drop Skybolt. By then, though, the Secretary had another fight with the Air Force on his hands over termination of a $10-to-15-billion program to build the next-generation strategic bomber, the B-70. In ensuing executive logrolling he overrode the committee's recommendations, but insisted on a "treaty" with his Air Force Secretary that development costs for Skybolt not exceed a $500-million ceiling that year.[4]

By next March the Secretary gave indication that he had doubts about proceeding with development of Skybolt. In testimony before a House subcommittee on defense appropriations, he expressed reservations about the missile's progress. At least partial failures of all four live-fire tests over the next six months confirmed those doubts.[5] Yet test performance had considerably less to do with the proposed cancellation than did cost effectiveness: the Pentagon's arsenal contained other weapons systems of proven capability which could take on the missions set out for Skybolt—for the moment, a shorter-range air-to-surface missile, the Hound Dog, and later on, Minuteman and Polaris, which would render defense suppression unnecessary—and McNamara was determined to halt the duplication of effort common in the services' past procurement practices.

By the time of the November 7 meeting, McNamara had made his decision to drop Skybolt from the fiscal 1964 budget. That decision, however, was not his alone to make: it was the President's, upon advice both of the military and of his Defense Secretary. Proper form dictated that the conclusions of McNamara's civilian staff be submitted to the Joint Chiefs of Staff for comment. Then their opinion and his own would be forwarded to the White House where, along with the rest of the defense budget, it would be thrashed out among White House and Budget Bureau officials in a conference slated for Thanksgiving.

When McNamara argued for cancellation at the meeting with Kennedy, the others who were present agreed. When he volunteered to alert the British, no one raised any questions. Their allies were, after all, "clever chaps"; given warning, they would study the situation and tell Washington what they wanted. The next day the Secretary called in the British ambassador, David Ormsby-Gore; a day later he telephoned the British Defense Minister, Peter Thorneycroft. To both, he indicated an inclination to scrap Skybolt, but he was deliberately vague. Why did he avoid telling them in precise terms that cancellation was a foregone conclusion? And if it was not, why bother to warn them so far in advance of formal presentation of the budget?

On November 27 a joint announcement provided the first official word that the President and the Prime Minister would meet at Nassau. The next day Lord Beaverbrook's *Daily Express* bore a banner headline, "Dec. 19-20—and on Big Two's Agenda: SKYBOLT TUSSLE." The lead, written by defense correspondent Chapman Pincher, forged a link between Nassau and Skybolt:

A determined attempt to eliminate Britain as an independent nuclear power is being staged by the U.S. State Department. Leading officials there are trying to secure cancellation of the American Skybolt H-bomb missile on which RAF Bomber Command will be totally dependent after 1965.... The fear that Britain may find herself in just that situation is believed to be a major factor behind Mr. Macmillan's decision to visit General de Gaulle and President Kennedy next month.[6]

The purposes behind "the State Department moves," Pincher further contended, were to prevent formation of a European deterrent independent of United States control, to keep NATO under American direction, and to eliminate Britain as a nuclear power. "If they succeed," he concluded, "Mr. Macmillan will be in serious difficulty because the Socialists have always maintained that Skybolt would never materialize." One day later came announcement of yet a fifth test failure.

On December 2, the *Sunday Times* of London ran a story from Washington by Henry Brandon, in point of service the senior British correspondent there. He wrote that "no decision has yet been taken here, but those who have for some time been skeptical about Skybolt are now in the ascendency."[7]

The basis of his assessment was unclear from his story: had someone in Washington passed a foreign correspondent information which American reporters did not yet have, or was Brandon banking on his fifteen years of experience in the capital to make an educated guess?

From London's perspective the plot now seemed to thicken. In the course of calling on the United States to press more vigorously for European economic and political integration and urging the Europeans to contribute more conventional forces to NATO, former Secretary of State Dean Acheson told an audience at the United States Military Academy that Britain was "about played out" as an independent actor in world affairs. Urging the British to join the Common Market, Acheson observed, "Great Britain has lost an empire and has not yet found a role."[8] This brought an angry rejoinder from Prime Minister Macmillan on the floor of Commons: first McNamara in a speech at the University of

Michigan had called into question the value of Britain's independent deterrent and now their old friend Acheson was raising doubts about Britain's relationship with the United States, the twin pillars of the Tories' foreign policy. From this point on, some Britons seemed to fix on Ann Arbor and West Point whenever they gazed westward toward Washington.

While Acheson was speaking, the Comptroller's Office at the Pentagon was notifying the services of Skybolt's demise. On December 7 *The New York Times* and United Press International carried stories attributed only to "qualified" and "informed" sources but quite similar in content. The *Times'* defense correspondent reported,

The Kennedy Administration has decided that the Air Force does not need the Skybolt ballistic missile as a strategic weapon. The Air Force disagrees. Thus another major public controversy over a military weapon is in prospect.[9]

The UPI dispatch read,

The Skybolt ballistic missile, chosen to be Britain's primary deterrent weapon and a mainstay of the United States Air Force in the mid-1960s, was reported last night to be near death as a major weapons project. . . . The future of the 1000-mile-range weapon, however, apparently has not been settled finally. Informed sources said it is the subject of top-level discussions here and in London.[10]

Both pointed out that no new appropriations were requested in the proposed defense budget. "Mr. McNamara," added the *Times*, "is expected to suggest to Britain that it may have to take over the cost of the Skybolt program." Were the two stories mere coincidence or not? If both reporters had the same "informed source," who was this person and why did he tell them what he did at this time?

This disclosure set off a volley of stories in the British press. A few took comfort in the official view of the Defense Department that no final decision had been made. As the *Daily Telegraph* of December 8 quoted a "well-placed" Pentagon spokesman, "We take a hard look at everything when we draw up a new budget—even motherhood." On December 9 Brandon reported, "I can now confirm that no new appropriation for development of the missile has been included in the Pentagon's budget for next year. This means that the United States Air Force inside the Pentagon has lost its fight for this missile."[11] Nonetheless he, too, saw some hope left for the independent deterrent:

The final decision on Skybolt has not yet been made by President Kennedy. Under the Anglo-American agreement on the missile, America has a certain obligation to supply Britain. So if Skybolt is kept on, it will be for political rather than military reasons. If it is abandoned, it is likely the President will offer Britain another weapon, possibly Polaris. . . . One thing is certain: America would not want to be blamed for having deprived Britain of her nuclear deterrent capabilities, even though the Kennedy Administration considers Britain's independent nuclear deterrent a waste of resources.[12]

The Observer's man in Washington, Godfrey Hodgson, had a slight variation of the same theme. "[T]he United States," he wrote on December 9, "is now considering offering Britain an alternative weapon system to maintain the British nuclear deterrent... but first will try to persuade Britain to put more money into Skybolt."[13] This was the view held by The Telegraph's air correspondent. Derek Wood. Had all three independently hit upon an American offer of a substitute, or was someone on one side of the Atlantic or the other floating this option as a trial balloon?

The Telegraph piece on the same day also alluded to "showdown discussions" between McNamara and Defense Minister Thorneycroft, slated to take place in two days' time:

It seems extraordinary that the British Government has not been kept fully informed of the American financial position on Skybolt or of any possible changes of policy. We have been working mostly in the dark over a joint program of the utmost importance. Clearly, hard speaking must be the order of the day when Mr. McNamara arrives. But doubts are felt in some quarters on whether Mr. Thorneycroft will be tough enough.[14]

Where did Wood get the idea that no one had alerted the British—from the same "quarters" worried about Thorneycroft's mettle?

The next day it was Chapman Pincher's turn to stiffen Thorneycroft's resolve. "It's Time To Stop Washington's Hidden Persuaders," admonished the Express headline. To Pincher the anticipated cancellation of Skybolt was "directly linked with the attack by Mr. Dean Acheson last week." It was all part of "a high-pressure public relations campaign of mounting intensity . . . to convince the world that Britain is 'played out' as an independent Power." If the Americans did not heed his pleas for Skybolt, Thorneycroft could "get equally tough," to the point of reminding McNamara that the agreement on Holy Loch "is no firmer than the Skybolt deal" and that if Skybolt went, the money to replace it would have to come from that allocated to keep British troops stationed in Germany. Above all, though,

[h]e must not fall now for any smooth McNamara offers of Polaris submarines, which would be no more likely to materialize than Skybolt and would involve U.S. veto on their use. He must reject any request that Britain should pay for the development of Skybolt by U.S. firms.[15]

The morning of McNamara's arrival, Pincher described Thorneycroft as "determined to be tough" in the negotiations.

When the Defense Secretary deplaned in London, he held an impromptu press conference. With Thorneycroft looking on, he offered a gloomy prospectus on Skybolt's future: "It is a very expensive program and technically extremely complex. It is no secret that all five flight tests attempted so far have failed and program costs have climbed sharply."[16] The two then hurried off to their talks. In Richard Neustadt's authoritative account of that encounter,

Thorneycroft was waiting for an offer of Polaris; McNamara was expecting him to ask for it. What McNamara offered was a crushing disappointment, and offensive to boot. How, as Henry Brandon notes, could Englishmen base "independence" upon something labeled Hound Dog? What Thorneycroft eventually was induced to ask he couched exclusively in terms of principles, no homework behind them, not a trace of cost-effectiveness analysis: would [the United States] publicly back Britain's nuclear independence, never mind the ways and means? McNamara's instructions barred an affirmative answer. He exceeded his instructions by implying that Polaris pledged to NATO might be feasible. Thorneycroft was having none of that. Polaris once in Britain's hands could be pledged if she liked; this was independence.[17]

In the morning papers Pincher summed up the exchange as "an attempt to fob Britain off with a second-rate H-bomb weapon called Hound Dog . . . until it could build a fleet of atomic submarines carrying Polaris missiles."[18] *The New York Times* made no mention of Hound Dog but did observe, "The proposal that the United States might offer Polaris submarines as an alternative nuclear deterrent brought the reply that this would mean an enormous change in the nation's defense system, from air to sea."[19] Defense correspondents for *The Guardian* and the BBC both pointed out that cancellation might lead to reexamination of the agreement on Holy Loch. While news accounts varied somewhat on the precise positions taken by the discussants, there was substantial agreement on the tone of Thorneycroft's presentation. The recurrence in report after report of phrases like "tough talks," the "serious" impact on Anglo-American relations, and warning of an "agonizing reappraisal" of British policy suggested that, while only *The Daily Telegraph* identified its source as "a Ministry of Defense spokesman," other correspondents had spoken to the same man. Who gave out this version of the talks and why?

One week intervened between the Thorneycroft-McNamara encounter and the opening of the Nassau conference. From Paris, where NATO defense ministers had gathered, came varied prognoses for Skybolt. From London came anti-American fulminations on Tory backbenches, growing louder with each item of news from across the Channel and the Atlantic. From Rambouillet, where Macmillan was visiting de Gaulle, came indications of a French veto of Britain's Common Market bid. And from Washington came still more unsettling words for already unsettled Britons. McGeorge Bundy, in a televised interview, denied that the United States had a "fixed obligation" to provide its allies with a substitute for Skybolt. Pressed on this point by a panelist, Bundy added that "if the Skybolt should be abandoned, after consultation, then the question which would face us and the British is a question which NATO has had on its plate now for four or five years, which is what is the best way of organizing missile . . . defenses for . . . NATO as a whole."[20] Then on the very eve of Nassau, the White House released the transcript of a year-end television interview with President Kennedy, in which Bill Lawrence of ABC had questioned the President about an advertisement promoting Skybolt which Douglas Aircraft placed in *Time* magazine. The project would cost $2.5 billion, Kennedy had commented, and "we don't think that we are going to get $2.5 billion worth of national security."[21] When Macmillan stepped off the plane at Nassau, Lawrence told him of the President's remark. It was the first that the Prime Minister had heard of it, but if he was stunned, he gave no indication.

Later that day Macmillan and Kennedy talked alone, as their aides busied themselves preparing position papers. Two days of formal talks followed, one more than originally scheduled. Theodore C. Sorensen, White House Special Counsel, summarizes the substance of the negotiations:

If the British still had faith in Skybolt, said the President, the project could proceed—and they need pick up only half of the development costs. No, said Macmillan, he now accepted U.S. evidence on the missile's performance. Perhaps, said the President, a joint study could be commissioned on how to fill the Skybolt gap. No, said Macmillan, he needed something more definitive; and he cited an angry letter he had received from 137 Members of Parliament from his own party. Possibly, said the President, the Royal Air Force could be adapted to use our shorter-range Hound Dog air-to-ground missile. No, said Macmillan, that won't work.[22]

When it was over, Macmillan had Polaris.

International agreements are usually distinguished for their imprecision, but the joint communiqué setting out terms and conditions of the deal was a masterpiece of ambiguity. Did it preserve Britain's "independent deterrent"? "[T]he President and the Prime Minister agreed that a decision on Polaris must be considered in the widest context . . . an opportunity for . . . new and closer arrangements . . . of strategic Western defense. . . ."[23] What did these "arrangements" entail? "The Prime Minister suggested . . . a start be made by subscribing to NATO some part of the forces already in existence. This could include allocation from . . . United Kingdom Bomber Command. . . . Such forces would be assigned as part of a NATO nuclear force and targeted in accordance with NATO plans." What about Polaris? "[T]he President and the Prime Minister agreed that the purpose of their two governments with respect to the provision of the Polaris missiles must be the development of a multilateral NATO nuclear force in the closest consultation with other NATO allies. They will use their best endeavors to this end." Those missiles sold to Britain, equipped with British warheads.

would be made available for inclusion in a NATO multilateral nuclear force. The Prime Minister made it clear that except where Her Majesty's Government may decide that supreme national interests are at stake, these British forces will be used for the purposes of international defense of the Western Alliance in all circumstances.[24]

Assessing the pact's meaning after Nassau, British officials pointed to a guarantee of nuclear independence contained in the clause, "except where Her Majesty's Government may decide that supreme national interests are at stake," at the same time as the Americans were portraying the agreement as a long stride toward nuclear interdependence in consigning Polaris to NATO. In London, meanwhile, Conservative M.P.'s howled their disapproval of the deal, just as the Cabinet in a hastily called session was giving its assent. Defense Minister Thorneycroft told reporters at London Airport that Skybolt "is thought to be lame," barely three hours before an Air Force spokesman at Cape Canaveral was pronouncing the latest test firing of the missile a "success"—an evaluation which in turn was challenged within the hour by a Defense Department source in Washington.

Within twenty-four hours various bits of information thus became public in widely scattered places. Out of such big blooming buzzing confusion, newspapers do not often try to discern a consistent pattern of reports. Instead, they act largely like transmission belts carrying information across international borders. The location of their reporters abroad, as at home, is critical in determining the information that newspapers acquire. What emerges at the other end of the line may vary markedly from news organization to news organization, and even from story to story on the very same page.

Foreign correspondence consists primarily of culling the local press and tapping routine channels of news. But there are other forces tending to "nationalize" news content. First, many of the sources for foreign correspondents, wherever they work, are their own countrymen, especially embassy personnel. Second, their notions of what is news are defined largely by audiences back home, in particular, by their editors and by the news sources in their own government who provide much of the news. The nature of foreign news coverage enables officials to exploit the press to affect outcomes in international politics even more readily than in domestic politics. Why they would do so is a function of their stakes and stands in any controversy.

Stakes and Stands

The Skybolt controversy seems simple enough on the surface. The United States had agreed to sell the British some Skybolt missiles if their development were successful. Having decided to renege on Skybolt, the Kennedy Administration proceeded to make good on its obligation by providing Polaris. What, then, was all the tumult about? Was the British press, spearheaded by Beaverbrook's *Daily Express*, merely creating a stir to sell newspapers?

On second glance, it was all an elaborate misunderstanding. Each side, misperceiving the other's stakes, misreading the other's intentions, acted accordingly, and was disappointed by the other's response. Partly this was due to the way each conceived of the other. Says Richard Neustadt,

So powerful, so nearly irresistible, at least for us, is the conception of a "government" as though it were a person, that even those who know better because they were inside one seem to have been incapable of consciously, consistently applying what they knew when thinking of the other they knew best in all the world, their "friend" in London.[25]

And "friendship," seemingly unrequited, induces paranoid reaction. In blunted expectation lies crisis.

Yet it was a misunderstanding only on the assumption that governments do act as though they were one man—a man who knows his own mind. As is evident from the differences in policy preferences among the principals in the drama, neither government was a unified whole. The national interest had as many versions as there were positions in government from which to view it.

In London, Harold Macmillan had taken office in the aftermath of Suez, a low point both for Britain's standing among the world powers and for Anglo-American relations. He thus sought to reassert Britain's place in the international arena and to reestablish what has come to be known as the "special relationship" between Britain and the United States. For the first, he relied upon development of an independent nuclear deterrent; for the second, upon cultivation of his friendship with President Eisenhower, an association seeded in wartime collaboration and not uprooted by Suez. From the outset, though, nuclear independence was entangled with transatlantic interdependence. In 1957, Macmillan persuaded the Eisenhower Administration to obtain an amendment to the McMahon Act in order to facilitate the sharing of American nuclear technology. Three years later, forced to cancel development of the Blue Streak missile, he again turned to Eisenhower, this time to provide the delivery capability for his nuclear independence.

With the coming of the missile age, independence was, for Britain, a sometime thing. Lacking the financial resources to keep pace with successive generations of sophistication in delivery and defense, the British had to depend upon others for research and development. A "European" deterrent was, perhaps, an eventual solution; but for the time, the others had to be American. Then too, there was the question of independent use. Whether or not the British technically could launch a nuclear attack without American assent, it was hard to conceive of situations in which they would do so. Moreover, if possession of nuclear weapons was supposed to entitle a nation to sit at the top table of international conferences and Western alliance defense policy-making, then October 1962, when the British were informed, not consulted, about American plans to compel removal of the Soviet missiles from Cuba, must have seemed a keen disappointment. To the Tories, presiding over not only dissolution of an empire but also a decline in Britain's own economic and political position, nuclear independence had become the very symbol of sovereignty, not as much to be brandished as to be polished and displayed—and held onto at all costs.

Skybolt was the Tory escutcheon, and Macmillan, its knight defender. Skybolt, not Polaris. Macmillan had considerable political capital invested in the missile, whatever its military value compared to Polaris. The deal with Eisenhower had been his. As time passed, the Macmillan Government's advocacy of it contained fewer and fewer cautionary notes. When the Opposition raised doubts about the Americans' intention to go through with it, he dispelled them; when they questioned the missile's effectiveness, he defended it.

Another consideration for the Prime Minister was the politics within the British military establishment. The RAF's aging V-bombers would soon be obsolete, unable to penetrate improved enemy defenses; with Skybolt they would remain serviceable until the late 1960s. The American missile was thus the guarantor of Bomber Command's strategic mission, and the RAF, the few to whom so many owed so much, had its fervent backers among Conservative M.P.'s as well as in the moribund aircraft industry. Land-based missiles would not do. Britain was a "tight little island," hardly the place to implant missiles which would be a prime target in a nuclear exchange. In any event, the RAF looked with disdain on "sitting in silos."[26] Polaris, on the other hand, would entail a takeover of the RAF's mission by the Royal Navy, a breach of the gentlemen's agreement among the services. Furthermore, the admirals wanted aircraft carriers, not submarines: "Who wants to make a career under the sea?" grumbled the First Sea Lord Casper John when Hyman Rickover had first tried to sell the British on the idea of Polaris back in 1959.[27]

Added to this was the question of cost. What had first attracted Macmillan to Skybolt was that the United States would bear the burden of research and development, charging him only what it cost to produce the missiles he ordered and to convert V-bombers to carry them. It was but a pittance compared to the expense of building and equipping a Polaris submarine fleet. The price of Polaris was bound to cause a stir among Cabinet members, whose departments were competing for their shares of an already strained budget. In short, as Macmillan himself would remark to the Commons a month after Nassau in defense of his original choice of Skybolt, "[I]t would get us through a long period of years with the least disturbance."[28]

Defense Minister Thorneycroft was hardly wedded to Skybolt or to the independent deterrent, but the vows were not his to take. It is the rare Cabinet minister who brings to his job both policy expertise and a program of action. Thorneycroft was no exception. Nor was the job itself conducive to ministerial activism. Lacking statutory authority and staff, a Defense Minister was subservient to the services. For his muscle a minister had to draw less upon his skill in administration than upon his standing in the party, and Thorneycroft had not much of that. He was new to his post, though not to the Cabinet. Once a "comer" in the party, he had served as Chancellor of the Exchequer earlier in Macmillan's tenure, but had quit in a dispute over the 1959 budget. He had pushed for deflation in opposition to those in the Cabinet, Macmillan among them, who were anxious to avoid cuts in welfare spending. In his letter of resignation he had violated orthodoxy by attacking the government's spending:

But Macmillan had the Cabinet behind him, and he knew politically deflation would not attract much support. He described the amount of money at issue—£50 million—as "chickenfeed," and was able to appear to the public as the guardian of social services: "Your resignation at the present time," he replied angrily to Thorneycroft, "cannot help to sustain and can only damage the interests which we have all been trying to preserve."[29]

Restored to the Cabinet on the suffrance of Macmillan in the reshuffle of summer 1962, Thorneycroft was hardly in a position to press the Prime Minister openly to go after the Polaris—least of all when this meant reallocating funds from social services to defense.

The principal opponents of Skybolt in the British government were in no position at all to do much about it. One was the Scientific Adviser to the Prime Minister, Sir Solly Zuckerman, whose advice was just that—advice—which he might or might not offer, and Macmillan might or might not take. A Scientific Adviser had no authority to compel anyone to listen. The other opponents were not in the government at all, but in the Opposition. Riven by internal argument over its stand on nuclear weapons, the Labour Party could not pose an effective challenge to Tory defense policies in 1960. Its parliamentary spokesman on defense, George Brown, personally had no quarrel with nuclear independence, but he did question the government's ability to deliver the goods. Two years later the party had closed ranks with the anti-disarmers still in the lead, but they were marching to a new tune—abandonment of the independent deterrent. Despite the Conservatives' disarray, Skybolt was not an issue on which the Opposition could do more than score some debating points.

For the Kennedy Administration, Skybolt crystallized what had been an amorphous, often evanescent debate about the future of transatlantic relations. Here was a concrete decision through which one of the several grand designs floating around Washington might come to realization, and it galvanized various bureaucratic factions into action. One group, concerned primarily with European military relations and centered in the International Security Affairs Division of the Pentagon, conceived of a single Atlantic community, built around NATO conventional forces and nuclear forces under American control. Europeanists in the State Department, concerned more with economic and political relations, had an alternative design in mind. It took the form of a "dumbbell," or partnership between the United States and an expanded Common Market. The Europeanists, recalls Arthur Schlesinger, Jr., "regretted the cancellation of Skybolt, fearing that it would overthrow the government in London committed to bring Britain into Europe. But, if Skybolt had to go, at least let it carry the special relationship down with it. . . ."[30] That relationship was incompatible with their design, but more than conceptual neatness was involved:

What worried the Europeanists was the thought that the United States by offering a replacement for Skybolt—Polaris, for example—would prolong the British deterrent, intensify Bonn's demand for a nuclear role and prove to de

Gaulle that Britain preferred the United States to Europe. Some Europeanists, like [Robert] Schaetzel, were chiefly concerned with the Common Market; others, like Walt Rostow and Henry Owen of the Policy Planning Council, with the MLF [multilateral force]. But both British entry into the Market and the MLF were now, in their view, at stake, and Skybolt offered the grand opportunity to terminate the special relationship and force Britain into Europe.[31]

These factions were not alone in their efforts to shape the outcome of the controversy. The threat to scrap Skybolt stunned the Strategic Air Command, still reeling from the loss of its B-70 bomber to Pentagon budget-cutters. To the missile's manufacturer, Douglas Aircraft, cancellation would further darken a profit picture already dim from "unrecovered expenditures" on development of a commercial jet.[32] They were certain to stir up their friends on Capitol Hill to save Skybolt.

This threat presented Defense Secretary McNamara with a political problem, which he attempted to solve by preemptive strike. Determined to bring defense procurement under control and given a Presidential mandate to do so, McNamara chose to eliminate appropriations for Skybolt from the fiscal 1964 budget, forcing its proponents in Congress to try adding on funds to a budget already showing a deficit. This legislative tactic presented the Administration with a diplomatic problem, to warn the British of impending cancellation without implying that the formal budgetary process had been circumvented and the advice of the Joint Chiefs of Staff not even sought. This problem, too, McNamara was delegated to solve, but by intimation rather than by firm declaration of intent. The reasons for his circumlocutions of November 8 and 9 are rooted in the nature of press and government relations between Washington and London.

The Politics of the Special Relationship

What was special about the "special relationship" was the close collaboration between officials at the operating level of the two governments. Not one permanent alliance, but several shifting alliances, linked the two capitals. Officials on one side of the Atlantic holding interests in common with those on the other were accustomed to acting in concert, sometimes quite openly, to achieve their common ends against officials within their own government who opposed them. So, an RAF group captain attached to the Pentagon kept abreast of new weapons developments of his American brethren; and while Skybolt was still on Douglas' drawing boards, even before Camp David, it was designed to meet the specifications of Britain's V-bomber.[33] So, too, when the U.S. Navy embarked on development of Polaris, Admiral Rickover visited London to describe its advantages to British admirals, who were not impressed, and to Whitehall civilians, who were. Among the latter was Sir Solly Zuckerman, who would remain its advocate over the next two years and relay discouraging reports on Skybolt from American government scientists to the Prime Minister.[34]

Somewhat less special, but no less persistent a feature of the Anglo-American relationship has been the use of each other's press to get messages transmitted outside routine diplomatic channels. The practice is not peculiarly Anglo-Saxon. Officials around the world have been known to feed information to foreign correspondents, or even to their own with the knowledge that foreigners will be monitoring the local press for just that sort of information. News traffic between Washington—or New York—and London has always been especially heavy, facilitated by common language and the number of news organizations with bureaus on both sides of the Atlantic. While America's economic and military importance for Britain would seem to account for the number of British news bureaus in Washington, the sizable American journalistic presence in London is partly a matter of tradition. Since colonial times, America has looked to England for news of the Old World. Editors, particularly on Eastern prestige papers, still sense among their readers a demand for "little England" vignettes, as well as for British perspectives on current affairs. Partly, too, it has become a matter of convenience. Into London flows news from a worldwide network of British correspondents. *The New York Times* leases a direct wire between its bureau in London and the foreign desk in New York, using London as a relay station for all European news and running a desk operation there much like the one in Washington. The difference in time zone permits most of the copy to be pulled together in London by early evening and cabled across the Atlantic by noon, New York time.

What extensive coverage makes possible, long-time practice makes probable. British officials are especially accommodating to American reporters; the Foreign Office even holds separate briefings for an American "group," dealing with topics of special interest to them and providing capsule summaries of global events on which those attending have come to rely. In two World Wars, moreover, officials have cultivated American correspondents in London in an effort to secure United States aid.[35] News management became so common in wartime London that when American correspondents sought to cable home reports that the United States was under severe criticism over its backing of Darlan in North Africa, the Foreign Office had censorship instituted, lest the State Department think the dispatches "had official sympathy in London."[36] Nor has use of the press been confined to British officials in wartime. Henry Brandon, for example, describes an invitation he got to interview Secretary of State Dulles just prior to the fall of Dien Bien Phu. After dropping word that American aircraft carriers were at that very moment steaming into the Gulf of Tonkin, Dulles indicated that, while he himself favored United States intervention in Indochina, President Eisenhower had made such action contingent on Britain decision to go in, too. Comments Brandon,

I knew, as Mr. Dulles must have known, that the British Cabinet was to meet in two days' time, on Sunday; a lot depended on that meeting, and I was certain, as I sat down to write my weekly dispatch to the *Sunday Times* (in which I could not quote from the interview), that in indicating such sensational developments Mr. Dulles was hoping to use one more avenue to influence the climate of opinion in London. . . .[37]

Special relationships called for special delicacy on McNamara's part. If he were to present cancellation as a fait accompli, word was bound to leak to the press that the Administration had made its decision without the requisite consultation with the Joint Chiefs of Staff, a breach of due process not to be countenanced in American military circles.

Yet McNamara's reliance on a privately communicated hint of cancellation would redound to his bewilderment when he met with Thorneycroft in London one month hence. Why had the British not undertaken any staff work in the interim and come up with a request for a substitute for Skybolt? It was not that the Defense Minister had failed to get McNamara's meaning over the telephone; he understood that Skybolt was out, but without a definitive statement to that effect, he could not get to work on finding an alternative. Both to his Prime Minister and to his Air Force he would have seemed a traitor, had he ordered a ministry study, and he lacked the staff to do his own contingency planning.[38]

Over the telephone the two Defense chiefs made plans to meet in London toward the end of the month to iron out arrangements. Timing was crucial, again because of the press. Formal consultation between the two was inadvisable before the President had given final clearance to his decision, expected on or about November 23. From that point on, it would be a matter of days before the Joint Chiefs would receive formal notice of cancellation through budgetary channels and word would leak to the outside. There were key Congressmen and the most influential of all hyphenated Americans within the foreign policy establishment, Anglo-Americans, to alert in Washington, and Tory backbenchers to arouse in London. Publication prior to consultation while perhaps damaging to the President, could be disastrous to the Prime Minister. Both governments agreed on that.[39]

Calculations went awry. The Cuban missile crisis had disrupted McNamara's schedule. Now, with other pressing matters to attend to, he put off his meeting with Thorneycroft until December 11. In the meantime the worst fears of the principals would be realized.

First came Chapman Pincher's story of November 28 warning of a "determined effort" by the State Department to wrest Skybolt, and with it, nuclear independence, from the British. Although this speculation bore some signs of parisan gamesmanship, probably George Brown's, Pincher had well-placed sources among American military attachés in the London embassy, particularly in the Air Force. As he subsequently acknowledged, his story had been based on "a deliberate U.S. leak."[40]

But the Pincher piece was contradicted the very next day by a *Daily Express* dispatch out of Washington. To every hint that all was not well with Skybolt, whether politically or technically, the response of the Air Force and Douglas had been the same: insistence that it would succeed. This occasion was no exception. If the British were convinced that they could continue to count on Skybolt, their conviction might, in the end, prove self-assuring. Here was another instance in which that conviction needed shoring up, and the Air Force saw to it. Brandon, meanwhile, guessed otherwise. From conversations in the White House and elsewhere he inferred correctly that Skybolt was in trouble although the final decision was still in the offing.

Hard upon Acheson's speech at West Point came the leak which McNamara and others had earlier anticipated. On December 7, three days after the Comptroller's Office gave notice to the Joint Chiefs, stories hit page one in Washington that the Administration was about to drop Skybolt over Air Force objections. The stories originated at an Air Force briefing.[41] In response, the official spokesman for the Defense Department took pains to emphasize, for the benefit of the British, that the decision was not yet final. There were even hints that Skybolt was still available if they wanted to pay for further development—a suggestion that could hardly be made for the record inasmuch as Congressmen might well question why if the missile was still good enough for the British, it was no longer good enough for the United States. To scotch British speculation that cancellation might be part of a plot to deprive Britain of its independent deterrent, Deputy Secretary of Defense Roswell Gilpatric called in British correspondents at week's end and told them that the United States recognized its obligation to the Macmillan government and would offer an alternative weapon system if the British did not wish to defray the cost of perfecting Skybolt.

In making public the internal battle, the Air Force had precisely achieved what it set out to do: its allies in London were rallying to the side of Skybolt. More than a few Tories were willing to accept the *Daily Express* theory that Acheson's musing about Britain's future role in the world, McNamara's prodding the European allies to increase their conventional force contribution to NATO while promoting centralization of nuclear control, and now Skybolt, were all somehow linked.

The RAF now put out the line that "the British Government had not been kept fully informed" about Skybolt, which was technically correct since they had been kept in the dark by Thorneycroft. They also played to the Defense Minister's political weakness by questioning whether he would show himself tough enough with McNamara. Thorneycroft's office moved quickly to allay RAF fears on this point: he was "determined to be tough," Pincher reported on the eve of the talks.[42]

The next day's session was billed by Arthur Schlesinger, Jr., as "a Pinero drama of misunderstanding."[43] Just as the Minister was bureaucratically constrained from asking for Polaris, so was the Secretary from offering it—or any American commitment to maintain the British deterrent. Europeanists in State had succeeded in drafting instructions that tied McNamara's hands for the moment.

When it was over, Thorneycroft's press aide, Brig. Godfrey Hobbs, called in reporters, Americans included, and presented a version of what had transpired which would dominate news accounts in London. "It has been really tough going," he asserted, echoing what was by now a familiar refrain. "Mr. McNamara is absolutely crystal clear to the British reaction to any cancellation of Skybolt because the Minister told him so."[44] Then, setting the stage for Nassau, Hobbs warned, "If Skybolt is withdrawn, there is going to be an agonizing reappraisal." He refused to specify what that reappraisal would encompass.[45] Subsequently he would suggest turning the Americans out of Holy Loch.[46]

If the talks had not been predictable, their outcome was. Richard Neustadt explains,

Understandably, suspicion mounted on both sides. Thorneycroft was playing to a gallery, as McNamara found out when he read the evening papers. But Thorneycroft was also in dead earnest. He felt betrayed. His expectations had been overthrown. . . . McNamara's feelings were not altogether different. He too had been surprised, and then lambasted.[47]

The scene then shifted to Paris, where both men had flown to attend a NATO ministerial conference. For the next week each provided reporters with information and misinformation aimed at strengthening his own side's bargaining position at Nassau. Thorneycroft and his aides, in not-for-attribution conversations with reporters, continued to fan the flames of Conservative discontent, while discreetly putting out hints that Polaris would do quite well as a replacement for Skybolt. It was "the official British view," reported the *Times* (London) defense correspondent from Paris, that "the American decision has come as a complete surprise to the Government. . . ."[48] "From the British side," added the *Guardian* defense man, also in Paris, "there is no willingness to concede that an American decision to cancel Skybolt would be anything but a major attack on the independent deterrent."[49] Two days alter *The Observer* had it "on good authority" that the government had "virtually abandoned hope" of obtaining Skybolt and was now "hoping that the Americans will maintain the British nuclear deterrent by supplying the Polaris missile. . . ."[50]

Across the Channel the RAF and the Royal Navy engaged in joint maneuvers to rescue Skybolt. *The Sunday Telegraph*'s air correspondent reported, "Government circles feel that the U.S. has been trying to mislead Britain over Skybolt. It is now known that the five recent firings of the missile which Mr. McNamara has described as 'failures' were, in fact, partial successes, with major steps forward." American estimates of the cost of completing the project, he added, were exaggerated since conversion of the V-bombers to carry the missile would run only a fraction of that needed for the B-52s.[51] At the same time, *The Telegraph*'s naval correspondent was putting the bill for a single Polaris-armed submarine at an exorbitant £41.1 million.[52]

These disclosures had a cumulative effect on Conservative restiveness. Tory backbenchers, who had come to associate nuclear independence with holding onto Skybolt, read the news reports and began to vent their rage at Washington. It was they who, in absentia, would give voice to Macmillan's best talking point with Kennedy one week hence: "Instead of pleading that his government would fall," notes Schlesinger, "he seemed to be saying that his party would accept anti-Americanism to keep itself in power."[53]

Against the barrage of self-serving disclosures from the British, McNamara strove to build an American brief: thus, from "authoritative sources eager to put the record straight" came a report that Skybolt was still available if the British were willing to spend $100 million a year for five years on research and development. "Nor, it is stated, was there anything in any agreement or memorandum between the two countries to justify the recent assertion by the B.B.C. that the United States agreed to give Britain an equity in Skybolt in return for the use of Holy Loch . . ."[54] The Secretary was seconded by McGeorge Bundy, who used a television appearance on "Meet the Press" to deny that the United States had any fixed commitment to come up with a substitute in the event Skybolt was scrapped.[55]

McNamara, however, failed to persuade even American editorial writers. *The New York Times* had already come out in favor of Skybolt's continuation, citing "serious political, as well as military, repercussions in the Macmillan government" and the missile's "importance" to the United States Air Force.[56] On December 15 *The Washington Post*, in an editorial quoted extensively in London, dwelt on the political concerns at the core of the affair: "Weaknesses of Skybolt as a weapon are less alarming and less disappointing than the weaknesses in the conduct of American foreign policy. . . ." Echoing leaders in London papers, the *Post* held that Skybolt "is not solely a weapons problem and it is alarming to see that this Administration is handling it as though it were."[57] *Post* publisher Philip Graham even paid a call on President Kennedy the day after to reiterate his position in person.

Elsewhere in Washington the Air Force was still pressing for a reversal of the Administration decision through background briefings for reporters and disclosures to friendly Congressmen. Eschewing more subtle methods, Douglas Aircraft took out a two-page spread in the December 14 issue of *Time* magazine to boost their product: "ON TARGET—Air Force Skybolt is expected to be one of America's most powerful deterrent weapons. This air launched ballistic missile will save *billions* in taxes by extending the useful life of our B-52 and British Vulcan II bombers." It also cited "several successful tests" carried out to date.[58] To head off any renewal of lobbying for Skybolt, President Kennedy pointedly refuted the Douglas ad in a year-end television interview:

Well, I think it was an attempt to influence our decision. I see nothing wrong with that. The fact of the matter is that this Skybolt is very essential to the future of the Douglas Company. . . . The only thing that we ought to point out is, we are talking about $2.5 billion to build a weapon to hand on our B-52's when we already have billions invested in Polaris and Minuteman. . . . How many times do you have to hit a target with nuclear weapons? That is why we are talking about spending this $2.5 billion we don't think that we are going to get $2.5 billion worth of national security.[59]

The White House released a transcript of the interview, which the press would insure greeted Prime Minister Macmillan when he arrived in the Bahamas.

The incident dramatizes the multiple-audience dilemma: a remark meant for domestic ears was bound to be picked up by the British. It would undercut the President's negotiating position. While he was willing to sell Polaris to the British, it did not follow that he wanted to. The deal would certainly cause problems in Washington on the Hill among the jealous guardians of America's nuclear secrets and in Foggy Bottom among Europeanists with different designs. It could not help Britain's cause in Paris, a cause the Administration wanted to succeed. When British Ambassador David Ormsby-Gore, on the plane to Nassau, proposed completion of Skybolt with a fifty-fifty split of development costs between the two governments, it seemed to Kennedy a face-saving solution.[a] To Macmillan, however, the President's interview had left little else to save. "The lady was violated in public," he commented upon hearing of the fifty-fifty offer.

To be more precise, the lady had not been "violated" in public; her reputation had been ruined. Press-government relations thus had special bearing on the outcome of the Skybolt affair. Political acts may or may not involve the allocation of resources to meet social purposes, but all political acts do have symbolic meanings. These meanings are attached both by the general public, often barely cognizant of what has transpired, and by various attentive publics, those in and outside government intensely aware of and concerned about political outcomes. Frequently, the symbolic meanings of an act transcend any importance it may have for resource allocation. Frequently, too, it is impossible to pin down any tangible referents for the symbolic meanings. The symbol is then an ideal source of political conflict, to wit, the independence of the British deterrent. Men disagreed over what they meant by "nuclear independence." They also differed on the significance that they ascribed to it. The lack of either agreed-upon or verifiable content to this term was at the root of the controversy. It mattered not as much *what* the Americans gave Great Britain as *how* they gave it. So it went with Skybolt's reputation. So, too, with Polaris: tied to NATO it would look from Tory backbenches like a diplomatic defeat for Macmillan.

---

[a]Ormsby-Gore's assessment of the bargain is that both men felt that it would be unacceptable to Macmillan, but that it was meant as "a clear token of American good faith" [Harlech "Suez SNAFU, Skybolt SABU," p. 46].

Given with no strings—or radio locks—attached, it would seem to undermine Administration efforts to achieve a "controlled response," to give away America's hard-won nuclear secrets, and to confirm de Gaulle's suspicions about Anglo-Saxons.

Once Macmillan opted for Polaris, both sides settled down to hard bargaining. News reports from Nassau reflected this shift. Conditioned to expect suspicion between the two, reporters hunted for signs of it. Most dispatches recorded that as President Kennedy inspected a guard of honor at the airport, a band played the tune, "Early in the Morning," which went, "Oh, don't deceive me,/Oh, never leave me,/How could you use a poor maiden so?" Some correspondents even found ulterior motives when Kennedy, in a light vein, greeted Macmillan by recalling their five previous meetings, "I am not sure the world is better off for them, but I am better off for the counsel and friendship you have shown me."

Much of the news was not the creation of the press corps. Arrangements for briefing the 400-odd reporters who descended on Nassau facilitated news management by the two sides. Significantly, Sir Harold Evans, public relations adviser to the Prime Minister, and Pierre Salinger, White House press secretary, were both on hand. As Evans describes the scene,

[W]hen one has these meetings with the Prime Minister and the President, and the British spokesman, customarily unattributable, unseen, has to face up the great international press gathering, with all the arc lamps and the cameras, even then you know that only certain questions are going to come up, certain obvious questions. None of the correspondents there are going to ask you questions which go really deep. He may ask a simple and obvious question, and you give a simple and obvious answer and then in the end, what do you do? You go off and give non-attributable briefings. I would be briefing the British correspondents. Pierre Salinger would do the same on his side. . . .[60]

Reporters at one briefing then swapped notes with their colleagues at the other.

London and Washington took advantage of the arrangements. Before the conference opened, for example, Salinger suggested that the United States regarded the festering Congo situation as top priority on the agenda. A British source countered by implying that tentative agreement on an alternative for Skybolt was a precondition to discussion of any other topic. Since no conflict over agenda ever arose in negotiations, this exchange seems to have been a feeding for domestic consumption. Hyperbole also was much in evidence at the outset. To one British aide, cancellation was "the biggest double-cross since the Last Supper."[61]

It was not until the talks were over, though, that the playing to domestic and international audiences began in earnest. What did the joint communiqué mean? The British put out one version, the Americans another. While Evans was portraying the deal as assuring Britain's nuclear independence, "a high Administration official"—Kennedy—was telling Carroll Kilpatrick of the *Post* that it "represented a giant step toward interdependence of the Western countries."

American officials dismissed the provision for Britain's "supreme national interest" as "no more than any sovereign nation would insist upon" and not applicable to "a Suez-type operation."[62] As one participant summed up the briefings,

There was a certain amount of gamesmanship. Both sides knew what the games were since they knew each other and each other's political problems. We could look with a measure of disinterested judgment on each other's efforts to cope with those problems.

Macmillan could depart from Nassau well pleased with the outcome. Had he not convinced the Yanks to sell him Polaris submarines, his alone to deploy whenever he felt "supreme national interests are at stake"? They were expensive, of course, but he had taken the extraordinary precaution of obtaining Cabinet approval before closing the deal. The pact might interfere with his Common Market bid, but after Rambouillet he had few illusions of success in that venture.[63] Then there were the services and the backbenchers to placate; but the admirals would get to like their new mission once they got used to it, and a new generation of Blue Streak air-to-surface missiles for Bomber Command would take the edge off RAF bitterness. With the services pacified, Tory rage would dissipate over the month-long Christmas recess, or would it?

Returning in the full flush of victory, Macmillan found himself excoriated by his own backbenchers for his "sellout" of the independent deterrent to Kennedy. Distrust of the United States, once aroused, proved difficult to set to rest.

Nor would reverberations from bureaucratic politics in Washington let it be. The Air Force announced, without prior clearance from the Pentagon, that in its sixth test Skybolt had scored a "success." Launched from beneath a bomber, it had flown 850 miles downrange, impacting less than a mile from the center of the target area. This performance appeared to contradict the Nassau communiqué which cited "doubts that had been expressed about the prospects of success of this weapons system" among the grounds for rejection of Skybolt.[64] That was not all. As *The Sunday Telegraph*'s readers learned from the December 23 edition,

It was no coincidence that the launch was made today. Reliable informants stated that both the Air Force and the Douglas Aircraft Corporation . . . had hoped to fire one during the talks in the Bahamas. . . . No official reason has been given for the abandonment of the earlier attempt, but most observers believe that they yielded to political pressure not to go on.[65]

Deputy Secretary of Defense Gilpatric moved quickly to undercut the Air Force announcement. "Today's single test," he said, "did not conclusively demonstrate the capacity of the missile to achieve the target accuracy for which the Skybolt system was designed."[66] Subsequent analysis would bear out this view. While the test had been a partial success, the missile, not equipped with a protective heat shield, had burned up on reentry. Had it not, it still would have overshot its target by fifty-seven nautical miles.[67] Told of the Air Force announcement at London Airport, Macmillan noted that he was glad of the success, but he still felt that Britain had gotten the better of the bargain. An Air Force officer at Cape Canaveral pronounced a prophetic elegy over Skybolt: "It may be dead, but it won't lie down."[68] By 1969, it had been resurrected under a new name, the SCAD.[69]

Meanwhile, still another inspired mix-up followed. At the close of the Nassau conference, the British had made public their understanding that the price of Polaris, like that of Skybolt, would include only production costs and none of the $2.5 billion needed to finance development.[70] At the end of January, just before Parliament was to take up debate on the pact, State Department officials let reporters know that while some details of the financial arrangements might not have been spelled out at Nassau, the United States insisted that Britain share the cost of development.[71] Pentagon spokesman Arthur Sylvester clarified the Defense Department's position. The United States had assumed all past expenses, Secretary McNamara said, but expected the British to contribute toward work on the latest version of Polaris missile, the A-3.[72] Curiously, the British embassy did not take issue with this position, and Macmillan told Commons that Britain had agreed to pay 5 percent over the final production price of the missile to cover additional development costs.[73] State's disclosure nevertheless added weight to arguments voiced in London that the deal was too costly.

Élysée Palace, too, issued confirmation of sorts for the Tory view. "From a profound study of the Bahamas, accord," reported Le Monde's diplomatic correspondent André Fontaine, "our leaders would conclude that Britain has accepted, in fact, to integrate completely her national defense in the American system."[74] This was but one of a series of unattributed statements from French officials depicting Britain as a potential Trojan horse within the European economic community—all leading up to President de Gaulle's veto of Britain's Common Market bid at his January 14 press conference.

British reporters had suspicions of their own about American intentions. When President Kennedy touched on alliance politics at a New Year's background briefing in Palm Beach, his remarks were construed as implying a new American willingness to act unilaterally:

He is willing to ignore allied criticism which apparently is accepted as the price for progress. The action in Cuba, the scuttling of the Skybolt program, and the dispatch of a military mission to the Congo, which were all undertaken without prior consultation, are apparently indications of the new tough policy toward the alliance.[75]

In writing his story, The Times' American correspondent Louis Heren identified the President as its source, technically not a violation of the ground rules since

Heren had not attended. Trying to amend the impression left by *The Times*, White House National Security Adviser McGeorge Bundy allowed Henry Brandon to quote verbatim from a transcript the following pertinent passage:

I think we are more aware probably that we are going to incur at intervals people's displeasure. This is sort of a revolving cycle. At least, I think the United States ought to be more aware of it; and I think too often in the past we have defined our leadership as an attempt to be rather well regarded in all these countries.[76]

The gesture angered American reporters but dissuaded few Tories.

"A diplomatic Dunkirk," one right-winger called Nassau; a "culminating humiliation," cried another. Air Commodore Sir Arthur Vere Harvey, chairman of the Conservative backbench defense committee, led a thirteen-man deputation of members to pay a call on Defense Minister Thorneycroft. Afterward, Sir Arthur paused only long enough to describe their session as "pretty tricky," before taking off for Washington to see for himself what had befallen Skybolt.[77] He returned still convinced it would have been the best weapon for Britain.[78] The Opposition, not surprisingly, was doing nothing to make life easy for the Government. One left-wing M.P. even introduced a tempting motion to annul the agreement on Holy Loch. It tempted few Tories. In the end they closed ranks. At the time of Nassau, 127 Tories had signed a motion demanding retention of the independent deterrent; by the beginning of February when an Opposition motion of no confidence was put to a vote, all but a handful of backbenchers heeded the Government whip.

The vote was not a full measure of Tory discontent over the outcome of Nassau. During the debate Macmillan had as many questions from his own backbenches as from across the aisle. Nor did suspicion of the United States subside. In mid-summer a *Newsweek* exposé on British security sparked accusations that President Kennedy had planted the piece in order to scuttle the Polaris deal.

For the Prime Minister, though, a little misunderstanding was just a minor cost in comparison to the benefit he saw himself deriving from Nassau. Henry Brandon ponders "whether the United States in quiet backstage negotiations could have been persuaded to give Polaris under the conditions agreed to at Nassau," and concludes, "It might not have been possible to forge this compromise except in the heat of a great crisis and at the summit."[79] Like most crises, it was generated by officials using the press. Not all the news managers on both sides of the Atlantic fared as well as the Prime Minister.

The man whose news exploits included the leaking of the Ems telegram, Otto von Bismarck once observed that "every country is at some time held to account for the windows broken by its press."[80] Generations of officials since have recalled his remark with approval, while ignoring its disingenuousness. It is as if a bright young boy trying to draw attention away from his own miscreance were to blame the liveliness of a ball he had just hit awry. Many a head of government since Bismarck has deemed it necessary to go outside formal bureaucratic channels to conduct foreign affairs. In recent years summit conferences, like that at Nassau, private exchanges of letters, like that between Kennedy and Krushchev over Cuba, and hot lines, like the one connecting the Cabinet Office with the White House basement, all attest to this need. By the same token, subordinates occasionally strike up special relationships with their counterparts abroad in order to advance their own policy goals back home. The press, too, is a vehicle for delivering messages outside channels. The vibrations that its use sometimes generates can, as in Skybolt, wreak not wholly unforeseen damage.

Notes

1. In addition to Richard Neustadt's authoritative account in ALLIANCE POLITICS and the investigative reporting of Henry Brandon in the SUNDAY TIMES, December 9, 1963, pp. 29-31, these include Schlesinger, A THOUSAND DAYS, pp. 544-66; Sorensen, KENNEDY, pp. 564-76; Robert Kleiman, ATLANTIC CRISIS (New York: Norton, 1964), Chapter 3; John Newhouse, DE GAULLE AND THE ANGLO-SAXONS (New York: Viking, 1970), Chapters 7-8; William P. Duff, "Skybolt" (unpublished senior thesis, Department of Government, Harvard University, 1968); and Lord Harlech, "Suez SNAFU, Skybolt SABU," FOREIGN POLICY 2, 2, (Spring 1971); pp. 38-50.

2. George J. Geiger, "Most Mobile Missile," ORDNANCE 47 (November-December 1962); 294-97; "Air Force and Douglas Accelerate Skybolt Ballistic Missile Program," AVIATION WEEKLY AND SPACE TECHNOLOGY 75, 18 (October 30, 1961); pp. 23-24.

3. Neustadt, ALLIANCE POLITICS, pp. 33-34.

4. Henry Brandon, "Skybolt," SUNDAY TIMES, December 8, 1963, p. 39.

5. "Skybolt's Fate Up to Kennedy, McNamara," AVIATION WEEKLY AND SPACE TECHNOLOGY 77, 25 (December 17, 1962); 26-27.

6. DAILY EXPRESS, November 28, 1962, p. 1.

7. SUNDAY TIMES, December 2, 1962, p. 1.

8. WASHINGTON POST, December 6, 1962, p. 1.

9. NEW YORK TIMES, December 7, 1962, p. 1.

10. WASHINGTON POST, December 7, 1962, p. A-3.

11. SUNDAY TIMES, December 9, 1962.

12. Ibid.

13. THE OBSERVER, December 9, 1962.

14. SUNDAY TELEGRAPH, December 9, 1962.

15. DAILY EXPRESS, December 10, 1962, p. 6.

16. NEW YORK HERALD-TRIBUNE (European edition), December 12, 1962, p. 1.

17. Neustadt, ALLIANCE POLITICS, pp. 47-48.

18. DAILY EXPRESS, December 12, 1962, p. 1.

19. NEW YORK TIMES (International edition), December 12, 1962, p. 1.

20. U.P.I. dispatch in the NEW YORK HERALD-TRIBUNE (European edition), December 18, 1962, p. 1.

21. WASHINGTON POST, December 18, 1962, p. A-12.

22. Sorensen, KENNEDY, p. 566.

23. U.S., Department of State, BULLETIN 48, 1229 (January 14, 1963); pp. 44-45.

24. Ibid.

25. Neustadt, ALLIANCE POLITICS, p. 138.

26. Ibid., p. 32.

27. Newhouse, DE GAULLE AND THE ANGLO-SAXONS, p. 193.

28. Great Britain, PARLIAMENTARY DEBATES (Commons) 670 (1962-63); 964.

29. Anthony Sampson, STUDY IN AMBIGUITY (London: Penguin Books Ltd,) p. 161. Reprinted by permission of A.D. Peters and Company.

30. Schlesinger, A THOUSAND DAYS, p. 860.

31. Ibid., pp. 860-61.

32. "Skybolt's American Shadow," THE ECONOMIST 206, 6229 (January 12, 1963); p. 127.

33. Brandon, "Skybolt," p. 29; THE TIMES, May 20, 1960, p. 13.

34. Newhouse, DEGAULLE AND THE ANGLO-SAXONS, pp. 192-93; Schlesinger, A THOUSAND DAYS, pp. 858-59; THE GUARDIAN, December 12, 1962.

35. H.C. Peterson, "British Influence on the American Press, 1914-1917," AMERICAN POLITICAL SCIENCE REVIEW 31, 1 (February 1937); 82-83, discusses World War I. In one of a number of similar incidents recorded since World War II, Joseph Alsop tells how a British attaché in Washington, John Foster, informed him of an exchange of telegrams between Prime Minister Churchill and President Roosevelt in 1940. Churchill, in need of destroyers, warned that the shortage might make possible a German landing in Britain, but the President replied "noncommittally but very discouragingly." Publication of the notes was part of a campaign which led eventually to transfer of the vessels to Britain. (Alsop and Alsop, THE REPORTER'S TRADE, p. 8.) Also, Robert E. Sherwood, ROOSEVELT AND HOPKINS (New York: Harper, 1950), pp. 372, 754.

36. Francis Williams, PRESS, PARLIAMENT AND PEOPLE (London: Heinemann, 1946), p. 71.

37. Brandon, ANATOMY OF ERROR, p. 10.

38. Neustadt, ALLIANCE POLITICS, p. 107.

39. Brandon, "Skybolt," p. 30.

40. DAILY EXPRESS, December 10, 1962, p. 6.

41. Kleiman, ATLANTIC CRISIS, p. 54.

42. DAILY EXPRESS, December 11, 1962, p. 2.

43. Schlesinger, A THOUSAND DAYS, p. 861.

44. Quoted without attribution, in the DAILY TELEGRAPH, December 12, 1962.

45. U.P.I. dispatch quoting a "British defense spokesman," NEW YORK HERALD-TRIBUNE (European edition), December 12, 1962.

46. THE GUARDIAN, December 15, 1962.

47. Neustadt, ALLIANCE POLITICS, p. 48.

48. THE TIMES (London), December 14, 1962, p. 12.

49. THE GUARDIAN, December 14, 1962.

50. THE OBSERVER, December 16, 1962.

51. SUNDAY TELEGRAPH, December 16, 1962.

52. DAILY TELEGRAPH, December 15, 1962.

53. Schlesinger, A THOUSAND DAYS, p. 864.

54. NEW YORK TIMES (International edition), December 14, 1962, p. 1; Reuter dispatch in the FINANCIAL TIMES, December 13, 1962.

55. THE TIMES (London), December 17, 1962, p. 8.

56. NEW YORK TIMES (International edition), December 12, 1962.

57. WASHINGTON POST, December 15, 1962, p. A-12.

58. TIME 80, 24 (December 14, 1962), pp. 70-71.

59. WASHINGTON POST, December 18, 1962, p. A-12.

60. Sir Harold Evans, "Government Public Relations and the Press," Report of the Proceedings of the Fifty-Fourth Annual Conference of the Commonwealth Press Union, London, July 15-16, 1964, p. 42.

61. "Old Allies—A New Stance," NEWSWEEK 60, 27 (December 31, 1962); 9.

62. WASHINGTON POST, December 22-23, 1962, p. 1; THE GUARDIAN, December 24, 1962.

63. Neustadt, ALLIANCE POLITICS, p. 52.

64. U.S., Department of State, BULLETIN 48, 1229, pp. 44-45.

65. SUNDAY TELEGRAPH, December 23, 1962.

66. Ibid.

67. DAILY TELEGRAPH, December 28, 1962.

68. SUNDAY TELEGRAPH, December 23, 1962.

69. NEW YORK TIMES, February 5, 1969, p. 18.

70. U.P.I. dispatch in the NEW YORK HERALD-TRIBUNE (European Edition), December 22, 1962.

71. WASHINGTON POST, January 28, 1963, p. 1.

72. NEW YORK TIMES, January 29, 1963. p. 6.

73. NEW YORK TIMES, January 31, 1963, p. 12.

74. Quoted in the NEW YORK TIMES, January 11, 1963, p. 1.

75. NEW YORK TIMES, January 2, 1963, p. 8. Cf., Ben H. Bagdikian, "The President Nonspeaks," COLUMBIA JOURNALISM REVIEW 2, 1 (Spring 1963); 43-46.

76. NEW YORK TIMES, January 6, 1963, p. 3.

77. DAILY TELEGRAPH, January 2, 1963; FINANCIAL TIMES, January 3, 1963.

78. THE TIMES (London), January 14, 1963, p. 13.

79. Brandon, "Skybolt," p. 31.

80. Sidney B. Fay, THE ORIGINS OF THE WORLD WAR (New York: Free Press, 1966), I, p. 29. Some examples of Bismarckian news management are presented in Erich Eyck, BISMARCK AND THE GERMAN EMPIRE (New York: Norton, 1964), p. 137.

9   The Press and Public Policy

If nothing may be published but what civil authority shall have previously approved, power must always be the standard of truth.

If every dreamer of innovations may propagate his projects, there can be no settlement; if every murmurer at government may diffuse discontent, there can be no peace; and if every skeptic in theology may teach his follies, there can be no religion. . . . The danger of such unbounded liberty and the danger of bounding it have produced a problem in the science of government which human understanding seems hitherto unable to solve.

Samuel Johnson [1779]

A number of different explanations have been offered to account for news content. One explanation focuses on the newsman himself as creator of news, choosing which bits of information to include in his story and which bits to ignore, which to emphasize and which to subordinate, and, implicitly at least, how to interpret the events of the day. Even in covering a fire, newsmen exercise selectivity in what they describe, whom they quote, and in what context they place events. They may choose, for instance, to emphasize the personal tragedy, the dilapidated condition of the building, the enforcement of housing codes, or the speed of firemen in reaching the scene. Yet an emphasis on journalistic judgment often leads to a concentration on the personal beliefs and social origins of newsmen as the primary explanation for news content. "Since absolute objectivity in journalism is an impossibility," writes Leo Rosten in his pioneering study, *The Washington Correspondents,* "the social heritage, the 'professional reflexes,' the individual temperament, and the economic status of reporters assume a fundamental significance."[1] This mode of explanation, however, tends to ignore that newsmen work not as individuals on their own, but in large-scale bureaucratic organizations.

Another fashionable explanation holds that technology determines content. It has been put in its starkest form by Marshall McLuhan in his slogan, "The medium is the message,"[2] that is, the most significant changes in the patterns of thought and behavior in the audience are the changes in perception produced by the medium itself rather than by whatever substance it transmits. A corollary is that certain media are best suited to transmit particular sorts of content: broadcast journalism, while capable of instantaneous transmission, excels at transmitting spot news and bulletins rather than deeper analysis; television best

179

disseminates information that lends itself to graphic portrayal; newsweeklies can feature a uniform interpretation of news—in Henry Luce's words, written "as if by one man for one man"—while newspapers transmit a "mosaic" of views.[3] Yet it is an open question whether or not the differences in news coverage by the media are more significant than the similarities and whether or not the differences among the media are greater than those among news organizations in any single medium. While technological imperatives do set some constraints on news organizations, the medium may be far from the whole message.

The starting point of a third explanation is that news organizations are business firms in oligopolistic markets whose revenues—and hence profits—derive primarily from the sale of advertising and secondarily from circulation. This theory has two main variants: one, that news responds to economic imperatives, particularly pressure from advertisers; two, that those who own newspapers dictate news content, and do so as members of the propertied class. As a 1947 report to the Commission on Freedom of the Press stated,

[T]here are special biases to which a large part of the contemporary press is liable because of its character (i) as a commercial enterprise whose terms of success are set by the business management, in view of the existing economy and the state of the public mind; (ii) as a large-scale enterprise interlocking both in finance and in personnel with the big industry of the nation; (iii) as an owner's enterprise in which much editorial ability is retained in the hire-and-fire relation of dependence; and (iv) as a competitive enterprise which through its growth and concentration tends to squeeze out of the productive picture many potential contributors of lesser stature or divergent trend.[4]

While the market place does impose severe constraints on newsmaking, to view newspapers strictly as business enterprises would be insufficient to account for news content at the *Times* and the *Post*, as well as some other news organizations.

Regardless of their differences, all these theories adopt a common approach to newsmaking: they all see news content as the result of the rational decisions of a unitary actor, either an individual newsman maximizing his personal preferences or an organization fulfilling its goals as if it were an individual, rather than as the result of a process that involves many people with various motives. By ascribing to news organizations an overriding motive, all these theories may explain why some information does not make the news, but each has its deficiencies in accounting for the information that does.

Newsmaking is a consensual process. The forming of consensus takes place within a context of shared values—conventions about news as well as conceptions of the newsman's role. The organization of newspapers and the location of newsmen structure the process. Hierarchical lines along which men communicate and action channels along which news copy flows within the organization determine who is in a position to make choices and to intervene and reverse them, and thereby to influence the content of the paper. Since the *Times* locates one-quarter of its national and foreign reporters and the *Post*, one-third of its, on government beats in Washington, officials in the U.S. government play an important part in newsmaking both as sources and as critics.

News in Washington can be seen as the product of the interaction of two bureaucracies—one composed of newsmen and the other of officials. From one theoretical perspective, news is the outcome of organizational politics. Bargaining along bureaucratic lines within the newspaper determines who covers a story, what changes editors make in the copy a reporter files, and how much play a story gets. Officials, in turn, disclose information largely as a by-product of their own bureaucratic politics—in an effort to muster and maintain support, both in and out of the government, for a particular course of action. The reporter and the official use each other to advantage in their own organizations: the former exploits his contacts in the government to obtain exclusives; the latter exploits the need for news to deliver messages to key audiences. From another perspective, news is the output of organizational routine. News organizations pick up most of their information through routine channels—official proceedings, press releases, and press conferences. Disseminating information through these channels has become a standard operating procedure within the government. In the first view, it is as if two ballgames were played on adjacent fields with the two sets of players bumping into each other and affecting the outcomes of both games; in the second, it is as if a mimeograph machine and a printing press were connected by a conveyer belt.

What gives organization its impact on news is the uncertainty endemic to newsmaking. Newsmen take their cues about news from the pattern of relations in the newsroom and on the beat: compared to the reality of the world outside, the need for social adjustment within the work environment is quite immediate. The routines of newsgathering yield certified news—stories that other news organizations will probably run concurrently or stories that replicate others run in the past whose validity went unquestioned. The conventions of newsmaking authenticate the news that they publish, as well as legitimating their procedures for obtaining it. So long as newsmen follow the same routines, espousing the same professional values and using each other as their standards of comparison, newsmaking will tend to be insular and self-reinforcing. But that insularity and self-reinforcement is precisely what newsmen need. It provides them with a modicum of certitude that enables them to act in an otherwise uncertain environment. The very routines and conventions that newsmen use to cope with uncertainty, though, are exploited by their sources either to insert information into the news or to propagandize.

The Impact of News and Newsmaking on Government

While it is difficult to formulate precise measures of the impact of news and newsmaking on government outcomes, the foregoing analysis does suggest some lines of speculation.

News and Power

Employed tactically to influence outcomes, the news can make or break reputations, affecting the power of governmental actors. Yet the process of newsmaking puts some actors at a disadvantage compared to others. "I'm the only President you've got," Lyndon Johnson used to drawl, but newsmen hardly needed the reminder. For the press, covering Washington means, above all, covering the President. By convention, he is the premier authoritative source: anything he says or does is news. The attention the press accords him and the in-fighting among reporters for access to him facilitate his efforts to put his views across in Washington and the nation.

The relationship between news and power manifests itself in the so-called "honeymoon period" a President enjoys when he first takes office. Inauguration Day sets off a scramble among officials in the government and correspondents from print and electronic media to gain access to the new incumbent and his immediate subordinates. In the early jockeying for position, bureaucrats are reluctant to snipe at the new administration and reporters are hesitant to record whatever criticisms they do pick up. Once the pecking order has been established, however, the officials and reporters who are not on top seek each other out. Gripes come out into the open, accompanied by complaints about the President's inaccessibility, tarnishing his image.

The President is the major though not the sole beneficiary of newsgathering practices. The relative ease with which other senior officials of the government can command coverage and their freedom to make use of it helps account for the frequency with which they, too, generate news. Officials who are more skillful and discreet in using the press than their colleagues can enhance reputations and garner prestige, and concomitantly enhance their ability to persuade others in the capital to go along with them. The contrast between John Foster Dulles and Dean Acheson as Secretaries of State or between Defense Secretary Robert McNamara and Secretary of State Dean Rusk may be instructive: their stature was not simply related to their closeness to the President.

The same applies to government bureaus: use of the press can improve a bureau's standing in the competition for budgets and programs. The sheer size of a bureau's public relations operation has some bearing on its power. The Arms Control and Disarmament Agency's platoon shrinks before the squadrons of military publicists, regardless of popular sentiment for arms control vis-à-vis military spending. Political support for the FBI and its autonomy within the Justice Department are due in no small measure to the favorable press it has won itself over the years. As James Clayton, who covered both the Bureau and the Department for the *Post*, observes,

The FBI runs its own public relations office quite independently from the Department of Justice and sets many of its own policies. It has a fine public relations operation; the reputation of the FBI and its director is the best evidence of that. The FBI will answer questions from most newsmen. And, upon occasion, it will leak to those newsmen whom it regards as its friends. Its leaks often produce some of the hottest news stories in Washington, but you can bet your last dollar that such stories appear where and when they do for certain specific reasons best known to the FBI.[5]

Perhaps the most clearcut impact that official use of the press has had on institutional relationships has been to accentuate impressions of the decline of Congress. While individual Congressmen, and sometimes committee staff members, can get a hearing for their views by establishing a close relationship with a reporter, Congressional impact on national—as distinct from hometown—news is diffused by a cacophany of voices and a multiplicity of views. The obverse of ineffective use is the dependence of the average Congressman on the press as a major source of information about doings in the capital and the country. On most matters outside the immediate purview of his committees, he relies for his information and his cues to voting on others—leaders of his party or his faction within the party, members of the committee that reported out a bill, lobbyists, like-minded colleagues whom he runs into in the cloakroom, or his own staff. Voting behavior in large legislative bodies is a social communication process, involving circulation of information, opinion leadership by a few members, and exchange of cues among men of similar views in a particular issue area, more among members than between members and their constituents.[6] In a body with such a diversity of backgrounds, representing such a variety of electoral districts, one common ground is the reliance on a rather small number of organizations for their news. This reliance makes the Congress more susceptible to leadership by the sources of news at the other end of Pennsylvania Avenue.

The Policy Process

Apart from its effects on the power of individuals and institutions, the news process can directly shape policy outcomes.

Officials have been known to tailor policy for its public relations value. For example, the pledge of a withdrawal of all U.S. forces from Vietnam "within six months" of an agreement became part of the American negotiating position as a result of President Johnson's desire for something "short and snappy" that would "get the headlines," according to one participant at the Manila Conference of October 1966.[7]

The omnipresent threat of leaks has also figured prominently in some important policy choices. For example, in the course of a meeting to decide whether or not to launch the Bay of Pigs invasion, CIA director Allen Dulles argued for going ahead: "Don't forget that we have a disposal problem. If we have to take these men out of Guatemala, we will have to transfer them to the United States, and we can't have them wandering around the country telling everyone what they have been doing." It was a telling point. "The determination to keep the scheme alive," writes Arthur Schlesinger, Jr., "sprang in part, I believe, from the embarrassments of calling it off."[8] Similarly, when the Nixon Administration was considering whether to hold up aid deliveries to India after the outbreak of the India-Pakistan war in December 1971, Maurice Williams, the deputy Agency for International Development administrator for the subcontinent, warned a National Security Council committee, "Word will soon get around when we do this. Does the President understand this?"[9] Henry Kissinger thereupon agreed to raise the question with the Chief Executive. In both cases the threat of public disclosure directly affected policy outcomes.

Yet the specific tailoring of policy to suit public relations purposes may have less significance than the structuring of the policy process to cope with the press; and the immediate effects on the process may stem less from the disclosures themselves than from anticipation of them.

Whenever leaks can alter outcomes, dissidents are excluded. In the words of national security adviser Kissinger, "One reason for keeping the decision to small groups is that when bureaucracies are so unwieldy and when their internal morale becomes a serious problem, an unpopular decision may be fought by brutal means, such as leaks to the press or to Congressional committees."[10] In addition to constricting the circle of advisers, the threat of leaks curtails the flow of information throughout the government. Thus, the classification system, which began as a method of keeping information out of the hands of enemies abroad, functions chiefly as a method of keeping it from rivals at home. Those whose job it is to classify information have a strong incentive to err on the safe side: few people will ever know that a document was overclassified, but if something damaging ever does get out, the subsequent investigations will leave nobody in the dark. In practice, moreover, most of the important documents are classified by senior officials, often the very men who have the greatest stake in keeping the information to themselves. The consequence is, as Justice Potter Stewart pointed out in a case involving the Pentagon papers, "[W]hen everything is classified, then nothing is classified, and the system becomes one to be disregarded by the cynical or the careless, and to be manipulated by those intent on self-protection or self-promotion."[11]

The compartmentalization that results from the attempts to seal leaks can interfere with policy implementation and coordination. It can confuse, if not confound, the conduct of foreign relations. While Henry Kissinger was in Peking in July 1971, engaged in negotiations that would culminate in President Nixon's visit to China, word of his mission was so closely held that no more than half a dozen officials in the U.S. government knew of it. On July 10, *The Washington Post* ran a lead story which began,

President Nixon is faced with a strong Pentagon recommendation to transfer American nuclear weapons from Okinawa to the island of Taiwan, the Nationalist Chinese stronghold. The Defense Department, it was learned, has urged that the President shift the weapons, which must be moved off Okinawa, to Taiwan.[12]

The leak came from State Department officials, unaware of Kissinger's whereabouts, who were making known their opposition to the transfer on several grounds, "including possible repercussions on the U.S. effort to improve relations with the People's Republic of China." The White House ultimately backed State, but the incident must have bewildered the Chinese.[13]

The possibility of subsequent disclosure, more than narrowing the range of options, may make officials hesitant to lay every option or argument on the table, lest their public standing be compromised. The plight of Adlai Stevenson in the aftermath of the Cuban missile crisis is best avoided by reticence in internal debate. If some things are left unsaid, others are said in private and never committed to paper, only complicating the problems of implementation. "My habit was that I did not go around writing a lot of memoranda," former Secretary of State Rusk once remarked, "I've been in government long enough to know it is not a good idea to spread papers all over the landscape."[14]

The decline of the Cabinet is due in no small measure to the quest for privacy. Over the tenure of most administrations, the Cabinet tends to fall into disuse as a forum for collective decision-making. Department heads hesitate to argue their case before their colleagues, preferring instead to talk to the President alone. As Cabinet meetings become formalities, they lose whatever utility they had, and busy Presidents dispense with them altogether. This pattern dates back at least to the days of FDR.[15]

The news process also can affect timing in the policy process. In the government crowded agendas combine with uncertainty to yield inaction. Either crises or deadlines can impart the urgency necessary to overcome inertia. Crises are a function of publicity. Whether in anticipation of or in reaction to bad news, officials feel the need to act. The realization that a mess will be spread across page one in the near future compels them to clean it up—or at least to cover it over and divert attention elsewhere. Deadlines are a function of routines. Issuing handouts, holding press conferences or background briefings entail commitments of governmental authority and hence invoke formal procedures. Like the preparation of the federal budget, the drafting of the State of the Union, or any other governmental routine, preparations for the authorized disclosure of information engage senior officials along preestablished action channels, deciding issues of public policy by a fixed point in time. For the government, then, the act of disseminating news fits the ideal-type of an action-forcing process. By creating crises and by imposing deadlines, newsmaking sets agendas for officials.

News Content and Policy-Making

Apart from the process of making it, the content of news itself affects policy-making. The news media, but especially the *Times* and the *Post*, constitute one network in the central nervous system of the U.S. government.

This network, unlike almost any other, transmits information throughout the government, and often with greater speed, than the internal channels of communication.[16] News organizations select the sights and sounds that Washingtonians will sense the next day. They thereby shape official perceptions of their environment.

Like a guided missile, any organization's ability to respond to changes in its external environment and to close in on its goals depends on the quality of information that is fed back into its decision-making process. "A society or community that is to steer itself," writes Karl Deutsch, "must continue to receive a full flow of three kinds of information: first, information about the world outside; second, information from the past, with a wide range of recall and recombination; and third, information about itself and its own parts."[17] The same applies to a government. What impact does the news have on information flowing into the government?

Two main factors make the press a source of much of the important information that the government gets about itself and its own parts. Publicity enhances the salience of information: it imparts heat as well as light. Moreover, subordinates ordinarily provide the bulk of the information that their nominal superiors require for making decisions. A subordinate, more censor than sensor, can use his expertise to manipulate communications and thereby exert control over those above him. The existence of rival government bureaus with alternative information and independent access to the news can reduce the likelihood of subordinate control. "The significant impact of the press upon the President," argues George Reedy, "lies not in its critical reflections but in its capacity to tell him what he is doing as seen through other eyes. . . . Virtually all other communications that reach him will be shaped either directly or indirectly by people who wish either to conciliate or [to] antagonize the Chief Executive."[18] If senior officials dominate the news, however, its utility as a disinterested source of policy-relevant information declines. As a repository of information about the past, the newspaper with its collection of official views from bygone days hardly seems an improvement over government files.

Newspapers do provide the government with a lot of current information about the society and the world. The more reporters get their information from inside the government, though, the more feedback resembles a closed circle. "Washington," one ex-official observes, "is a terribly isolated city, insulated against opinions from the outside. Those of us who work in the capital are responsible for that a great deal. We talk to each other in Washington."[19] Within the capital the press may be an important means of circulating dissenting opinions, but primarily those of officials, not of outsiders. Listening to the news for the sound of public opinion, officials hear echoes of their own voices. Looking for pictures of the world outside, they see reflections of their own images.

Personal beliefs circulated privately in the bureaucracy and reinforced publicly in the press become the presuppositions of the government. Reiterated day after day, they crystallize and become inured to change. The result can be a rigidification of policy, a loss of flexibility, a deadening of "the nerves of government." Yet the alternatives to the press as providers of information to officials are the formal channels within the government and the rumor mill around the capital. Compared to the shortcomings of newspapers, theirs may be as great or greater.

Newsmaking and the News

A newspaper's picture of the world necessarily remains incomplete, with some details etched in bold relief and others barely delineated. What typically engages the machinery of the press are surface manifestations, not the social forces at play beneath them. The disintegrative impact of ethnicity on many countries today, the processes of economic development and growth, the migration of rural populations to urban centers, and the effects of these forces on the lives of ordinary people—all these trends will tend to go unnoticed in the routine gathering of news. Not only events but also individuals receive differential treatment in the news. As Alfred Friendly, managing editor of the *Post*, told his staff in 1964, "There is a chilling suspicion that while *The Washington Post* as presently constituted would have reported what Russell and Palmerston said and did in 1848 and 1859 in Commons, it might not have noted a publication by Marx and a book by Darwin in those years."[20]

Readers, whether government officials or interested citizens, tend to lose sight of the point that news is not reality, but a sampling of reality. As large organizations, all that newspapers can do is to establish some standard operating procedures for sampling what is happening. Whatever procedures they adopt will bias the selection of information. No procedure can guarantee a sampling that will satisfy every reader; no procedure can even guarantee a sampling that excludes outright lies.

Knowing how the news gets made—the organization and politics of newsmaking—is a prerequisite for understanding what the news means. Just as interpolating the history of ancient Egypt requires both an ability to read hieroglyphics and a sensitivity to the context in which that history was transcribed, so, too, sensitivity to the context from which today's news emerges is essential for newspaper readers.

Limitations on manpower and money, even in financially sound enterprises like the *Times* and the *Post*, permit reporters to witness very few events firsthand. In gathering information, they must depend on news sources. Newspapers are organized to tap some sources and not others. To the extent that the *Times* and the *Post* array their staffs in existing bureaus and beats and rely on routine channels for newsgathering, national and foreign news will remain what government officials, principally those in the U.S. government, say it is. Their agenda will dominate the front page. Whether the topic is the military balance in Europe or poverty in Appalachia, a skyjacking over Miami or Soviet missiles launched from beneath the sea, it is likely to break into the news when it appears on the desks of senior American officials and not until then. Apart from when a subject makes the news, what the *Times* and *Post* report about it will reflect to a considerable extent what officials say about it. News is thus less a sampling of what is happening in the world than a selection of what officials think—or want the press to report—is happening.

An analyst of Soviet policy-making, Myron Rush, has employed the concept of *esoteric communication* to denote the seemingly minor changes in the ritualistic language of articles in *Pravda* and *Izvestia* whereby shifts in power and policy stands are transmitted to Soviet bureaucrats. Having rather large incentives to gauge the prospects of success of any leaders or policy proposals before committing their careers to them, Soviet officials develop considerable skill in discerning the subtlest alteration in wording.[21] While the cloaking of partisan conflict lacks the ideological justification that Marx and Lenin have given it in the Soviet Union, most American administrations regard overt public expressions of internal dissension as politically taboo. The language may not be as ritualistic, its transcription by the reporter not as faithfully monitored, and the news media hardly as centralized, but Washington makes as much use of esoteric communication as Moscow. From a close reading of the press, U.S. officials can glean the information and the cues they need in order to take action. With experience they learn to distill what a story means for them out of what it says about events and issues. Outsiders must do the same in order to reconstruct what is going on in the government.

The basic principle of newsmaking is that the government seldom speaks with one voice. While the air may resound with echoes of the administration line, it also carries contrapuntal themes, varying in pitch and intensity, but usually audible to the careful listener. This principle has a corollary: news tends to emerge as a by-product of policy change or dispute. Interpreting it requires determining what the change or dispute is all about. It requires making inferences about the source of the information and his position in public life, the face of the issue under consideration as he would see it, the target of his words, and his possible reason for uttering them.

Present journalistic practices, by disguising the origin of stories and not correcting mistakes, often interfere with understanding the news. As William White pointed out in 1958, "Often reporters handle a leaked story with a solemn uncriticalness. The documents, or whatever, are ceremoniously produced for the public—which at times must scratch its head in perplexity as to what the devil they are all about. But the motivation for the leak usually is not mentioned, although that may be the most significant part of the story."[22]

Newsmen can aid their readers by telling as much as they can about the origins of a story, at least by identifying the reporter, his beat, the channel through which the information was passed, and the source, whenever these details could further their understanding. All too often reporters do not insist as hard as they might that officials speak on the record. The most egregious examples of this lapse are the background briefings held for the entire White House or State Department press corps: the identity of officials who appear at these sessions is soon an open secret around Washington, but not in the country at large. If newspapers appoint their own ombudsmen, it might give them a task to perform: reconstructing where important news came from. The *Post* has done this on occasion in editorials headlined "F.Y.I." which explain some of its newsmaking practices.

Newspapers have also shown reluctance to correct mistakes, almost as if the acknowledgment of error would itself undermine credibility: as Joseph Pulitzer expressed it, "Accuracy is to a newspaper what virtue is to a lady." "Of course, a newspaper can always print a retraction," was Adlai Stevenson's rejoinder. The *Times* has recently instituted a corrections column appearing regularly in the daily index to acknowledge some of its mistakes. Beyond this step, newspapers can explicitly revise interpretations and "news analysis" as new information becomes available.

Access: The Key to Newsmaking

What the news is depends very much on who its sources are. If each day's front page were like a single frame in a movie, the composite series of still frames would necessarily contain some distortion. What is the nature of the distortion? While the camera might belong to newsmen, the lights are in the hands of their sources, who tend to aim them in directions which they find advantageous, leaving many things in shadow and still more in total darkness. Moreover, if every other news source had a flashlight to point wherever he chose to, senior officials would have a spotlight and the President, a beacon.

In the past, sources have made the news to the extent that they were in a position to pass along information to reporters engaged in routine newsgathering. Within the government, senior officials, by dint of their virtual monopoly of access to the routine channels of news and their means of controlling subordinates' disclosures, can dominate press discussion of issues by the sheer volume of their own emanations. Outside the government, some individuals and groups have gained a hearing at official proceedings—legislative hearings and trials—routinely covered by reporters. Some have gained coverage when their concerns have impinged on reporters assigned to regular beats; labor, farm, and business groups or the Council on Foreign Relations are examples. These groups could call press conferences and grind out press releases, much as officials do. Others, not to mention the unorganized, could not. Their only recourse was to adopt flamboyant tactics like demonstrations in order to capture attention and make the news.

The structure of newsgathering can thereby affect the public impression, as well as the array and emphasis, of various proponents and opponents of policy alternatives in and out of government. Some have a chance to be heard, but not others. Some gain a hearing only at the risk of appearing disruptive to the newspaper audience. If the late 1960s were a precursor and not an aberration, opposition to government policy may take the form of ad hoc mass movements and not gradual shifts among elites. In that event, the decentralization of these movements, their lack of a unique official spokesman, and their need for symbolic action in order to grab the headlines may make any opposition seem less than respectable, programmatically inchoate, and unlikely to succeed—in comparison to a government which can schedule press conferences and grind out press releases.

Nevertheless, a greater variety of Americans than ever before have learned how to obtain news coverage for their points of view. A half century ago only a handful of public relations men knew how to package and purvey information for the press. By the late 1930s industrial union organizers had mastered these techniques. The civil rights movement in the South made a major breakthrough, which was capitalized on by other social movements from Wallaceites to Yippies, from Italian-Americans in Columbus Circle to Buddhist bonzes in Saigon pagodas. The range of political discourse in the press has thus broadened somewhat, at the expense of Washington officialdom.

But not without resistance. The press has always been a sore subject among officials, particularly those at the top of the government. They too are readers, perhaps the most devoted that the press has, and along with other readers they share an outlook: they seek confirmation of their own beliefs in whatever they read. When the fail to find what they are looking for—when they get "bad news" as they see it—they tend to distrust its source. Like Greeks killing the bearers of bad tidings, they spread doubts about the performance of the press. The virulence of their recent attacks on the press may stem in part from a desire to retain the amount of coverage their predecessors had. The irony may be that in their zeal to obtain more favorable coverage by attacking the fairness and objectivity of the press, officials may do themselves a disservice by reducing the credibility of their own messages, which dominate the news.

At present, news space is still more readily available to high administration officials than it is to spokesmen of any other organization or institution in the society. So long as news organizations concentrate large staffs in their Washington bureaus, so long as newsmen adhere to the existing routines and conventions of newsgathering, so long as editors hesitate to counteract absorption on the beat, in short, so long as the organization and politics of newsmaking remain as they are, the press will primarily offer news from official sources passed through official channels.

During the coming decade several trends may cut into official predominance in the news. First, the major news organizations, to the extent that they open new bureaus around the nation and the world, expand their national and foreign staffs, and elaborate their networks of "stringers" elsewhere, may broaden their range of news sources.

Second, the news industry has become less competitive in most localities in the course of this century. Somewhat paradoxically, however, declining competition, insofar as it promotes financial stability among the remaining firms in the industry, may improve the quality of national and foreign coverage by providing the wherewithal for expansion of newsgathering operations. Beyond the local level, the threat to diversity in the news may stem less from declining competition in the industry than from monopoly at the source. It is the medium-sized newspaper with a one- or two-man bureau in Washington that is most susceptible to dominance by senior offials. A newspaper must generate considerable revenues to support enough manpower in Washington to tap sources beneath the top echelon of the government as well as to maintain enough bureaus outside the capital to be accessible to nongovernment sources. Yet even relatively prosperous newspapers such as the *Times* and the *Post*, dominant firms in their local markets, are at the mercy of economic forces beyond their control. Population shifts dispersing their readership encourage suburban newspapers to compete for advertising. Rival media compete for audience. Most newspapermen have been conscious of the challenge of television; fewer have noticed the proliferation of specialized journals targeted at relatively discrete audiences, but carrying a variety of timely articles on national and foreign affairs. Some are journals of opinion, like *The New Republic* and *The National Review*, catering to distinct political groups; others, like *Fortune* and *Business Week*, are primarily business and financial organs; still others, like *Foreign Affairs, Science,* and *Aviation Weekly*, address themselves to audiences with technical specialties. The substitution of magazines for newspapers may curtail the growth of readership and, hence, revenues that newspapers might allocate to newsgathering. A memorandum from the publisher to the staff on November 5, 1971 may have been a sign of things to come at the *Times*: ". . . [T]here's no doubt that the recession has something to do with our problems. But . . . we are overmanned in too many areas."[23]

Third, the routines of newsgathering at the *Times* and the *Post* have undergone some change over the past two decades. For instance, coverage of Congressmen speaking to the party faithful during the Lincoln's Day recess, a staple of page one in years gone by, had moved off the front pages by 1964 and almost out of the newspaper by 1972. Television's capacity to cover spot news has pushed the two newspapers into more trend and background stories. The introduction of clusters in the *Times* newsroom, freeing reporters from deadlines, beats, and other routines to pursue news somewhat more idiosyncratically, may advance in-depth coverage of social trends, as well as widen the range of news sources.

Fourth, recruitment of reporters may also change. The experience of the Depression was still fresh in Leo Rosten's mind when he concluded,

The intensification of social crisis precipitates discontent with the circumlocutions of "respectable" political parties in the intellectuals of the middle class, caught between the hammer of industrial capitalism and the anvil of proletarian violence. Dissatisfaction is communicated to the sons of intellectuals in the atmosphere of homes characterized by rising insecurity of middle-class men who handle symbols for a living. The sons of lawyers, clergymen, journalists, and teachers may well be possessed of heightened reformist energies to embark upon a career which throws them into vital contact with the organ of the body politic, and which opens the possibility of "tearing away the veils of pretense and hypocrisy," exposing politics and politicians in the disenchanted light of "hard-boiled" journalism.[24]

The seeds of the present social crisis may lie elsewhere, but they may yield similar outcroppings. Even so, it will be a decade before the latest recruits work their way onto the national and foreign staffs of the *Times* and the *Post*, a decade in which the routines and conventions of newsmaking will be assiduously grafted onto the attitudes which first attracted them to the occupation. Among young reporters, discontent with old practices is endemic. Advocacy journalism, organized opposition to editorial policy, demands for promotion of women and blacks—all manifest the rise of a new generation of reporters as a self-conscious occupational class pressing for changes within the industry and outside it. If the movement were to gain momentum, it could force revision of present-day news practices; but the experience of the Depression generation leaves little ground for such expectations.

Changes in news conceptions are likely to be glacial. Habits of mind resist change. If inertia is characteristic of individual beliefs, it is all the more so for organizational routines. Establishing new procedures takes time, a scarce resource for newsmen with daily deadlines to meet. Uncertainty about the nature of news compounds the difficulty. If no one knows what news is, newsmen attain at least a measure of security from their reliance on the same channels and sources and on common values. Uncertainty makes any change in routines and conventions a scary prospect.

Technological developments may rapidly outstrip any changes in newsmaking practices. The futurists' vision is one of rapid transmission of information by new means of telecommunication, its storage in computers for retrieval by editors sitting at consoles, a speed-up in composing and printing, and new modes of distribution. Yet wedding twentieth-century production and distribution capabilities to seventeenth-century methods of news gathering makes official domination of news all the more pernicious. If the news techniques of packaging and delivering information which some forsee do prove economically feasible, they will only make the question of access more acute. Who gets to appear in the news and who provides the information that readers get are the basic questions of a democratic polity. If these questions are addressed in the future as they have been in the past, journalistic practices will continue to foreclose access to the many and grant it to the few, and the few will be the holders of political power, not their opponents.

Access remains an issue in two senses: access for the press and access to the press. Access for the press is essential if the governed are to exercise any measure of control over their governors. Access to the press, in particular to the principal national suppliers of news such as the *Times* and the *Post*, is essential if freedom of expression is to have any meaning.

A number of proposals to reform the press and the government have been offered to deal with problems of access; among them have been the reassignment of news staffs, additional staff to assist reporters in investigation and research, legislation to protect the confidential relationship between newsmen and their sources, a revamping of the classification system, and a shifting of the burden of proof onto the government to show damage to the national security in trials of officials accused of leaking information to the press. Without delving into the merits of the various proposals, it is possible to stipulate the primary criterion by which they all should be evaluated: ensuring maximum diversity of opinion in the news on issues of public policy.

The standard is not unambiguous. Does it necessitate providing access to every individual or group who requests it, to anyone who claims to advocate a viewpoint not already covered, or to those whom newsmen judge worthwhile? Should the criterion apply to news coverage alone, or to advertising and editorial space as well? Should the press grant access to foreign views or just to domestic, to those not organized to put forth their views or unable to hire a public relations man or a lawyer to represent them? Does the criterion imply equality of access, and if so, how can equality be measured? Whatever its ambiguities, this criterion is the fundamental premise underlying the First Amendment and democratic government.

Democracy and the Press

The defining characteristic of Western democracy is the existence of an institutionalized opposition, entrenched in the political system and having a reasonable opportunity of taking over the government. Often the locus of opposition is parliament, but in a system with power as dispersed as in the United States, an opposition group can contend with the government on a number of fronts.

The press, by circulating information, plays a major role in rendering opposition effective. Internal and public opposition tend to go hand in hand. It is more than covariance; it is symbiosis. Informed public and congressional debate on many an issue, if it is to exist at all, would be doomed to sterility without a nest of opposition within the federal bureaucracy: interested groups outside would have little way of making a timely intervention in the internal debate. On the other hand, external, though not always public, support is virtually indispensable to internal opposition in overturning existing policy. By providing a two-way communication link, the press promotes policy debate.

To perform this function, the press must remain independent of government and free from its coercive power. The draftsmen of the Constitution regarded the existence of conflicting interests and opposition groups—what they called "faction"—as inherent in society, and their elimination as incompatible with democracy. It was to control the effects of faction that they contrived a government based on republican principles: interest would continue to rival interest with elected representatives serving as brokers. *The Federalist Papers* offer a succinct statement of this position. Its authors assumed that mediation was possible and harmony attainable, but above all, that institutional autonomy was essential. For the health of society, government had to permit social groups of divergent interests to remain free of coercion while curbing their excesses—a difficult but critical distinction. In the case of the press, though, special care was taken to insure its freedom from government coercion.

But along with the massive social changes that have marked this nation's passage through two centuries has come a shift in the relationship between the state and the society. Instead of remaining outside the government pitted against each other in a struggle to use the government for their own ends, social groups have entrenched themselves in the bureaucracy. The Departments of Agriculture, Commerce, and Labor are the most visible manifestations of this entrenchment. Yet, and this was another side to their design, the Federalists had been the first group to entrench themselves—in an independent judiciary which they drew up as a counterweight to a legislature soon to fall into the hands of small farmers, artisans, and assorted easy-money types.

Mirroring the gradual entrenchment of groups within the government has been the gradual intrusion of government into private organizations in society. No less than newsmen, industrialists and academics have immersed themselves deeply in the policy process while encouraging government involvement in business and university life. The interpenetration of government and private institutions has created a formidable problem of social control, both of entrenched private groups and of government encroachment. No less than newsmen, industrialists and academics who have become involved in government may cease performing vital functions as external critics, as well-springs of effective opposition. In the case of the press, this trend has received doctrinal sanction in the "fourth branch" theory, portraying the press as a coordinate branch of government.

The history of journalism in America records a change in emphasis of government efforts to control the news media from censorship and regulation to news management. Licensing of newspapers, criminal prosecution for sedition, censorship of dispatches have each in turn given way before the onslaughts of newsmen. While resistance to direct forms of control has hardened in the press, susceptibility to news management has spread. Concerted efforts have penetrated the veil of secrecy donned by officials, but usually with the complicity of other officials. Newsmen resist, even resent, the blandishments of officials to play along with them, but often fall prey to the more insidious temptations of becoming insiders, of having influence. The routines and conventions of their work incline them to accept the words of officials without probing beneath them on their own. Finally, with freedom, the press has taken on responsibilities, responsibilities foisted upon them by the well-intentioned to do more than report the news as accurately and fairly as they can. These responsibilities only make the press more vulnerable to manipulation by the government.

Freedom to express dissenting views was precisely what those who asserted the freedom of the press two centuries ago sought to protect, and the expression of dissenting views is precisely what arouses the hostility of those in power. In the first edition of the first newspaper published in the Colonies *Publick Occurrences*, newspaperman Benjamin Harris defined his responsibilities as follows:

That something may be done toward the Curing, or at least the Charming of the Spirit of Lying, which prevails amongst us, wherefore nothing shall be entered but what we have reason to believe is true, repairing to the best fountains for our Information. And when there appears any material mistake in anything that is collected, it shall be corrected in the next.

Moreover, the Publisher of these Occurrences is willing to engage, that whereas, there are many False Reports, maliciously made, and spread among us, if any well-minded person will be at pains to trace any such false Report, so far as to find out and Convict the First Raiser of it, he will in this Paper (unless just Advice be given on the contrary) expose the Name of such Person as a malicious Raiser of a False Report.[25]

That appeared in 1690, in an age of simpler epistemological premises and greater consensus on basic values, an age of one-man newspapers and small government, an age of blunt speaking and blunter action. Yet the fate of Harris' venture might serve as a caution to those who take the freedom of the press for granted. Volume I, number II, of *Publick Occurrences* never did reach Boston newsstands; the Governor and Council of Massachusetts had it suppressed.

As the size of officialdom has grown, its interests as a class have multiplied and have diverged from the public's interest, affecting relations with the press. The framers of the Constitution seemed to anticipate this conflict in drawing up a Bill of Rights prohibiting legislation abridging freedom of the press. They recognized it was a slim guarantee. As Alexander Hamilton pointed out in the *Federalist Papers*, No. 84, responding to objections that the original draft of the Constitution contained no Bill of Rights,

What signifies a declaration that "the liberty of the press shall be inviolably preserved?" What is the liberty of the press? Who can give it any definition which would not leave the utmost latitude for evasion? I hold it to be impracticable, and from this I infer that its security, whatever fine declarations may be inserted in any constitution respecting it, must altogether depend on public opinion, and on the general spirit of the people and of the government.[26]

Notes

1. Rosten, THE WASHINGTON CORRESPONDENTS, p. 150.

2. Marshall McLuhan, UNDERSTANDING MEDIA (New York: Signet, 1964), Chapter 1.

3. Ibid., p. 185.

4. Hocking, FREEDOM OF THE PRESS, p. 142.

5. James E. Clayton, "News from the Supreme Court and Justice Department," THE PRESS IN WASHINGTON, ed. by Ray E. Hiebert, p. 195.

6. Robert A. Dahl, CONGRESS AND FOREIGN POLICY (New York: W.W. Norton, 1964), Chapters 9-10; Raymond A. Bauer, Ithiel de Sola Pool, and Lewis A. Dexter, AMERICAN BUSINESS AND PUBLIC POLICY (New York: Atherton, 1963), Part V; Donald R. Matthews, U.S. SENATORS AND THEIR WORLD (New York: Vintage, 1960), pp. 204-06; and Lester W. Milbrath, "Lobbying As a Communication Process," PUBLIC OPINION QUARTERLY 24, 1 (Spring 1960): 32-53, adopt this theoretical perspective on congressional behavior.

7. Chester L. Cooper, THE LOST CRUSADE (New York: Dodd, Mead, 1970), p. 315.

8. Schlesinger, A THOUSAND DAYS, p. 242. Morton Halperin called my attention to this example.

9. Reprinted in NEW YORK TIMES, January 6, 1972, p. 16.

10. Henry A. Kissinger and Bernard Brodie, BUREAUCRACY, POLITICS AND STRATEGY, Security Studies Paper No. 17 (Berkeley: University of California Security Studies Project, 1968), p. 5.

11. THE NEW YORK TIMES COMPANY v. U.S., 403 U.S. 713 (1971).

12. WASHINGTON POST, July 10, 1971, p. A-1.

13. James McCartney, "What Should Be Secret?" COLUMBIA JOURNALISM REVIEW 10, 3 (September/October 1971): 40-41.

14. NEW YORK TIMES, June 28, 1971, p. 6.

15. Schlesinger, THE COMING OF THE NEW DEAL, p. 519.

16. Cooper, THE LOST CRUSADE, pp. 229-30.

17. Karl Deutsch, THE NERVES OF GOVERNMENT (Glencoe: Free Press, 1963), p. 129.

18. Reedy, THE TWILIGHT OF THE PRESIDENCY, pp. 99-100.

19. Pierre Salinger, "The Press and Presidential Leadership," Address at the University of Minnesota Newspaper Guild Forum, November 9, 1961.

20. Alfred Friendly, memorandum to the staff of THE WASHINGTON POST, November 16, 1964.

21. Myron Rush, THE RISE OF KHRUSHCHEV (Washington: Public Affairs Press, 1958), Appendix 2.

22. William S. White, "Trying to Find the Shape—If Any—of the News in Washington," HARPER'S 217, 1299 (August 1958):79. Copyright © 1958, by Minneapolis Star and Tribune Co., Inc. Reprinted from the August 1958 issue of HARPER'S MAGAZINE by permission of the author.

23. Quoted in Ben Bagdikian, "The Myth of Newspaper Poverty," COLUMBIA JOURNALISM REVIEW, 11, (March/April, 1973), p. 19.

24. Rosten, THE WASHINGTON CORRESPONDENTS, p. 158.

25. PUBLICK OCCURRENCES (Boston), September 25, 1690, p. 1.

26. Alexander Hamilton, THE FEDERALIST PAPERS, No. 84.

References

References

Abelson, Robert P.

1959. "Modes of Resolution of Belief Dilemmas." JOURNAL OF CONFLICT RESOLUTION 3 (1959): 343-352.

Abrams v. U.S., 250 U.S. 616 (1919).

Adams, Sherman.

1961. FIRSTHAND REPORT. New York: Harper.

Adler, Ruth.

1971. A DAY IN THE LIFE OF THE NEW YORK TIMES. Philadelphia: J.B. Lippincott.

"Air Force and Douglas Accelerate Skybolt Ballistic Missile Program." AVIATION WEEKLY AND SPACE TECHNOLOGY 75 (October 30, 1961):23-24.

Allison, Graham T.

1969. "Conceptual Models and the Cuban Missile Crisis." AMERICAN POLITICAL SCIENCE REVIEW 63 (September):689-718.

1971. ESSENCE OF DECISION. Boston: Little, Brown.

Allison, Graham T., and Halperin, Morton H.

1972. "Bureaucratic Politics: A Paradigm and Some Policy Implications." WORLD POLITICS 24 (Spring):40-79.

Alsop, Joseph and Stewart.

1958. THE REPORTER'S TRADE. New York: Reynal.

Alsop, Stewart, and Bartlett, Charles.

1962. "In Time of Crisis." SATURDAY EVENING POST 235 (December 8):16-20.

American Society of Newspaper Editors.

1949. "Canons of Journalism." In MASS COMMUNICATION. Edited by Wilbur Schramm. Urbana: Univ. of Illinois Press.

Armacost, Michael.

1969. THE POLITICS OF WEAPONS INNOVATION. New York: Columbia Univ. Press.

Bagdikian, Ben.

1963. "The President Nonspeaks." COLUMBIA JOURNALISM REVIEW 2 (Spring):42-46.

1967. "What Makes a Newspaper Nearly Great?" COLUMBIA JOURNALISM REVIEW 6 (Fall):30-36.

1970. Panel discussion at the Institute of Politics, Kennedy School of Government, Harvard University, Cambridge, Massachusetts, May 19, 1970.

1971. THE INFORMATION MACHINES. New York: Harper and Row.

1973. "The Myth of Newspaper Poverty." COLUMBIA JOURNALISM REVIEW 11 (March/April):19-23.

Baker, Russell.

1961. AN AMERICAN IN WASHINGTON. New York: Knopf.

1963. "Fourteen Clues to Washington News." NEW YORK TIMES MAGA-ZINE (April 7): 31ff.

Baldwin, Hanson W.
1963. "Managed News: Our Peacetime Censorship." ATLANTIC MONTHLY 211 (April):53-59.

Bauer, Raymond A.; Pool, Ithiel de Sola; and Dexter, Lewis A.
1963. AMERICAN BUSINESS AND PUBLIC POLICY. New York: Atherton.

Bent, Silas.
1927. "Two Kinds of News." YALE REVIEW 16 (July):691-709.

Berger, Peter L., and Luckmann, Thomas.
1967. THE SOCIAL CONSTRUCTION OF REALITY. New York: Double-day.

"The Big Flap." NEWSWEEK 60 (December 17, 1962):17-20.

Boylan, James.
1966-67. "A Salisbury Chronicle." COLUMBIA JOURNALISM REVIEW 5 (Winter):10-14.

Bradlee, Benjamin C.
1972. "Backgrounders: A Conspiracy in Restraint of Truth." WASHINGTON POST (January 2):B-7.

Brandon, Henry.
1963. "Skybolt." SUNDAY TIMES (December 8):29-31.
1969. ANATOMY OF ERROR. Boston: Gambit.

Breed, Warren.
1955. "Newspaper 'Opinion Leaders' and Processes of Standardization." JOURNALISM QUARTERLY. 32 (Summer):277-84.

Brownlow, Louis.
1955. A PASSION FOR POLITICS. Chicago: Univ. of Chicago Press.

Brucker, Herbert.
1962. JOURNALIST. New York: Macmillan.

Burns, James MacGregor.
1956. ROOSEVELT: THE LION AND THE FOX. New York: Harcourt, Brace.

Butler, David E.
1968. "Political Reporting in Britain." In STUDIES IN BRITISH POLITICS. Edited by Richard Rose. New York: St. Martin's Press.

Cater, Douglass.
1959. THE FOURTH BRANCH OF GOVERNMENT. New York: Vintage.

Catledge, Turner.
1967. "Forward." In HOW I GOT THAT STORY. Edited by David Brown and W. Richard Bruner. New York: Dutton.
1971. MY LIFE AND THE TIMES. New York: Harper and Row.

Chase, Harold W., and Lerman, Allen H.
1965. KENNEDY AND THE PRESS. New York: Crowell.

Clapper, Raymond.
1944. WATCHING THE WORLD. New York: McGraw-Hill.

Clayton, James E.
1966. "News from the Supreme Court and Justice Department." In THE PRESS IN WASHINGTON. Edited by Ray E. Hiebert. New York: Dodd, Mead.

Cohen, Bernard C.
1963. THE PRESS AND FOREIGN POLICY. Princeton: Princeton Univ. Press.

Collier, Bernard Law.
1971. "The Joe Alsop Story." NEW YORK TIMES MAGAZINE (May 23): 72-73ff.

Cooper, Chester L.
1970. THE LOST CRUSADE. New York: Dodd, Mead.
1972. "The C.I.A. and Decision-Making." FOREIGN AFFAIRS 50 (January):223-36.

Cornwell, Elmer E., Jr.
1960. "The Presidential Press Conference." MIDWEST JOURNAL OF POLITICAL SCIENCE 4 (November):370-389.
1962. "The Press Conferences of Woodrow Wilson." JOURNALISM QUARTERLY 39 (Summer):292-300.
1965. PRESIDENTIAL LEADERSHIP OF PUBLIC OPINION. Bloomington: Univ. of Indiana Press.

Corry, John J.
1964. "Confessions of an Unrepentent Deskman." NIEMAN REPORTS 18 (December):10-11.

Cutler, Robert.
1965. NO TIME FOR REST. Boston: Little, Brown.

Dahl, Robert A.
1964. CONGRESS AND FOREIGN POLICY. New York: W.W. Norton.

Deutsch, Carl.
1963. THE NERVES OF GOVERNMENT. Glencoe: Free Press.

Duff, William P.
1968. "Skybolt." Senior thesis, Department of Government, Harvard University.

Edelman, Murray.
1967. THE SYMBOLIC USES OF POLITICS. Urbana: Univ. of Illinois Press.

Eisenhower, Dwight D.
1963. MANDATE FOR CHANGE. New York: Doubleday.

Evans, Sir Harold.
1964. "Government Public Relations and the Press." Report of the Proceedings of the Fifty-Fourth Annual Conference of the Commonwealth Press Union, London, July 15-16, 1964.

Eyck, Erich.
1964. BISMARCK AND THE GERMAN EMPIRE. New York: W.W. Norton.

Fay, Sidney, B.
1966. THE ORIGINS OF THE WORLD WAR. Vol. I. New York: Free Press.

Filvaroff, David.
1968. "Origins of the Civil Rights Act." (Mimeographed.) Institute of Politics, Kennedy School of Government, Harvard University.

Ford, Paul L., ed.
1894. THE WRITINGS OF THOMAS JEFFERSON. Vol. II. New York: G.P. Putnam's Sons.

Friendly, Alfred.
1965. "Attribution of News." In REPORTING THE NEWS. Edited by Louis Lyons. Cambridge: Belknap Press of Harvard University.

Fryklund, Richard.
1966. "Covering the Defense Establishment." In THE PRESS IN WASHINGTON. Edited by Ray E. Hiebert. New York: Dodd, Mead.

Galbraith, John Kenneth.
1965. "Why Diplomats Clam Up." In REPORTING THE NEWS. Edited by Louis Lyons. Cambridge: Belknap Press of Harvard University.
1969. AMBASSADOR'S JOURNAL. Boston: Houghton Mifflin.

Geertz, Clifford.
1964. "Ideology As a Cultural System." IN IDEOLOGY AND DISCONTENT. Edited by David Aptor. New York: Free Press.

Geiger, George J.
1962. "Most Mobile Missile." ORDNANCE 47 (November-December):294-97.

Gelman, David and Kempton, Barbara.
1969. "The Trouble with Newspapers: An Interview with Murray Kempton." WASHINGTON MONTHLY, 1 (April): 24-35.

Gershen, Martin.
1966-67. "The 'Right to Lie.'" COLUMBIA JOURNALISM REVIEW 5 (Winter): 14-16.

Gieber, Walter, and Johnson, Walter.
1961. "The City Hall Beat: A Study of Reporter and Source Roles." JOURNALISM QUARTERLY 38 (Summer):289-297.

Goulden, Joseph.
1970. "The Washington Post." WASHINGTONIAN 6 (October):55ff.

Goulding, Phil G.
1970. CONFIRM OR DENY. New York: Harper and Row.

Graber, Doris A.
1968. PUBLIC OPINION, THE PRESIDENT, AND FOREIGN POLICY. Chicago: Holt, Rinehart and Winston.

Great Britain, PARLIAMENTARY PAPERS, vol. 1 (REPORTS), "The Civil Service," Cd. 3638, June 1968.

Halberstam, David.
1965. THE MAKING OF A QUAGMIRE. New York: Random House.

Hall, Max.
1961. "Leads Grow Shorter." NIEMAN REPORTS 15 (October):18-19.

Halloran, Richard.
   1970. JAPAN: IMAGES AND REALITY. Tokyo: Charles E. Tuttle.
Halperin, Morton H.
   1971. "How Bureaucrats Play Games." FOREIGN POLICY 1 (Spring):70-90.
Harlech, Lord.
   1971. "Suez SNAFU, Skybolt SABU." FOREIGN POLICY 2 (Spring):38-50.
"Hellbox." MORE 1 (September 1971):2.
Henry, John B., II.
   1971. "March 1968: Continuity or Change?" Senior thesis, Department of Government, Harvard University.
Hersh, Seymour.
   1967. "But Don't Tell Anyone I Told You." NEW REPUBLIC 157 (December 9): 13-14.
   1970a. "How I Broke the Mylai Story." SATURDAY REVIEW 53 (July 11):46-49.
   1970b. "Mylai 4." HARPERS 240 (May):53-84.
Hilsman, Roger.
   1967. TO MOVE A NATION. Garden City, N.Y.: Doubleday.
Hocking, William E.
   1947. FREEDOM OF THE PRESS. A Report from the Commission on Freedom of the Press. Chicago: Univ. of Chicago Press.
Hohenberg, John.
   1967. BETWEEN TWO WORLDS. New York: Praeger.
Hoxie, R. Gordon, ed.
   1970. THE WHITE HOUSE: ORGANIZATION AND OPERATIONS. Proceedings of the 1970 Montauk Symposium of the Center for the Study of the Presidency.
Hughes, Emmet John.
   1963. THE ORDEAL OF POWER. New York: Atheneum.
Ickes, Harold L.
   1954. THE SECRET DIARY OF HAROLD L. ICKES. Vol. I. New York: Simon and Schuster.
Jackson, Henry, ed.
   1965. THE NATIONAL SECURITY COUNCIL. New York: Praeger.
Jones, Joseph Marion.
   1964. THE FIFTEEN WEEKS. New York: Harcourt, Brace and World.
Kahn, Roger.
   1965. "The House of Adolph Ochs." SATURDAY EVENING POST 238 (October 9):32ff.
Kalb, Marvin.
   1966. "Covering the State Department." In THE PRESS IN WASHINGTON. Edited by Ray E. Heibert. New York: Dodd, Mead.
Kennedy, John F.
   1961. "The President and the Press." Speech to the Bureau of Advertising,

American Newspaper Publishers Association, New York City, April 27, 1961. In VITAL SPEECHES 27 (May 15, 1961): 450-52.

Kissinger, Henry A., and Brodie, Bernard.
1968. BUREAUCRACY, POLITICS AND STRATEGY, Security Studies Paper No. 17. Berkeley: Univ. of California Security Studies Project.

Kleiman, Robert.
1964. ATLANTIC CRISIS. New York: W.W. Norton.

Kraft, Joseph.
1966. PROFILES IN POWER. New York: New American Library.

Kraslow, David, and Loory, Stuart H.
1968. THE SECRET SEARCH FOR PEACE IN VIETNAM. New York: Vintage.

Kristol, Irving.
1967. "The Underdeveloped Profession." PUBLIC INTEREST 6 (Winter):36-52.

1966. IN THE NATION. New York: McGraw-Hill.

1968. MEMOIRS. New York: Funk and Wagnalls.

Lane, Robert E.
1962. POLITICAL IDEOLOGY. Glencoe: Free Press.

Leacacos, John P.
1968. FIRES IN THE IN-BASKET. New York: World.

Lee, Alfred McClung.
1937. "Freedom of the Press: Services of a Catch Phrase." In STUDIES IN THE SCIENCE OF SOCIETY. Edited by George P. Murdock. New Haven: Yale Univ. Press.

Liebling, A.J.
1948. "Goodbye, M.B.I." NEW YORKER (February 7). Reprint in THE PRESS. New York: Ballentine Books, 1964.

Lewis, Anthony.
1968. "Newspapermen and Lawyers." In REPORTING THE NEWS. Edited by Louis Lyons. New York: Atheneum.

Lindley, Ernest K.
1961. In THE ROLE OF THE MASS MEDIA IN A DEMOCRATIC SOCIETY. Edited by DeWitt C. Reddick. Austin: Univ. of Texas Public Affairs Press.

Lippmann, Walter.
1920. LIBERTY AND THE NEWS. New York: Macmillan.

1965. PUBLIC OPINION. New York: Free Press.

Lyons, Louis M.
1964. "Calvin Coolidge and the Press." NIEMAN REPORTS 18 (September):6-8.

McCartney, James.
1968. "The Vested Interests of the Reporter." In REPORTING THE NEWS. Edited by Louis Lyons. Cambridge: Belknap Press of Harvard University.

1971. "What Should Be Secret?" COLUMBIA JOURNALISM REVIEW 10 (September/October): 40-44.

McConnell, Grant.

1963. STEEL AND THE PRESIDENCY—1962. New York: W.W. Norton.

McGuire, Delbert.

1967. "Democracy's Confrontation: The Presidential Press Conference." JOURNALISM QUARTERLY 44 (Winter):638-44.

McLuhan, Marshall.

1964. UNDERSTANDING MEDIA. New York: Signet.

MacNeil, Robert.

1968. THE PEOPLE MACHINE. New York: Harper and Row.

Mailer, Norman.

1968. THE ARMIES OF THE NIGHT. New York: New American Library.

Malinowski, Bronislaw.

1954. "Myth in Primitive Societies." in MAGIC, SCIENCE AND RELIGION AND OTHER ESSAYS. Garden City, N.Y.: Doubleday.

Mannheim, Karl.

1936. IDEOLOGY AND UTOPIA. New York: Harcourt, Brace.

Markel, Lester.

1972. "So What's New?" A.S.N.E. BULLETIN 556 (January):9ff.

Marx, Karl.

1847. THE POVERTY OF PHILOSOPHY. New York: World, 1963 edition.

Marx, Karl and Friedrich Engels.

1932. THE GERMAN IDEOLOGY. New York: International, 1970 edition.

Matthews, Donald.

1960. U.S. SENATORS AND THEIR WORLD. New York: Vintage.

Mecklin, John.

1965. MISSION IN TORMENT. Garden City, N.Y.: Doubleday.

Medaris, John B.

1960. COUNTDOWN FOR DECISION. New York: G.P. Putnam's Sons.

Merton, Robert K.

1952. "Bureaucratic Structure and Personality." In READER IN BUREAUC-RACY. Edited by R. Merton, et al. New York: Free Press.

Meyer, Karl E.

1957. "Ordeal by Leak." NEW STATESMAN (London) 64 (December 14, 1962):858-60.

Milbrath, Lester W.

1960. "Lobbying As a Communication Process." PUBLIC OPINION QUAR-TERLY 24 (Spring):32-53.

Millis, Walter.

1958. ARMS AND THE STATE. New York: The Twentieth Century Fund.

Mollenhoff, Clark.

1962. WASHINGTON COVER-UP. New York: Doubleday.

Mott, Frank Luther.

1941. AMERICAN JOURNALISM. New York: Macmillan, 1950 edition.

Neustadt, Richard E.
1960. PRESIDENTIAL POWER. New York: Wiley.
1970. ALLIANCE POLITICS. New York: Columbia Univ. Press.
New York Times Company v. U.S., 403 U.S. 713 (1971).
Newhouse, John.
1970. DEGAULLE AND THE ANGLO-SAXONS. New York: Viking.
"News Under Kennedy." COLUMBIA JOURNALISM REVIEW 1 (Spring 1962):11-20.
Niebuhr, Reinhold.
1963. "The Role of the Newspaper in America's Function As the World's Greatest Power." In THE PRESS IN PERSPECTIVE. Edited by Ralph D. Casey. Baton Rouge: Louisiana State Univ. Press.
Nietzche, Friedrich.
1968. "On Truth and Lie in an Extra-Moral Sense." In THE PORTABLE NIETZCHE. Translated by Walter Kaufman. New York: Viking.
Nimmo, Dan D.
1964. NEWSGATHERING IN WASHINGTON. New York: Atherton.
Oberdorfer, Don.
1971. TET! Garden City, N.Y.: Doubleday.
"Old Allies—A New Stance." NEWSWEEK 60 (December 31, 1962):9.
Osborne, John.
1972. "The Nixon Watch: Toilet Training." NEW REPUBLIC 166 (January 1-8): 16-17.
Peterson, H.C.
1937. "British Influence on the American Press, 1914-1917." AMERICAN POLITICAL SCIENCE REVIEW 31 (February): 79-89.
Peterson, Theodore.
1963. "The Social Responsibility of the Press." In FOUR THEORIES OF THE PRESS. Edited by Fred S. Siebert, Theodore Peterson, and Wilbur Schramm. Urbana: Univ. of Illinois Press.
Philby, Kim.
1969. MY SILENT WAR. London: Panther.
Phillips, Cabell.
1955. "Questions and Answers on the Press Conference." NEW YORK TIMES MAGAZINE (February 13):62-63ff.
Phillips, Wayne.
1968. "Information and the Newsman." In THE VOICE OF GOVERN-MENT. Edited by Ray E. Hiebert and Carleton E. Spitzer. New York: Wiley.
Pincus, Walter.
1971. "Before the Pentagon Papers: Why the Press Failed." NEW YORK 4 (July 19):34-38.
Pulitzer, Joseph.
1904. "The College of Journalism." NORTH AMERICAN REVIEW 178 (May):658.

Raymond, Jack.
 1964. POWER AT THE PENTAGON. New York: Harper and Row.
Reedy, George.
 1968. "Speaking for the President." In THE VOICE OF GOVERNMENT.
 Edited by Ray E. Hiebert and Carleton E. Spitzer. New York: Wiley.
 1970. THE TWILIGHT OF THE PRESIDENCY. New York: World.
 1971. "Moynihan's Scholarly Tantrum." MORE 1 (September):6.
Reston, James.
 1966. "The Press, the President, and Foreign Policy." FOREIGN AFFAIRS
 45 (July):553-73.
 1967. ARTILLERY OF THE PRESS. New York: Harper and Row.
Riker, William H.
 "The Firing of Pat Jackson." Inter-University Case Program No. 1. Mimeographed.
Rivers, William L.
 1962. "The Correspondents After 25 Years." COLUMBIA JOURNALISM
 REVIEW 1 (Spring):4-10.
 1964. THE OPINIONMAKERS. Boston: Beacon Press.
 1970. THE ADVERSARIES. Boston: Beacon Press.
Rosten, Leo.
 1937. THE WASHINGTON CORRESPONDENTS. New York: Harcourt,
 Brace.
Rothchild, John.
 1971. "The Stories Reporters Don't Write." WASHINGTON MONTHLY 3
 (June):20-27.
Rush, Myron.
 1958. THE RISE OF KHRUSHCHEV. Washington, D.C.: Public Affairs Press.
Salinger, Pierre.
 1961. "The Press and Presidential Leadership." Address at the University of
 Minnesota Newspaper Guild Forum, November 9, 1961.
Sampson, Anthony.
 1967. MACMILLAN: A STUDY IN AMBIGUITY. Hammondsworth, Eng-
 land: Penguin.
Schlesinger, Arthur, Jr.
 1958. THE COMING OF THE NEW DEAL. Boston: Houghton Mifflin.
 1965. A THOUSAND DAYS. Boston: Houghton Mifflin.
Shapiro, Fred C.
 1972. "What's News in New York's Newspapers." COLUMBIA JOUR-
 NALISM REVIEW 10 (March/April):48-52.
Sherwood, Robert E.
 1950. ROOSEVELT AND HOPKINS. New York: Harper.
Sidey, Hugh.
 1968. A VERY PERSONAL PRESIDENCY. New York: Atheneum.
Sinclair, Robert.
 1949. THE BRITISH PRESS: THE JOURNALIST AND HIS CONSCIENCE.

London: Home and Van Thal.

Skardon, James A.

1967-68. "The Apollo Story." COLUMBIA JOURNALISM REVIEW 6 (Winter): 34-39.

"Skybolt's American Show." THE ECONOMIST 206 (January 12, 1963): 127.

"Skybolt's Fate Up to Kennedy, McNamara." AVIATION WEEKLY AND SPACE TECHNOLOGY 25 (December 17, 1962): 26-27.

Sorensen, Theodore C.

1963. DECISION-MAKING IN THE WHITE HOUSE. New York: Columbia University Press.

1965. KENNEDY. New York: Harper and Row.

Stampp, Kenneth M.

1950. AND THE WAR CAME. Baton Rouge: Louisiana State Univ. Press.

Stark, Rodney W.

1962. "Policy and the Pros: An Organizational Analysis of a Metropolitan Newspaper." BERKELEY JOURNAL OF SOCIOLOGY 6: 11-31.

Steed, H. Wickham. 1938. THE PRESS. Harmondsworth: Penguin.

Stone, I.F.

1952. THE HIDDEN HISTORY OF THE KOREAN WAR. New York: Monthly Review Press.

"The Stranger on the Squad." TIME 80 (December 14, 1962): 15-18.

Sullivan, Mark.

1930. OUR TIMES. Vol. III. New York: Charles Scribner's Sons.

Sullivan, Walter.

1966. "Two Times Reporters Share a Troublesome Secret." In THE WORKING PRESS. Edited by Ruth D. Adler. New York: G.P. Putnam's Sons.

Sumner, William G.

1965. FOLKWAYS. New York: Blaisdell.

Sutton, Francis X., et al.

1962. THE AMERICAN BUSINESS CREED. New York: Schocken.

Szulc, Tad.

1967. "THE NEW YORK TIMES and the Bay of Pigs." In HOW I GOT THAT STORY. Edited by David Brown and W. Richard Bruner. New York: Dutton.

1969. THE KINGDOM AND THE POWER. New York: World.

Tocqueville, Alexis de.

1835. DEMOCRACY IN AMERICA. Translated by Henry Reeve.

Truman, Harry S.

1955. MEMOIRS, I: YEAR OF DECISIONS. Garden City, N.Y.: Doubleday.

1958. MEMOIRS, II: YEARS OF TRIAL AND HOPE. New York: Doubleday.

Tuchman, Gaye.

1972. "Objectivity As a Strategic Ritual: An Examination of Newsmen's

211

Notions of Objectivity." AMERICAN JOURNAL OF SOCIOLOGY 78 (January):660-679.

Tunstall, Jeremy.
1970. THE WESTMINSTER LOBBY CORRESPONDENTS. London: Routledge & Kegan Paul.

U.S., Advisory Commission on Civil Disorders, REPORT. New York: Bantam, 1968.

U.S., Congress, House, Committee on Government Operations, HEARINGS, GOVERNMENT INFORMATION PLANS AND POLICIES, 88th Cong., 1st Sess., 1963.

U.S., Congress, Senate, Committee on Foreign Relations, HEARINGS: NEWS POLICIES IN VIETNAM, 89th Cong., 2nd sess., August 17, 1966.

U.S., Department of State, BULLETIN, no. 44, 1145 (June 5, 1961), p. 841.

U.S., Department of State, BULLETIN, no. 48, 1129 (January 14, 1963), pp. 44-45.

Villard, Oswald Garrison.
1925. "The Press and the President." CENTURY 89 (December):193-200.

Viorst, Milton.
1972. "William Rogers Thinks Like Richard Nixon." NEW YORK TIMES MAGAZINE (February 27):12-13ff.

Walker, Stanley.
1934. CITY EDITOR. New York: Stokes.

Weaver, Paul.
1968. "How the Times Is Slanted Down the Middle." NEW YORK 1 (July 1):32-36.
1969. "The Metropolitan Newspaper As a Political Institution." Ph.D. Dissertation, Department of Government, Harvard University.

Weinstein, Martin E.
1971. JAPAN'S POSTWAR DEFENSE POLICY, 1947-1968. New York: Columbia University Press.

Welles, Chris.
1972. "Harder Times at 'The Times.' " NEW YORK 5 (January 17):38-47.

White, Llewellyn, and Leigh, Robert D.
1946. PEOPLES SPEAKING TO PEOPLES, A REPORT ON INTERNATIONAL MASS COMMUNICATIONS FROM THE COMMISSION ON FREEDOM OF THE PRESS. Chicago: University of Chicago Press.

White, Theodore H.
1961. THE MAKING OF THE PRESIDENT—1960. New York: Atheneum.

White, William S.
1958. "Trying to Find the Shape—If Any—of the News in Washington." HARPERS 217 (August):76-80.

Williams, Francis.
    1946. PRESS, PARLIAMENT AND PEOPLE. London: Heinemann.
Witcover, Jules.
    1965. "Surliest Crew in Washington." COLUMBIA JOURNALISM REVIEW
    4 (Spring):11-15.
Wolfe, Tom.
    1972a. "The Birth of 'The New Journalism.' " NEW YORK 5 (February
    14):30ff.
    1972b. "Why They Aren't Writing the Great American Novel Anymore."
    ESQUIRE 78 (December):52ff.
Worthy, William.
    1972. "Debriefing the Press: 'Exclusive to the C.I.A.' " VILLAGE VOICE
    (December 7):1.
Yarmolinsky, Adam.
    1971. THE MILITARY ESTABLISHMENT. New York: Harper and Row.
Young, James.
    1966. THE WASHINGTON COMMUNITY. New York: Columbia University
    Press.
Ziman, John.
    1968. PUBLIC KNOWLEDGE: THE SOCIAL DIMENSION OF SCIENCE.
    Cambridge: Cambridge University Press.

Index

Index

About the Author

Leon V. Sigal recently joined the research staff of the Twentieth Century Fund. A native of New Haven, Connecticut, he received the B.A. from Yale University in 1964 and the Ph.D. from Harvard University in 1971. He was a Rockefeller Younger Scholar in Foreign Policy Studies at the Brookings Institution in 1971-72. He currently lives in New York City with his wife, the former Anne B. Frank.

REPORTERS AND OFFICIALS
The Organization and Politics of Newsmaking

At a time when the biggest thing in the news is the news media themselves, **REPORTERS AND OFFICIALS** looks inside two of the biggest newsmaking institutions in the country, *The New York Times* and *The Washington Post*.

REPORTERS AND OFFICIALS examines the structure of these two mammoth, influential, and bureaucratic organizations and details how the news gets made within them. Leon V. Sigal explores and analyzes the organizational routines followed by the newsmen of the *Times* and the *Post* in gathering and transcribing information here and in foreign bureaus.

Drawing on several case studies involving the *Times* and the *Post*, he describes the internal politics of these newspapers and the impact they have on key decisions such as the make-up of Page One. **REPORTERS AND OFFICIALS** explores these other questions:

To what extent does the profit motive effect the structure and operation of the news organization?

What of accountability within the organization: who has ultimate responsibility for the news?

How do manpower and staff distribution affect the reporting of the news?